Columbus
And The
Ends Of The Earth

Columbus
And The Ends Of
The Earth

Europe's Prophetic
Rhetoric
As Conquering
Ideology

Djelal Kadir

UNIVERSITY OF CALIFORNIA PRESS
Berkeley • Los Angeles • Oxford

University of California Press
Berkeley and Los Angeles, California

University of California Press
Oxford, England

Copyright © 1992 by The Regents of the University of California

Library of Congress Cataloging-in-Publication Data

Kadir, Djelal.
    Columbus and the ends of the earth : Europe's prophetic rhetoric
as conquering ideology / Djelal Kadir.
      p.   cm.
    Includes bibliographical references and index.
    ISBN 0-520-07442-4 (cloth)
    1. Columbus, Christopher. 2. America—Discovery and exploration.
3. Prophecy (Christianity) 4. Europe—Territorial expansion.
I. Title.
E111.K15   1992
970.01′5—dc20   91-13558
                                          CIP

Printed in the United States of America

1 2 3 4 5 6 7 8 9

8791569

pco

*There has never been a document of
culture which was not at one and the
same time a document of barbarity.*

—*Walter Benjamin,
"Theses on the Philosophy of History," VII.*

Contents

Preface

In the historical plot of the European tradition, Columbus is the finder of a New World. This World was dubbed "New" because until 1492 it was generally known only in the cosmological desires and philosophical speculations of Europe's imaginative and visionary savants. But besides being a "finder," Columbus is also a founder and, like most founders, he personifies an intricate web of convictions that determine his vision, his actions, and his reactions. This same set of beliefs also sustains his determination and his tenacity. As such a personification Columbus is more than a "biographical" subject. He is a dramatic character in the plot of a particular historical drama. In that capacity, he is an emphatic embodiment of the conceptions, goals, desires, and ambitions of the cultural complex that constitutes the theater in which, and on behalf of which, he acts and reacts. Since he also carries with and within him those particular precepts and principles that give legitimacy to particular courses of action and authorize specific moves, gestures, and articulations, I shall often range beyond the immediacy of Columbus in an attempt to convey the context he exemplifies. To extend my theatrical metaphor just a bit, Columbus was a consummate actor within the particular historical drama in which he found himself. In fact, he was a better actor than he consciously knew, inasmuch as he acted out of the unshakable conviction that he was the protagonist of a drama that was *the* universal and ultimate production in the cosmos. He was also convinced that the Ultimate Playwright of all dramas had cast him as the elect hero and privileged emissary to play out the last and climactic act of this cosmic theater. To serve as protagonist in the plot of a particular drama means to epitomize the values, language, and other expressive modes of that drama. An epitome of something is the most emphatic symptom of it. Columbus is indeed such a blatant representation and, as such, he personifies not only the history of the drama in which he acts, but he epitomizes, as well, the actors and the actions of those acts that, unexpectedly, come after him. The drama, in other words, extended well beyond what was thought to have been the last act with Columbus as its final protagonist. In this expectation and unexpected extension, Columbus foreshadows those who would see themselves also as the culmination of the cosmic plot. Our study, therefore, will also focus on those who followed Columbus to the New World impelled by the same convictions.

Now, to see yourself as occupying the first and foremost position on a world stage and, at the same time, to be convinced that you are also playing out the last role in the grand finale could lead you to the certainty of enjoying a uniquely privileged position in the cosmic scheme. That certainty, in turn, could enable you to undertake certain projects, and to do so with such cocksure and righteous authority that all difficulty, impediments, and considerations are diminished to insignificance, if not dismissed altogether. This sort of empowerment, in the final analysis, could put all means beyond questioning, leaving the ends of the End as the only criteria by which to judge your actions and justify your course.

This is the sort of enterprise in the New World that Columbus epitomizes most consistently, and this is what the present study aims to trace in and through Columbus. I say "in and through" because Columbus is viewed here not as an independent and discrete entity, but as a cultural phenomenon. He is treated as the embodiment of the complex or web of certain notions, cultural forms, and conditioning ideas that furnish the enabling requirements and provide the legitimating protocols for a world-transforming enterprise. That undertaking would entail a people's movement and incursion into the cultural and geographical terrain of another people with profound consequences for all.

As much as Columbus himself, the subject of this book is the culture and context that engendered Columbus, as well as the particular culture, or more accurately, the certain phases of a culture, that he augured in the New World (primarily in New Spain and in New England). More specifically yet, the present study focuses on a particular mode of language and the ideological formations that underwrite that language. In more technical parlance, my concern is with a particular kind of discourse, its formations, and its deployment for particular ends. In limning out the "archaeology" of these formations, I have consciously attempted to take as little for granted as possible, and I have endeavored to read the archive itself that contains, and is contained by, that archaeology. Given the cultural diversity and plurality of languages (discourses and disciplines) in which we live, it would be self-deluding to presume a shared understanding of such key terms as, for example, "prophecy," "typology," "eschatology," "millennium," or, for that matter, "history," terms all whose shared understanding among the contemporaries of Columbus would not be in question. Thus, I have sought, even at the risk of rehearsing what for some might be commonplaces, to obviate the etymology of certain notions, usages, and presuppositions that underlie the enterprise that Columbus headed, and that belie the self-justifications of those who felt themselves to be acting in the name of transcendent ends and transcending imperatives.

In weaving this text out of the threads that form the web that wove Columbus's world, I have aimed to begin in the beginning and to end there too. I have done so in the full realization that any knots tied with the ends of those threads are ultimately knots of water, as elusive as the oceanic byways Columbus sought to convert into the anchored waystations of his worldly and otherworldly pilgrimage, only to discover that even the anchors and the ropes with which he sought to tie his vessel into havens of faith were prone to endure the caprices of (historical) currents and liquid currency. Inasmuch as Columbus embodied all this, I always begin and end, inevitably, with Columbus.

Acknowledgments

My initiation into the readings and writings of Columbus began in the New World and its New Haven at an age of starry-eyed enthusiasm under the tutorship of José Juan Arrom, to whom I acknowledge my debt. I am equally indebted, from that formative period of my apprenticeship, to Richard M. Morse, whose subtle irreverence taught me to wink back at history's truth-claims; and to Harold Bloom, whose stentorian decalogues on reading vision and transgression echo, ineluctably, in whatever I still read, alas. More recently, I have been the fortunate beneficiary of Allen Mandelbaum's friendship and of his avuncular injunctions on reading poetry and writing prose. *Grazie, Maestro, tante grazie!*

The notes at the end of this book reflect particular intellectual debts. I should own, nonetheless, to my general indebtedness to a number of writers whose pervasive conditioning of our contemporary cultural environment extends to my own work as well. From Edward Said and Roberto Fernández Retamar I have learned a good deal about the reading of colonial discourses. Hayden White has made it possible for me and my contemporaries to engage the historical canon on terms other than its own canonicity. Stephen Greenblatt has opened new venues to/for the historical archive.

I am materially grateful to Dean David A. Caputo of the

School of Liberal Arts at Purdue University and to the Center for Humanistic Studies for making it possible for me to complete work on this project with a Center Fellowship. My debts to colleagues are too numerous to be listed individually. I would be remiss in excess, however, if I did not acknowledge my gratitude to my friend and colleague William L. Rowe of the Philosophy Department for reading and commenting on an early draft of my first chapter. To my colleagues Vincent Leitch and Virgil Lokke from English, G. Richard Thompson and Harold Woodman from American Studies, Floyd Merrell from Spanish and Latin American Studies, and Calvin Schrag from Philosophy, many thanks for years of conversation, continued support, and collegiality. I also wish to note my appreciation to Lester Cohen, former colleague in American Studies and now a distinguished attorney, for his genuine friendship and lucidity in all matters. A special thanks is due to my classicist colleagues Keith Dickson and John Kirby for persuading futuristic machinery to print in ancient character. And to all my colleagues who took on the administrative responsibilities of the Comparative Literature Program while I saw this project to completion, I am grateful.

A good deal of the material in chapter 2 comprised the text of my lecture in the Provost's Distinguished Lectures Series of Ball State University. I am grateful to Provost Warren Vander Hill for that occasion and for his agreement to my use of that material here. I have had valuable reactions and commentary to various phases and related concerns of the current book from colleagues and graduate students at various institutions beyond my home university—University of Chicago, University of Colorado, Washington University, the Woodrow Wilson International Center for Scholars. My thanks to all.

Finally, my heartfelt gratitude to my keenest critic, my wife Juana Celia, for her endless support. To my daughter Aixé I am deeply grateful for her understanding and philosophical acceptance of the competing demands such projects have always made on *our* time.

CHAPTER I

Emergent Occasions

Of Prophecy and History

Christopher Columbus was a Hermetic character and he knew it. He made sure we would become party to his insight when he underscored his Mercurial vocation by habitually signing his name in its Greek etymological form, Xpo-Ferens—the bringer of the anointed one, the bearer of the Messiah. It would seem he knew full well that he mediated more than between two geographical hemispheres. He was aware, it would appear, of his existence on the cusp of two temporal worlds—the Medieval and the Renaissance. Just as significantly, we know from his writings that he viewed his ferryman's responsibility as one that encompassed the passageways between this world and the other world.

To say that any man was a man of his time is a bald-faced tautology. But, in the case of Columbus, perhaps we can indulge in that redundancy since Columbus's were particularly extraordinary times that obsessively reached after their extra-territoriality. Or at least that is how our historical canon has taught us to understand them. Our historiography has made a commonplace of the symmetrical notion that the oceanic/geographical crossroads traversed by Columbus have their temporal/ideological correlatives in the historical junctures that nurtured and versed the Mariner. These claims too are less than wholly immune to the charge of a tautology logically implicit in all true symmetries. I invoke this time-honored canon not to reassert or impugn its validity necessarily, but to point through it in the direction of what has been studied least in Columbus, namely, his self-perceived role as providential agent with divine election and a prophetic task. In his writings, among them a compilation of a *Book of Prophecies,* Columbus understood his historic accomplishment in terms of this appointment. In doing so, he epitomized the ideological crosscurrents of his epoch and prefigured, too, a significant strain in what would become a tradition of the New World on whose shores he was to be discovered: a New World that discovers itself in his and in the natives' mutual befuddlement on the occasion of that initial encounter. The shape of this ideal embodied by Columbus partakes of the many facets, some contradictory, others paradoxical, that mark the passage of the Medieval epoch across the threshold of the Renaissance—a cultural crossing where the world views of Medioaevum and Renaissance mingle and become compounded. At this juncture, I must offer a broader context to the individual project of Columbus in order to recapitulate a number of historical commonplaces. Thus, I hope to end up with a frame of reference that governs Columbus's self-perception and that passes with him into the New World to become a cultural framework for the New World's own self-apprehension.

Consonant with the elusiveness of the prototypical messenger Hermes/Mercury, Columbus's many biographers find their subject a study in enigmas, a predicament that historians cannot escape when they know too much or too little about their subject. As for the historical epoch coincident with Columbus's life, it manifests its own conundrums, perforce symptomatically, in the enigmatic figure of the Admiral of the Ocean Sea. Having lived and dreamed at a temporal junction of Medieval twilight and Renaissance dawning, it is inevitable that Columbus should embody the paradoxes of that confluence: as cartographer and hemispheric surveyor, Columbus charted and sallied toward new horizons, but fundamental principles that governed his prescience and scientific convictions had their firm grounding in Classical Antiquity and the cosmological arithmetic of the ancients. In this sense, Columbus partakes of that fundamental irony that the very term "Renaissance" connotes, a predicament that Frances Yates, an acute student of the period, aptly characterizes when she notes that the "great forward movements of the Renaissance all derive their vigour, their emotional impulse, from looking backwards."[1] However, as spiritual itinerant on a Christian pilgrimage, Columbus exemplified, too, the stress of polar tensions that marked the autumnal ripeness of Europe's Medieval Age. For at least once during his vigorous life, and on his pitiful deathbed, he donned the garb of apostolic poverty, the habit of those spiritually aflame who sought Christianity's past golden age in evangelical primitivism in order to propitiate eschatology's yearned future. Because, to those such as Columbus for whom emergent occasions were always devotional waystations, as John Donne would have it, the future was always at a high premium and the ultimate prize. But what is peculiar to Columbus and his time is the fact that even for its strain of cyclical Antiquity, which the Renaissance sought to recoup, the progress of the soul was no longer toward a Golden Age of yore but in an investment in the features of futurity, whether Elysian fields or Arcadian *eutopias*. Classical Antiquity's premium on happy returns fell in line with the pilgrim's progress, and the incipient Renaissance of Columbus's time already is a prospector in the by-and-by rather than the bygone, even if the means, as Frances Yates points out, pertain to the ancients. It would be overly simplifying to attribute that shift in outlook wholly to Antiquity's Judeo-Christian baptism. For, as we learn in studies such as A. Bartlett Giamatti's *The Earthly Paradise and the Renaissance Epic*,[2] the Classical ethos was well on its way to providence under its own powers and in its own time. Works, now become homilies, such as Horace's Sixteenth Epode and Virgil's Fourth Eclogue not only mark a temporal shift from nostalgia to expectation, but they also point the Oceanic way and cardinal direction in which Columbus was to sail. Such directional pointers, of course, antedate both Horace and Virgil and extend back to Homer's *Odyssey* (book 4, lines 561–568) and to Hesiod's *Works and Days* (lines 169–179), albeit still centered in a temporal locus of a mythological past. But for Columbus's

frame of mind, engendered as it was by the typological mindset of
the Medieval ethos, *all* past was but a premonitory sentience that
augured his providential calling. As such, all history has a symmetry programmed by God's design, and all men's deeds and sentences were but fitting versicles of a transcendental opus. In this
sense, all occasions were emergent occasions or, if I may deviate
from John Donne's phrasing, they were penultimate emergencies
that prefigured the final future. Thus, when I say that Columbus
had a sense of his own election, it is tantamount to saying that
Columbus had a sense of history and his appointed role within it.
His uncompromising tenacity before courts and men of lesser
vision drew its obstinate nourishment from a conviction well-
rooted in a blueprint of history whose design had already been
inalterably shaped. We shall be taking up Columbus's explicit
pronouncements in this regard in due course. For now, I should
like to recall that inexorable relation between history and prophecy, a linkage that is key to understanding Columbus's itinerary
and the prophetic enterprise of New World culture. In the process, I hope to clarify the particular sense of a number of key
terms employed throughout this study.

My suggestion that Columbus's perception of his own prophetic role may well have been identical with his sense of history
derives from an appreciation of a long tradition in which prophecy and history run concurrently and not always in strictly parallel paths. The historical and prophetic modes of apprehending the
course of the world and of human destiny often illumine each
other in reciprocal fashion. Thus, when we read, for example,
Columbus's own characterization of his historic achievement, the
deeds of history become meaningful only when viewed in the
light of prophecy: "Ya dise que para la hesecuçión de la ynpresa
de las Yndias no me aprovechó rasón, ni matemática ny mapamundos, llenamente se cunplió lo que diso Isayas [I have said
already that for the execution of the enterprise of the Indies neither reason nor mathematics nor map serve me, plainly Isaiah's
prophecy was fulfilled."[3] Columbus's letter of 13 September
1501, partially cited here, to the Spanish sovereigns augurs as
prototype the pronouncements on the New World enterprise,

pronouncements in which the connubium of history and prophecy becomes the overarching criterion by which America's prophetic tradition can be appreciated. Without that criterion our readings in such New World figures as Gerónimo de Mendieta, John Winthrop, Antonio de Vieira, William Bradford, Gonzalo Tenorio, Edward Johnson, and Cotton Mather—among others we shall allude to in the course of this study—would be left starkly impoverished. In the very term "New World" then, history and prophecy are of a piece, as Columbus's own suggestive allusion to Isaiah 65 pointedly implies.

If we were to be guided strictly by etymology, history and prophecy would appear to be diametrically contrary modes of apprehension. Literally speaking, history is a "re-search," a looking into the past, whereas prophecy is a projection into the future. But, of course, Greek etymology is only a starting point and, once we set out, our departure itself takes on its own connotations that render the neat lexicon of etymologies highly problematic. In the complex of typological explanation, this is so with history and prophecy, for what are initially antonymous terms become functionally synonymous, with their original meanings exchanged and mutually substitutable. Thus, history, which is more assuredly knowable by virtue of referring to what ostensibly occurred in the past, ends up as object of divination. Whereas, prophecy, which is enigmatic discernment through the opacity of the visionary's dark glass, becomes the surest and least controvertible mode of knowing. This differentiation is not grounded on abstract philosophical principles of epistemology. It is founded, rather, in the empirical contexts of a certain system of beliefs that actually governs the experience of a particular culture—the Western Judeo-Christian culture that undertook the New World enterprise. And within the particular contexts of this tradition, the peculiar interchange of history and prophecy renders the first a complex of prefigurations to be divined, discerned, and thus fulfilled in "a present," and the latter an irrevocable certainty, since prophecy, if it truly be prophetic, must prophesy the inevitable. The first, history as constellation of prefigurations, comprises the study of typology. The latter, prophecy as precognition of the inevitable, is a viewpoint of eschatology. The *forthgathering* of typological promise and the *foregathering* of eschatology's last things underwrite the grand unveiling, the final acts of disclosure that legitimate the promises of the past and the promise of the future. This ultimate vindication of expectancy's steadfastness consists in the revelations most commonly known by the Greek term *apocalypsis*. We can say, then, that typology, eschatology, and apocalypse are the triune members through which prophecy finds its articulation as coterminus integer of history. I should like to take each of these ternary components of prophecy in turn, particularly as they engender and sustain that symbiotic relationship between the historical and the prophetic.

Typology may well be one of the most radical modes of reconstituting and reading history. A drastic form of historical revisionism, the typological mode is essentially a New Testament, Christian instrument by which the past is made significant and justified. Through this mechanism, all history, pagan or Hebraic, attains to a status of sacred history by virtue of having arrived at its appointed destination. That *terminus ad quem* consists in the miraculous life of the Christian community. As such, all pre-Christian history is figured as a blueprint that finally reaches its fulfillment in being realized as the edifice that is the Christian Church. The history that antedates the Christian era comprises the promise, in other words, the *type,* that arrives at its consummation, that is, the *antitype,* with the incarnation, crucifixion, and resurrection. In this schema, all history, then, is rendered object of a visionary exercise, forthgathered through a *re*-visionary act. The community that gathers forth all history to itself understands itself as privileged by virtue of being divinely elected to carry out this task and, concomitantly, considers itself enabled to engage in this act of forthgathering because it views itself as God's own (Galatians 6:16; 1 Peter 2:9). On the double mirror of this self-fulfilling legitimacy, history runs out its course and finds its justification, finally. The Pauline interpretation of universal history, on which many subsequent assessments ultimately rest, pretty much sealed the fate of historical continuity by the paradoxical twist of deeming the sinful and shadowy past a necessary prerequisite to the divine grace that finally derails history for all time and depletes all time once and for all—God's divine gift to His people of the end-time. The Christian community, then, has the unique privilege of being out of time and running out of history. This culmination of history notwithstanding, however, the obstinate continuity of the end-time endowed the community's ahistorical existence with a historicity, *malgré lui*. Typology then is born, in part, of the necessity to deal with the history of existence in "non-history." As an instrument designed to interpret occurrences in a time after time, typology ends by inversely historicizing the miraculous, albeit in a nongeneological, nondevelopmental way. By casting all history as adumbration of what occurs in non-history and as fulfillment of that foreshadowing, typology serves as mediating instrument for an inter-testamental connection. Rather than a natural development, the linkage is miraculously created by a Divinity for His new people. History, the Old Testament, and the historical life of His "old people" stand in a special relationship to the end-time, the New Testament, and the ahistorical life of His "new people." The peculiarity of this connection consists in the reversal of the causal relationship between promise and fulfillment, augury and event, prescience and ascertainment. In this reversal, typology emerges as instrument of back-formation by which the explanation of the cause ensues from the result, the nature of the fulfillment explains promise, and the eventual occurrence interprets its auguration. Typology, thus, is not only a necessity born of the end of history, but it is also a decidedly antihistorical mechanism in its *modus operandi,* a mechanism that works by inverting the order of interpretative historical sequence and continuity.

By privileging the adjective in a *New* Testament, a *New* Covenant, and a *New* World, the typological *sensus comunis* made an Old Testament, an Old Covenant, and an Old Dispensation indispensable. Indispensable too became a shift in interpretative strategies for reading the Old Testament and "old" Israel's history. It has often been noted, for example, that exegetical focus shifted from the Torah (the Law) to the Nebiim (the Prophets) in the targumen of early Christian hermeneutics[4]—clearly, because those prophecies from the past now find their "adumbration" and true sense in becoming realized. Jeremiah's promise (31:31) of a New Covenant for the time of the end, for example, becomes object of (re)visionary insight at prophecy's other temporal end (1 Corinthians 11:25; 2 Corinthians 3:6 ff; Galatians 4:24; Hebrews 7:8 ff). All promises of the Old Testament, in fact, become truly prophetic for they finally have arrived at their significance as meaningful and purposive revelations in which the latest things of the end-time that is finally here and now were foreseen and foretold. In other words, those old prophecies have now become truly prophetic by being vindicated in the inevitability of their predications. Prophecy, then, is not at all prophetic by virtue of being a pre-vision of the future. Rather, prophecy, in the typological schema, is what it is by virtue of being a re-vision of an insight and utterance of the past. And necessarily so, since for the incipient Christian community that saw itself as the culmination of history and at the end of time there was no distant time other than the past time. Therefore, all visionary projection into temporal distance had to be directed toward the past. The future was not yet, but it was felt to be all too close and imminently closing in. The basic tenets of this typological schema became the foundations on which successive generations elaborated a framework of diverse ideologies that range from the Pauline to the Johannine, from Augustinian to Joachite, and from the orthodox to the heretical. By Christopher Columbus's time, these tenets had become a *forma mentis,* a mental habit. This, in part, may help us appreciate why Columbus searched so anxiously in the scriptures and in the writings of the Church fathers, as well as in pagan sources such as Seneca, for example, to find the prophetic promises of his own achievement. We shall see later how, in this vein, prophecy *post eventum* becomes the dire unction for cosmological insecurity in the New World.

I have already suggested that whereas typology engages in a forthgathering of the past, eschatology aims at a foregathering of the future and, as the root etymon of the term implies, it is a reaching after ultimate things of the last times. Insofar as the early Christians considered themselves the people of the end-time

(1 John 2:18; Matthew 12:28), they formed, in their own view, an eschatological community. Indeed, for those who believed that the incarnation, crucifixion, and resurrection spelled the culmination of history and its worldly time, their lives were already being lived in a "realized eschatology." A couple of factors mitigate the clear-cut nature of this early eschatological reckoning, however. First, the notion of eschatology, unlike typology, is not even ostensibly Christian. Second, the last times tenaciously hold on, exacerbating duration and exasperating those who are convinced that the end is not only imminent but also immanent.

Eschatology is the historicizing of the ancients' nonhistorical, cyclical movement of the cosmos and its "world-years." The paradoxical becomes inescapable, once more, when we have to speak of the historicizing of a nonhistorical concept by a people who believed itself to be beyond time and extra-historical. Nevertheless, this is precisely what does happen. The periodic cosmic aeons, or *status,* of Antiquity are reduced to the history of the world; the recurrence at the end of a cosmic era becomes understood as the opening up to a time of unending welfare. The Church fathers and their exegetes, in fact, continue to employ the nonhistorical vocabulary of Antiquity to refer to these historicized notions, notably, the term ἀποκατάστασις (apokatastasis), meaning *restoration,* which in astrological literature "refers to the periodical return of a star to its starting point, and consequently to the Stoic philosophers' use of the word for the return of the Cosmos at the end of a world-year to the origin from which a new world-year starts. But in the Acts of the Apostles (3:21) and in later Christian language, following Origen, ἀποκατάστασις (apokatastasis) became a technical term for eschatology."[5] Equating the definitive end with a recursive and recurrent term such as "restoration" may well compound incongruity. But, with time, the paradox proves a masterful stroke, most efficacious for justifying the tardiness of the imminent finality and the historicity accruing to ahistory, at the end of which a "second coming" as *restitution* becomes indispensable. The difficulty of this paradox in Christian thought emerges as pivotal point of an oscillation between those who believe that the Christian era is already a "realized eschatology," a millennial kingdom already at hand (the primitive Christian community and, later, St. Augustine) and those who persist in the expectation of an end-time, a millennial kingdom at the end of this world or in the last days of its history (John the Divine and, much later, Joachim of Fiore). Alternatively, we see a metaphorization of the problem of eschatology that ultimately translates into an amillennialist anthropology. This alternative already has its incipient outlines in Paul and what is referred to as Pauline theology.

Paul faced the problem of an end-time that would not end, an ahistory that was itself becoming historical, and he dealt with the difficulty directly. His procedure basically entails a further historicizing of world history by transforming the cosmic into a human dimension. By individualizing the promise of eschatological expectation, he renders cosmology into anthropology and the promised end of the world into promised ends awaiting the individual. Eschatological world history thus becomes modified into the historical (everyday) circumstances of the individual's existence as a new creature by dint of baptism (2 Corinthians 5:17) "in the fullness of time" and by the grace of God (Galatians 4:4). Paul's hortatory preaching serves, then, as parenetic assurance, in other words, as exhortation to ethical behavior. The individual Christian, according to Paul, should thus turn from his expectation of a world eschatology toward attaining his own eschatological ends in his liberation from history (Romans 12:2; 1 Corinthians 6:12, et passim). The decisive event has already come to pass for the believer who is "in Christ" (2 Corinthians 6:2) and history need no longer enslave the believer since Christ is the end of the law (Romans 10:4) and, with that, history reached its end—temporally and teleologically speaking. These eschatological pareneses in Paul's anthropology of individual ends help us, in part, to understand the terrific sermon of Puritan jeremiads in New England and the equally dire eschatological advertences of a Gerónimo de Mendieta in New Spain. But more about them in a later chapter.

The key to the liberation Paul recommends to the people lies in the strength to free oneself from the past. The past for Paul and, as we noted already, for the early Christian community in general, belongs to the old, sinful aeon that was miraculously interrupted. (This contrast between old and new resonates endlessly in the New World ethos of America vis-à-vis Europe, as one reads in writers that range from Mendieta in the sixteenth century to Henry James in the nineteenth, and to proponents of liberation theology in the twentieth century. The deepest roots of this antithesis may well lie in Pauline theology itself and its rhetoric of liberation. We shall return to the New World manifestations of this ideological complex in due course.) Analogically, the individual's past must also be overcome continuously. Man must be free of his past decisions when confronted with new circumstances so that he may heed the call of God in new situations. Only in this freedom can the individual become continuously "the one he is to be." Justified by faith, the individual is set free from the past and his sinful self (Romans 12:2; 1 Corinthians 6:12). Clearly, Paul's anthropological historicism leads the individual to a continuous dialectical existence, an existence at a shifting point between the abandoned past and the anticipated future. From a static end-time that was viewed as cosmic hypostasis, Paul's eschatology of history precipitates the individual and the community into a dynamic life. The motion of that dynamism configures a dialectical pilgrimage on a path that continuously leads from the "no longer" to the "not yet," a being on the way to becoming. In this way, Paul reorients universal eschatology and its end-time toward the individual ends of salvation, without abandoning the prevailing view of an end-time focused on a "second coming." Thus, for example, Greek terms like *parousia* take on a futuristic connotation, as well as referring still to the event of the incarnation; and salvation becomes linked with a *parousia* in a final form, a "second coming" whose immediate consequences will be the deliverance and vindication of the faithful. Consequently, the restorative resonance in the Greek lexicon for astrological recurrence, ἀποκατάστασις, becomes meaningful as an eschatological theophany with which the expectant people of the end-time are reassured (Romans 11:25–26; 1 Corinthians 15:51–52; 1 Thessalonians 4:16–17; Revelation 16:15, 21:6–8, 22:12–15). The

arithmetic for that anxiously expected *final* end of last things has
been variously calculated, in the Old World and in the New
World, by Columbus and by the Puritans. I leave discussion of
that elaborate prophetic abacus for our next chapter. For now, I
merely wish to note that the itinerary of the dialectical pilgrimage
delineated by Paul is fundamentally an individualized project.
The main current of Christian thought, in fact, points to the
disparity between the victory of good over evil in the salvation of
the individual soul, whereas the collective society and its institutions are generally headed not for victory but toward a progressive deterioration that presages the expected end (Matthew
24:12; St. Augustine; St. Cyprian, et al.). We shall explore this
disparity between individual itinerary and collective waystations,
as well as an alternative view with radical implications for the
history of the New World specifically in due course.

What I have referred to as an eschatological theophany ac-
quired a technical term of its own following the incorporation of
the last book into the New Testament canon. The genre of this
last inclusion about last things has been the subject of lengthy and
enduring debate. What is beyond question, however, is the
book's own self-characterization. Within its first three verses, it
declares itself to be simultaneously apocalypse, prophecy, and
epistle. The masterful symmetry of canonizing as last a book
about last things, a book that guarantees its own lasting status by
including a terrible admonition against future increments or
emendations (Revelation 22:18), has awed the faithful and de-
lighted generations of secular exegetes. Equally fascinating is the
book's historiographic significance, for it has served as foundation for a formidable constellation of diverse philosophies of history, ranging from the Montanist to the Marxist. In this regard,
no reader can fail to notice the historical irony of John's book: as
parenetic and admonitory exhortation that promises the fervently
expected and enjoins its imminence to break forth, John's can-
onized injunction achieves the institutionalization of the transitional (the ahistorical end-time), thereby endowing the *status eva-
nescentiae* with canonical *standing*. Thus, what Paul had
achieved earlier with eschatology, that is, a shifting historicist

perfectum praesens as dialectic predicated on an individualized anthropology, John of Ephesus at Patmos exacerbates and "cosmologizes" once more as an inherently dialectical foundation of a world history. The "realized eschatology" of early Christianity which became personal, individual fulfillment in Pauline theology becomes in John cosmological "promise" once more. For what is revealed in this apocalypse is what awaits, the promise implicit in *nondum,* the "not yet," but not just for the individual, as in Paul, rather, for the world of the end-time at the conclusion of its (transitional) history. The desideratum beyond that *nondum* is what makes history meaningful as history. In other words, it is what makes for the necessity of a philosophy of world history. Thus, product of a desideratum, history is the history of desire, born of and about desire, which is the yearned-for "inevitability" that is to vindicate all prophecy, thereby proving that it is truly prophetic. John arrives at his achievement through a radical strategy that revolutionizes the prophetic/apocalyptic tradition in which he is writing. He does so by subsuming that tradition and subjecting it to a drastic revisioning worthy of the strongest latecomer and authorial successor.

A belated phenomenon in the Hebraic Testamental tradition of prophecy, the apocalyptic genre evolved a set of procedures, understandably self-conscious given the genre's belatedness, which John strategically violates in his (re)visionary gambit. In doing so, he implicitly acknowledges the prototypical precursors of his project, thereby forging a role for himself as *antitype,* or fulfillment, of his typological antecedents. As a visionary writer working at the very "end" of a latter-day tradition whose supreme instrument of self-legitimation is typology, John astutely partakes of the legitimacy founded on that sanctioning schema. Thus, his deviations from the norms of the apocalyptic genre find their symmetrical self-vindication. John's epistolary revisionism and its reassuring promise to the people of the seven Asiatic churches become a purposive appropriation of the scriptural mantic tradition and purposive, too, is the brand of history that is born of this "incongruous" canon. We shall examine the nature of this purposiveness in history shortly, and later we shall see its serviceability for the justification of "discovery and conquest" when the Old World takes the New World as its object. For now, I wish to elaborate on John's willful appropriation and his radical revisionism as it skews the apocalyptic tradition in which he is writing. As we shall see further on, both history's purposiveness and John's generic revisionism become key ideological paradigms for Columbus and the revisionist project of New World history, an enterprise that sees itself as a new historical dispensation in contradistinction to the Old World's old and corrupted history.

More than any other mode of prophecy, apocalypsis is a historical genre. Its historicism derives from the fact that apocalypsis inevitably has a specificity grounded in actual sociopolitical contexts. It emanates, we could say, from a pragmatic necessity and carries with it the sense of urgency born of concrete and pressing historical situations. Daniel and John exemplify this sense of urgency. The first and last, and the only two full-fledged apocalypses to have been incorporated into the canon, they both issue as responses to social and religious circumstances of distress and they may well be prophecy's version of "pamphleteering." Daniel's target is Antiochus Epiphanes, John's Domitian, and the baneful legend of Neroredivivus. Although John evinces the commonality of this historicist contextualism with his precursors, a drastic breach separates him from them. I believe this difference could be adequately elucidated by recourse to the intertwined ternary fulcrum of *reference, deference,* and *concealment.* Scriptural hermeneutics has traditionally "explained" the first as the ploy of "pseudonymity," the second as "parenetic patience," and the third as "esotericism." John's strategy scuttles this triune ploy and in that willful severance he may well be the prophetic precursor to the severity with which the New World tradition views its own prophetic/historical novelty. We shall be expanding on that suggestive connection by and by.

"Pseudonymity," or what I have termed *reference,* consists in a strategy of recursive attribution. Authorial proprietorship of apocalyptic prophecy is ascribed to a commanding voice already legitimated by tradition. Thus, even though Hebraic apocalypses are penned in a period that extends roughly between 200 B.C. and

A.D. 100, they are attributed to pious and heroic figures of an earlier and a more venerated epoch. Ascription to such venerable forefathers as Enoch, Abraham, the Twelve Patriarchs, Moses, Solomon, Ezra, and Baruch became a traditional mechanism for legitimating later apocalyptic prophecy.[6] By contrast, John arrogates to himself the authority and authenticity of a divine commission (1:9–20) and an apostolic ministry to mediate divine revelation to the seven churches. As a faithful servant (1:6; 5:10), he is empowered to speak directly from what is his "here and now" to the believers of a corresponding "here and now" contemporaneous with his ministry. For John, then, prophet and faithful Christian become coterminous (22:6, 9).[7] In foregoing pseudonymous attribution, John effectively does away with the concomitant necessity of recursivity, of prophecy *ex-eventu*. That is, he abolishes the need to recur to a history surveyed and cast as prophecy of a future that has now matured as the confirming present of that retrospective "pre-vision." As a result, the present is not genealogically bound to the past and its plenitude emanates from the grace of its own vision rather than the provisional determinacies of prevision. Both consequences of John's revisionary deflection of referential pseudonymity (every faithful Christian a prophet and the present as divine wonder through the direct grace of God) will eventually find their distant resonances in the New World, as we shall see, where the roles of "sainthood" and "prophet" become "democratically" generalizable and Wonder-Working Providence makes its graces evident to the people of "God's country" directly.

The urgent immediacy characteristic of John's message undermines as well the urgings of patience and abeyance that traditionally accompanied Hebrew apocalypses. The *deference* I speak of is best exemplified in the opening lines of Enoch. Deferred there is the present for a more promising present still in the future, for the prophet's vision, we are told, is "not for this generation, but for a remote one which is for to come" (1:2). Eschewing authorial deference by spurning pseudonymity, John also rejects temporal deferral and ends with an imperative pleading. He calls for the awaited *eschaton* of his visions to break forth and overtake the dire situation of a persecuted people whose apocalyptic prophet himself has to carry out his apostolic ministry by way of the epistle from his exile on Patmos. Neither diffident, nor deferrent, John communicates with certainty his vision that judgment and redemption are imminent and that the yearned-for time *is* at hand (1:3; 22:11–12). Embedded within the quickening pace of John's prophetic injunctions is the eschatological impatience whose high-pitched echo resounds in the New World as "Apocalypse now!" starting with Columbus's Tertiary arithmetic, Antonio de Vieira's Joachite dreams, and John Davenport's chiliastic enthusiasm, as we shall see in a later chapter.

Hebrew apocalyptic prophecy becomes "esotericized" by willful occlusion. Although John's book may well prove amply "esoteric" even for the initiate, the deliberate concealment that characterizes apocalyptic genre is consciously undermined. Although not free from historical incongruity, as I have already noted, John avoids the paradox that haunted the Hebrew prophet, a paradox in which apocalypses had to revert to anacalypses. I am referring to the standard decree that the apocalyptic prophet seal his message until the end of time (e.g., Daniel 8:26 and 12:9; Enoch, referred to as the Slavonic Enoch, 33:10; 2 Esdras, referred to as 4 Ezra, 12:37). Such deferral through concealment, of course, would not be in keeping with the urgency of the *last* canonical prophet of the end-time. For John, the end of time is now (20:11) and he stands at the Sabbath of the world, at the very end of the world week. It logically follows, then, that he should receive his apostolic commission and apocalyptic vision on Sunday, on "the Lord's day" (1:10).

We can never know with certainty the motivations that underlie the esotericizing through concealment of the Hebraic revelation. We can only speculate that such re-veiling of the revealed and the deferral of its discernment to a temporal remove may well have constituted a strategy that served to deflect disconfirmation. For John, there was no need for such a safety device since this apocalyptic vision was ultimate confirmation and was coterminous with the awaited eschatology. Having committed himself to that equation, John's anxieties have to be of a different order.

They are summed up in the concluding plea, the "Maranatha," uttered with all desire and the frenzy of a pace quickened by direful alarm, lest history overtake the race of climactic consummation. In this terrific apprehension, John prefigures, as well, the anxious foundations of a New World, whether New Spain, New England, or New Portugal, where God's promise to His people ends up as a hare/tortoise race between prophetic impatience and plotting history, a race, as we shall see, that repeatedly culminates with the generalization of the imminent into the immanent and the transumption of temporal eschatology into its geographic and political corollaries. Having envisioned and pleaded for a foreshortening of history, a twist of irony wrought by implacable time undermined John's fervent pleading. It converted the utterance of his prophetic visions into beacons of an epistemology that would extend, not curtail, the path of history by endowing it with philosophical meanings. Paradoxically, then, what was envisioned as *the* ultimate antitype ends up as a prototype, a targumical instrument that adumbrates historical existence. This is especially so in the New World, whose eruption into the Old World's historical consciousness signaled the tolling of the apocalyptic Eleventh Hour for men like the Minister-General of the Franciscan Order Father Francisco de los Angeles. It is a New World whose geographical vicissitudes are eschatologically characterized, after Psalm 19:4, as "the ends of the Earth" in such works as Cotton Mather's *Magnalia Christi Americana*. As we shall see, the providentialist ethos of both the Anglo and Latin Americas derives its ideological impetus from John's book as much as it educes its typological justification from the Hebrew prophets. Columbus himself, convinced of his messianic mission that leads him to the gates of the Earthly Paradise—the Paria of his third voyage—and all too conscious of the telling simultaneity between his initial sally and the Spanish Jews' exodus into yet another Wilderness in 1492, embodies the prototypical exemplum of New-World providentialism.

Providentialism, especially in its New World context, is a shorthand designation that codifies into a single term prophecy's ternary schema of typology, eschatology, and apocalypse. That code functions as a philosophy of history, as a formulaic spectrum whose reflections shed a particular light, thereby making history meaningful in a particular fashion. That meaningfulness is, above all, deterministic in nature, and the force of its determinacies serves not only to "explain" and justify historical events but, also, to imbue those occurrences with metaphysical and transcendental significance. As such, historical life within the providentialist ethos becomes tantamount to a vocation and that vocation to a task of universal meaning. The daily contingencies, the historical events of the task's attempted completion become secondary to the transcendent purpose of the task. The historical acts born of that calling, in other words, become way stations for a pilgrimage greater than the tasks themselves, and the human agents who follow the calling are but elected instruments deployed for that greater purpose. History, in this sense, becomes purposive, and it is meaningful only insofar as it moves toward its appointed purpose. This oblique way of saying that history is teleological describes the kind of history that is born of/by prophecy's tradition, and its most salient, for being the most explicit and most definitive, formulation and primal example is John's book. It is under the aegis of this paradigm that teleological terms such as "end," with which we describe providential history, equivocate simultaneously as "goal" and as "culmination." Similarly, certain Romance terms, such as the French *sens* and the Spanish *sentido,* bifurcate in the same vein to signify at once spacio-temporal "direction" and semantic "meaning." Providential history is thus meaningful because it is purposive and its "ends" serve as directional beacons that orient its progress toward a final and transcendent goal. Although this progress is a movement in time, for those "pilgrims" who sailed West in God's name and under the banner of His purposive ends, this is also a progress in space and geography, and the deeds of God's elect carry with them the sanction of their divine calling. In practical terms, this is an unquestionable form of enablement that justifies all acts and sanctifies all means. The results of this form of ideological empowerment, of course, have proved fatal to many who would stand in the way or who would become targets of such

providential missions. The political ethos and international policies of God's country in the New World still evince the profound
symptoms of this founding ideology and the degree to which it is
engrained in the national fabric.

A number of studies link our progressivist ideologies to the
secularization of providentialist notions.[8] But for Columbus, the
Franciscans, and for the enthusiastic Puritans whom we shall be
discussing, providentialism is free from our modern illusions of
progress. Because, for them, the meaningful end of history meant
just that, *an end* to be precipitated by an interventionist Providence for whom historical determinacies were already final preparations for an eschatological goal. In this sense, those early New-
World providentialists, like their distant precursors of primitive
Christianity, had more in common with the ahistorical "fate" of
Greek life that utterly negated modern ideas of "progress" than
with our post-eighteenth-century notions of *endless* melioration.[9]
I speak now of "secular" notions, inasmuch as any notion could
achieve a truly "secular" ground, unlike the more ideologically
grounded progressivism of Marxist teleology and Liberationist
theology, both of which still resonate sharply with echoes of
John's apocalyptic enthusiasm in the modern New World.

Thus, providentialist history, by which Columbus himself was
driven, as we shall see, is purposive and meaningful, but only
insofar as it constantly verges on an eschatological edge. Before
we can appreciate the significance of this end-time experience in
the New World, we need to examine, however cursorily, the background of that tradition that Heinrich Bullinger, in his 1556 *A
Hundred Sermons upon the Apocalipse of Iesu Christ,* attributed
to those men "whom the endes of the world haue ouertaken."

Anxious Foundations

To dwell in/on prophecy is to dwell nomadically. Always at the junctures of discontinuity, the prophetic ethos shades out of time and place. Emphatic yearning for an "other place" and an "other time" is synonymous to ecstatic affliction, and *ecstasis*, of course, literally translates as outward dislocation and as chronic displacement. Rupture and rapture, too, become synonymous, and the prophetic impulse exhorts peregrination to the peripheries, to the thresholds or liminalities of time-space that shade into sublime. Sublimity means living on the edge, and prophetic edginess is a most precarious existence. It obliges one to live beyond one's present in and for a time as yet inexistent and in an untenable terrain, deterritorialized by dint of a calling from a habitation not yet realized except as yearning. *Uchronia* and *utopia* (no-time and no-place), then, are the anxious dimensions whose frontiers recede ever beyond reach to receive those who heed prophecy's call and to compound, in the process, anxious expectancy's sublime edginess. Expectancy's anxiety is a desire for what one fears most, or a terrific anticipation of what one most desires. Prophetic impatience invests its energies in unequivocal futures. The prophet inevitably declaims "truth or consequences." Implacably convinced of the first, he dwells on and in the consequential.

Consequence too is a dwelling at the farther side, a cohabitation with an aftermath at the verge of the horizon.

Prophecy's declamation, then, proclaims its own charter to chart the unpastured sea, and the prophet's cartography traces the topology of a New World. Thus, the historical conjunction of the prophetic tradition with the transoceanic voyaging may not be the symmetry of a logical necessity. But the coalescence of prophecy's impulse and geography's traversal inevitably compels. Inasmuch as prophetic ends are trained on eschatology's promise, the cosmic End itself, we should not be surprised at the conjugation of the "discovery" of the New World with the end of the world, as Marcel Bataillon phrases it.[1] By this prophetic arithmetic, we in the New World are would-be phantom souls inhabiting a post-apocalyptic ghostland that goes on outliving the life of an end-time calculus and its anxious expectations.

"Ghostland lies beyond the jurisdiction of veracity."[2] So wrote Hawthorne sometime between 1853 and 1857. He served as consul in Liverpool at the time, representing his New World homeland in the Old World home of his ancestors. Hawthorne, of course, was irremediably haunted by his Puritan forebears. So much so, that his obsession drove him to seek the imperatives of his New England inheritance in the jurisdiction of veracity's fictions. I do not think, then, we would be conjecturing unduly were we to suppose that Hawthorne was writing of America when he noted his observations on "Ghostland" in his *English Notebooks*.

In a time closer to our own, the poet Wallace Stevens sought, not unlike Hawthorne, to ascertain an order for a "jurisdiction of veracity," only to discover that the frontiers of such jurisdiction faded no less into "Ghostland's" originary mirage of prophetic visions and phantom voices. Thus, he would conclude "The Idea of Order at Key West" with that clamoring stanza that echoes the beset prophet's voice in the wilderness:

> Oh blessed rage for order, pale Ramon,
> The maker's rage to order words of the sea,
> Words of the fragrant portals, dimly-starred,

And of ourselves and of our origins
In ghostlier demarcations, keener sounds.[3]

Prophetic reckoning has proved a congenital obsession; and admonitions against the impulse have been equally timeless. As early as the time of that ancestral school master whom we identify as the Ecclesiastes, we are warned that "of making many books there is no end; and much study is a weariness of the flesh" (Ecclesiastes 12:12), a caveat that has gone unheeded sempiternally. Even conservative church fathers who, like St. Augustine, endeavored to check the arithmetic impulse by pointing to such admonitory scriptures as Matthew 24:36, "But of that day and hour no one knows, . . . but the Father only," and Acts 1:7, "It is not for you to know the times or the seasons," have inadvertently inflamed apocalyptic calculus in ways that adumbrate the most powerful notions and the most brazen emblem of the New World: the eagle, bold and embaldened in America's self-conception as prophecy's fulfillment and piety's epitome that managed to baptize even Jupiter's thunderous arrows with righteousness. I am referring to St. Augustine's Eighty-first Sermon: "The world is passing away, the world is losing its grip, the world is short of breath. Do not fear, thy youth shall be renewed as an eagle" (81:8). St. Augustine is echoing the fifth verse of the hundred-third Psalm, and the Book of Psalms, as already noted, is the first book to be printed in New England's New World. (The eagle, emblematic also of another North American nation, Mexico, derives from native antecedents, the founding sources, equally anxious, of Aztec cosmology.)

The compelling imperatives of apocalyptic arithmetic served as threshold to the New World, and its reckoning is what has kept life on the edge for almost half a millennium now. This is because our historic year of 1492 figures prominently on the prophetic abacus of those early millenarian calculators who did not hedge on figures. To them, 1492 stood for urgent stakes of cosmic consequence. It meant the end of this world, the closure of history, the beginning of a New World, and the opening to a celestial reign.[4] Instead, of course, they ended up with the earthly bathos of *our* New World and our not-so-celestial glories. Halfway between the

fall of Constantinopolis in 1453 and Columbus's 1492 dis-
oriented landfall, the apocalyptic arithmetic becomes more precise. In his 1472 *Chronography,* Gennadius Scholarius, the first
patriarch of Constantinopolis under Turkish rule, laid bare the
figures: the Sabbath of the world, its seventh millennium when
the curtain would rise on a heralded new age, was scheduled for
the year 1492, that is, seven thousand years after its creation
according to the Byzantine and Roman eras. In this reckoning, the
first year of the creation extends from the first of September, 5509
B.C. to the first of September of 5508 B.C. which, subtracted from
7000 yields the unquestionable figure of 1492. Or, in the summa-
tionist progression of the Holy Patriarch's inexorable providence,
5508 plus 1492 adds up to the reckoned hour. This horological
arithmetic finds its echo in the interpolated Slavonic version of
Pseudo-Methodius, what is commonly referred to as the Revelation of Methodius of Patara,[5] cited by Christopher Columbus in
his *Book of Prophecies*[6] to which we shall refer again shortly.

But both Gennadius Scholarius of Byzantium and the Slavonic
Pseudo-Methodius are latecomers to the computing tables. The
tallying tradition already is under way by the second century
when, as we have seen in our previous chapter, the imminently
expected end-time tarries beyond the imminent and expectation
lingers long enough to take on mathematical weight, augmenting
the factor of one by a thousand-fold. Thus, expectations of a here
and now projected into the future recombine with enduring promises from the past to become factors of a millennial ledger. I shall
explain and, in doing so, I shall rehearse some fundamental commonplaces of Old World accounting that would form the chrono-
metric foundations of our New World cultures and their temporal anxieties.

Although it has pagan antecedents and heretical offshoots, millenarianism, as we know it, is scripturally founded.[7] Confounded
by the tardiness of the promised New Age, the second century
probes the past for news of the heralded future, and those tidings
are not lacking. I and II Thessalonians, I Corinthians, and later,
of course, the Revelation of John the Divine announce the cosmic
hiatus. Referred to as a Time of Rest in II Thessalonians (1:7) and

as the Millennium in Revelation (20:4), this intermediate status is
to ensue from Christ's second coming, the Parousia that effects
the defeat of Antichrist (II Thessalonians 1:8; Revelation 19:19),
the resurrection of the dead saints, (I Corinthians, 15:23; I Thessalonians 4:16; Revelation 20:4), and the transfiguration of
saints still living (I Corinthians 15:51). After a thousand years'
reign with Christ on earth, there comes the Last Judgment and
the passage of the righteous into the incorruptible other life (I
Corinthians 15:25; I Thessalonians 4:17; Revelation 20:11–15).
These testamental proclamations of the Messiah's triumph, His
reign, and the New Creation are prefigured, in turn, in Hebraic
prophets such as Ezekiel and in noncanonical scripture of apocalyptic and paradisiacal eschatology such as I Enoch, II Esdras
(6:20–28), and II Baruch (29:4–8).

The classical text of millenarian arithmetic is Psalm 90:4,
where "with the Lord one day is as a thousand years." The
passage from this equation to a typology of the week in which the
six days of creation represent the time of this world and the
seventh day the time of the world to come derives from the Jewish
tradition founded on Genesis. The extrapolation of this typology
to the arithmetic of seven millennia as the total time of the world,
however, is not Jewish. It is founded rather on Hellenistic mathematics of the seven planets in conflation with the Babylonian
notion whereby each of the seven planets reigns over a corresponding cosmic era. In the synergism of this summation, the sum
of Jewish and Hellenistic-Babylonian coefficients yields a whole
greater than the accretion of those parts, thus giving us an eighth
day that follows the millennium and comprises the beginning of
another world. The earliest Christian manifestation of this
conflation occurs in the second-century computations of the
anonymous Epistle of Barnabas. The unknown Greek author
from Egypt writes:

> Of the sabbath he speaketh in the beginning of creation: And God
> made the works of his hands in six days, and he ended on the seventh
> day and rested on it. . . . Behold the day of the Lord shall be a
> thousand years. Therefore, . . . in six days, that is in six thousand
> years, everything shall come to an end. . . . He says to the Jews, it is

not your present sabbaths that are acceptable (unto Me), but the Sabbath which I have made, in the which, when I have set things at rest, I will make the beginning of the eighth day which is the beginning of another world. (XV.3–8)[8]

Although the Epistle of the Egyptian-Greek Barnabas is telling with regard to the arithmetic of last things, his aim, as Daniélou notes, was primarily to purify Christianity from residual elements of Judaism in his catechesis. It was another church historian, the Syriac Theophilus of Antioch, who, in the second century, placed millenarian computations in the context of ancient cosmology. In this context, Theophilus was among the first historians of theology to be seduced, in turn, by the theology of history. And his tabulations would prove most influential in church fathers like Iranaeus whose work entitled *Against Heresies* plays a decisive role within the development of the patristic tradition, the mainline millenarian tradition. In Theophilus's computations, the birth of Christ corresponds to the world's 5500th year. This being the middle of the sixth millennium, the 6000th year should initiate the messianic reign of the seventh millennium, with the 7000th year marking the end of the world and the beginning of the New World. Theophilus's calculus extends the end to the year 1500, granting this world a reprieve of eight years beyond the 1492 hour of reckoning figured by Byzantium's Greek Patriarch. Theophilus's arithmetic is echoed in Hippolytus, a Roman priest by some accounts,[9] a Syrian bishop, according to varying opinion.[10] Hippolytus has left us the first complete Christian exegesis to have survived. His *Commentary on Daniel* packs more than the ostensible aims implied in the title of his work. The Greek treatise targets apocalyptic impatience, seeking to dampen the eschatological zeal that raged at high pitch in the beginning of the third century. Hippolytus's arithmetic attempts to fend off imminent expectations by simultaneously echoing Theophilus and recapitulating the Epistle of Barnabas through a strategy of allegorical reading. He writes:

Now the ark has five cubits and a half in length, and these are the 5500 years at the end of which the Lord came. From his birth, then,

500 years have still to pass to make up the 6000, and then shall be
the end. (IV. 24)

Hippolytus, then, is a reluctant tabulator, and in that reticence
he prefigures a long line of orthodox moderation compelled to
intercede, numerically, on the side of patient anticipation as
against enthusiasts who would precipitate the end with prophetic
injunction and numerical invocation.

The Syrian tradition represented by the anonymous author of
the Barnabas Epistle, by Theophilus, and by Hippolytus is a milder
form of millenarianism. Its contemporaneous counterpart identified with Asia Minor counts in its ranks the third-century Tertul-
lian, a radical millenarian who could be considered the father of
Puritan nonconformity, and Lactantius, a converted Roman rhetorician often referred to as the "Christian Cicero." Focused primarily through Phrygia and the enthusiastic acolytes of Montanus, this
Asiatic tradition compounds numerical arithmetic with earthly
delights and fructiferous hyperbole, giving the millennium yet
more tempting urgencies as tantalizing as any in the fertile imagination of a Hieronymus Bosch. If the Syrian tradition identifies its
millenarianism with the more quiescent "Time of Rest" (II Thessalonians 1:7), the Asiatics are closer in line with the more frenzied
activity of abundant multiplication and yield of paradisiacal materiality. The millennium in this context spells an earthly inheritance
that proved a problem for early church fathers, but an inheritance
whose impulse survived their vigilance to justify the enticements of
New-World chiliasm (as millenarianism is often referred to by this
Greek variant in the New World) in the Vineyard of Franciscans in
New Spain and in the milk-and-honey-dipped New Canaan of
New England's Puritan divines. This paradisal inheritance was, in
fact, identified as Judaic and spurned as such by the church fathers.
(In this sense, too, the referral to various geographies of the American New World as New Israel was not accidental.) But, in its acts
of indictment and admonition, the more moderate tradition unwit-
tingly extended the life of millenarian materialism in the very act of
calling up visions and earthly delights to impugn and to admonish
those who envisioned them. Disapproving recension, then, ends up

as reiteration. The earliest target of this censure was also the proto-type of the later millenarian poor, portrayed in their zealous squa-lor by Norman Cohn's now-classic study, *The Pursuit of the Mil-lennium*. They were the Ebionites, adherents to Judaic messianism who impatiently anticipated the temporal cornucopia promised for the time of that awaited Kingdom. Although not the first, St. Jerome is the most explicit in the condemnation of this error: "The Jews and the Ebionites, heirs of the Jewish error, who have taken the name of the 'poor' through humility, understand all the de-lights of the thousand years in a literal sense" (LXVI.20; cited in Daniélou). What Jerome censures in the fourth century is what Iranaeus had admonished before him, namely, the tendency to transfer the plenitude promised by Hebrew Testament prophets such as Isaiah (65:20–25) and Amos (9:13) from the next world to a messianic millennium in this world. That irrepressible foreshort-ening would prove a sempiternal foundation for millenarian apoca-lyptics and their hungry hosts who would progressively narrow the temporal gap between their direful "here and now" and the prom-ised "then" with frenzied celerity. And understandably so, since what the good father Iranaeus rehearses in his second-century tract *Against Heresies* was bound to excite the appetite more than in-duce parenetic patience or forbearing contrition:

> The days will come in which vines shall grow, each having ten thou-sand branches and each branch ten thousand twigs, and in each twig ten thousand shoots, and in each one of the shoots ten thousand clusters and on every one of the clusters ten thousand grapes, and every grape when pressed will give five and twenty metretes of wine. And when any one of the saints shall lay hold of a cluster, another shall cry out, "I am a better cluster, take me; bless the Lord through me." In like manner . . . a grain of what would produce ten thousand grains, and every grain would yield ten pounds of clear, pure, fine flour. (III.33; cited in Daniélou)

Such irenic attempts to keep faithful expectations alive and to check enthusiastic impatience at the same time become institu-tionalized of necessity. Assurance of an end is a cornerstone of the Christian edifice put in place by Christ himself; and the purposive movement of Christian history has that end as desired goal, made more desirable at times by rift and dissonance that historical life introduces between the ultimately promised and the immediately endured, between deliverance and vicissitude. That institutionalization, like all institutions, aims at assuaging the conflictive stress and contrariety in competing impulses: faith and realization, expectancy and immediacy, patience and enthusiasm, abnegation and desire. Both elements of the binary are optimally valued and the institution must optimize the orderly unfolding, concert the disconcerted and the disconcerting, tame heterodoxy into orthodox orderliness without dulling the edge of faith or anesthetizing the edginess of fervent expectation. Clearly it is a precarious balance, and institutional hierarchies, whether in the Old World or the New, have succeeded only variably in the balancing of the millenarian impulse, usually through its incorporation by tacit acquiescence or outright appropriation. The American New World, especially its Puritan patrimony, is the unpredictable outcome of such mixed success (or variable failure, if one be so inclined). For at least half of the New World is founded on schismatic principles of protestation and its Protestantism, whereas the other half made its foundations spiritually plumb and theologically justified often by an adversary perspective toward the institutional orthodoxies of the moment. This does not mean, of course, that a millenarian explanation of the New World exhausts all that needs explaining. But it does mean that the articulated millenarian professions by its finders and founders must be duly countenanced, even when those finders and founders themselves may have been lost or foundering. Their belief in the course and outcome of their pilgrimage and its enterprise had the force of conviction rather than the wishfulness of probability. Or, to echo the frame of Hawthorne's phrasing with which we began, the way stations of their pilgrimage were indisputably within the jurisdiction of veracity, even if those jurisdictional boundaries circumscribed a "Ghostland." A *u-topia* or "Ghostland" it might have been, but to them it was undeniably a jurisdiction and a geography imbued with the spirit of the Holy Ghost and its promissory Ends.

The end, like most things in the New World, begins with Columbus. In his *Book of Prophecies* and dire epistles, Columbus articulates a number of topoi that throughout the Middle Ages, to which he so inextricably belonged, shaped millenarian expectations into conventional form. One of these conventions was the theme of *translatio,* a topos originally devised to explain the gradual passage of imperial authority and rule from East to West.[11] By the twelfth century, the theme of *translatio* we now call "Westering" itself becomes subsumed by those conventions as metaphor for a spatial displacement, a geographical corollary through which a spiritual pilgrimage leads this world to its appointed end, transporting its expectant faithful from the unregenerate Old World to the promised millennial New World. In his hopeful writings, *The Mystical Ark of Noah 4.9,* Hugo of St. Victor who, as canon of his Parisian monastery between the years 1115 and 1133 transformed St. Victor into a stronghold of orthodoxy, sums up the tradition with clear conviction:

> The order of place and the order of time seem to agree almost completely in the course of events. Thus it appears to be established by divine providence that what was done at the beginning of the ages, at the outset of the world, took place in the East, and finally, as time runs along to its End, the completion of events should penetrate even as far as the West. Hence we may acknowledge that the End of the world approaches because the sequence of events has reached the geographical end of the world. The first man was placed in the East, in the Garden of Eden already prepared, so that from this source his posterity might spread throughout the world.[12]

Hugo of St. Victor's "geographical end of the world," whose attainment had to translate into the temporal End as well, was Europe's Atlantic shore. Christopher Columbus, of course, came a bit farther and, in doing so, by his 1498 third voyage he was convinced that he had reached the end of the Orient, well beyond the starting point of Hugo's visionary pilgrimage. And, in believing himself East of Eden, surely the End, the temporal correlative of this geographical encirclement could not be very far off. That was, as I mentioned, on Columbus's third voyage. The year was 1498, the year of Savonarola's public burning in Florence in an attempt to quell the fires of prophetic zeal, the year in which

Albrecht Dürer completed his *Four Horsemen of the Apocalypse,*
and one year after John Cabot reconnoitered for England the
eastern shores of the North American continent.

Although the spirituality of Columbus's enterprise would inten-
sify with each successive voyage, there was an unmistakable sense
of mission and apostolic election in the mariner, even before he
first sailed West for the ends of the East which, for him, stood in
both literal and allegorical terms for the scriptures' "ends of the
Earth." In fact, the scriptural citation, Psalm 19:4 in our Revised
Standard version and 18:5 in the Latin Vulgate edition of the
Bible Columbus was using, figures no less than five times in his
Book of Prophecies.[13] As Columbus cited it, it reads: "In omnem
terram exivit sonus eorum, et in finis orbis terrae verba eorum."
In our Standard version it is rendered as: "Yet their voice goes
out through all the earth,/ and their words to the end of the
world." To paraphrase Heinrich Bullinger's 1556 *A Hundred
Sermons uponn the Apocalipse* that became so important to English Puritans, we could say Columbus was overtaken by the
"ends of the earth," even before he convinced himself of having
overtaken those ends when he *knew* he had reached the threshold
of Terrestrial Paradise at the mouth of the Orinoco River. In
general consensus, the historical canon points to the year 1489 as
clearly the documentable first instance in which Columbus manifests a spiritual mission and a crusader's commitment in the enterprise of the Indies which he was proposing to the Spanish Catholic monarchs at the time. In that year, Columbus was in the city of
Baza where the royal court was pursuing its own messianic crusade, the reconquest of the Iberian peninsula from the Moors.
Two Franciscan emissaries from Pope Innocent VIII, one of the
two being Father Antonio Millan, prior of the Monastery of the
Holy Sepulcher, brought threatening tidings from the sultan of
Egypt. He threatened actions of dire consequences against the
Holy City if the Spanish monarchs continued their campaign
against the Muslim community of Spain.[14] From that encounter
between Columbus and the two Franciscan fathers beneath the
city walls of Baza, the enterprise of the Indies, as the Genoese
mariner called it, must be devoted to the subvention of the con-

quest of Jerusalem and the restoration of Zion's Holy Temple. Columbus notes the assurances he received to this effect from the Catholic monarchs starting with a diary entry of 26 December 1492 during his first voyage. He does so repeatedly on or right after each of his subsequent three voyages, in his original will drafted between his second and third sailings, and, of course, in his *Book of Prophecies,* as well as in his letter of February 1502 to Pope Alexander VI.

Columbus's commitment to the recovery of Jerusalem was of a piece with his conviction that he had reached the "ends of the earth" East of Eden. It is of a piece, too, with Columbus's sense of an apostolic mission to carry the Word of the Gospel to parts of the world unknown until his Oceanic crossing. And all of these pieces come together in the *Book of Prophecies* to which I have so often alluded and should finally describe. Here, then, is the opening of *El libro de las profecias:*

> Incipit liber sive manipulus de auctoritatibus, dictis, ac sententiis, et prophetiis circa materiam recuperande sancte civitates, et monte Dei Syon, ac inventionis et conversionis insularum Indie, et omnium gentium atque nationum . . .

> [Here begins the book of a handful of authors, sayings, pronouncements, and prophecies concerning the recovery of the Holy City and God's Mt. Zion, and the discovery and conversion of the islands of the Indies and all peoples and nations.]

The *Book of Prophecies* was begun in 1501 with the help of a Carthusian monk, Father Gaspar de Gorritio, and was destined for the Spanish monarchs. Its end, like many prophecies, was never realized, and Their Royal Majesties never did receive it. To Columbus's typological understanding of history and historical events, it was imperative that his accomplishment be the proof of prophetic prognostications, the realization of visionary expectations long harbored. And it was important, too, to prove that this actualization of what had been prophesied for the agency of Columbus was indeed a step toward the eventual culmination of all prophecies' object, namely, the climactic end and the millennial beginning. In the terse overture just cited, Columbus encompasses the three key elements woven through the long prophetic tradition we have traced and its expectant scanning for the hopeful signs of the promised end: to wit, the recovery of Jerusalem, the geographical incorporation of all parts of the earth, and the conversion of all humanity to the light of the "true" faith. This worldwide inclusion would mean the realization of the "Universal Church" and would translate into prophecy's formulaic *unum ovile et unus pastor*—one flock and one shepherd—at which time a World Emperor (who, for the Iberian messianism of the moment had to be Ferdinand of Aragon) would engage and defeat the Antichrist on Mt. Zion, after which an Angelic Pope of a *renovated* church would lead the faithful flock into the promised time of a thousand-year bliss before the Last Judgment. This, in simple form, is the general plot of the Medieval tradition that Columbus knew so well and incorporated so diligently into his *Libro de las profecias* by way of citation, reference, and allusion. It is in this vein that he invokes an array of Classical and Hebraic authority, of scripture (canonical and apocryphal), and sundry ecclesiastical voices as diverse as St. Augustine and the Calabrian Abbot Joachim of Fiore, Pseudo-Methodius, and Cardinal Pierre d'Ailly, Nicholas of Lyra and Peter Lombard. The plot is tightly wrought and broadly documented. And, of course, this latest, and certainly the *last,* production of the cosmic drama could not play itself out except through the instrumentality and the providentially elect and amply prophesied, and most aptly named *Christoferens,* "the transporter or bearer of Christ" across the waters to the far shores of prophetic ends that abut the gates of a New Heaven and a New Earth. (Not to be outdone by the of course divinely determined symmetry between Columbus's "christopheric" name and his providential role, Cotton Mather, in his *Magnalia Christi Americana* [1702], would characterize John Winthrop, the first and, most symbolically, seven-time governor of the Massachusetts Bay Colony, as *Hermes Christianus,* after the Greek messenger god, duly baptized, of course.)[15] As already pointed out, Christoferens is how Columbus became progressively accustomed to signing his name as part of the enigmatic sigla of his signature.

In 1500, writing to the nurse of the ill-fated Prince John, heir-apparent of the Catholic monarchs, Columbus confesses:

> God made me the messenger of the New Heaven and the New Earth of which he spoke through St. John in the Apocalypsis, after having spoken of it through Isaiah; and He showed me to that location.[16]

A year later, in the cover letter that was to accompany the *Libro de las profecias,* Columbus reminds their highnesses of his providential appointment in nearly identical terms (pp. 79–89). And with this most humbly confessed admission, Columbus does more wonders for the New World "spot" he found than the Puritans' "Wonder-Working Providence" will have been willing to grant God's other chosen people and elect messengers in their more northerly New Earth. The "found" New World becomes articulated in its primal finder's confession in terms that make it consubstantial with the millennial dispensation of Isaiah's and John the Divine's "New World." A number of years later, the New World would be descried in analogous terms in the prognostications of Increase Mather, New England's ardently convinced millenarian (or chiliast, as was his wont) for whom the awaited end was most certainly and most literally imminent. I cite from a manuscript of Mather discovered in 1976. It is entitled "New Jerusalem" and dates from 1687:

> *Againe,* when New Jerusalem comes down from heaven, it is saide that the heaven and earth that now are, shall be no more, but a new heaven and a new earth: Rev. 21:1,2. There will then be a *New World,* another world wonderfully differing from what this is at present where we now live. (29)[17]

Columbus, of course, is fully cognizant of the steps and turns through which the prophetic script must arrive at its own and the world's apocalyptic last act. Accordingly, he rehearses the calculus with ingenuous faith and ingenious strategy, a combination undoubtedly founded in providential prompting. He calculates in earnest and the integers of his abacus span the sacral range of orthodoxy's gamut, lest anyone think to impugn his prophetic arithmetic with suspicions of heretical impatience. In the process, he marks the reckoned hour at a safe enough distance, a prudence

his New-World inheritors in New England and in Latinate America will not always emulate. He is, as you will remember, doing
his arithmetic in 1501, one year after Theophilus of Antioch's
second-century calculations would have all but mooted the need
for further figuring. I translate, once more, from Columbus's still
nearly Medieval and almost Renaissance Spanish in this section
of the *Book of Prophecies:*

> The sacred Scriptures attest in the Old Testament through the
> mouth of the prophets and in the New Testament through our Savior
> Jesus Christ that this world has to have an end. The signs for when
> this end should occur have been told by Matthew, Mark, and Luke.
> The prophets, too, had abundantly predicted it.
>
> From the world's creation, or from Adam till the Advent of our
> Lord Jesus Christ, there are five thousand three hundred, forty-three
> years, and three hundred eighteen days, according to the accounting
> of King Alfonso [Alfonso X, "the Wise," of Castille], which account-
> ing is held to be most certain. Following Pierre d'Ailly, in his
> *Elucidario astronomice concordie cum theologica et hystorica
> veritate,* Xth verba, and adding one thousand five hundred and one,
> we have six thousand eight hundred and forty-five. According to this
> calculation, there are but one hundred and fifty-five years remaining
> to complete seven thousand, at which time, as I said above following
> the cited authorities, the world will have to come to an end. (p. 81)

In closing Hugo of St. Victor's geographical circle, Columbus
thus closes the time of the world's pilgrimage, announcing the
good news of the end. Being the news that was long awaited, its
impact is myriad. For the most part, however, Columbus's
achievement spells a closure both of a time and of a geography.
His compatriot Amerigo Vespucci also knew he had reached a
New World and his editor cleverly entitled Vespucci's letters announcing his find *Mundus Novus,* after the usage first employed
on October 20, 1494 by Peter Martyr of Anghier in a letter to his
friend Borromeus. The usage, by the way, does not figure in
Columbus until August 1498, that is, during his third voyage. But
a world of difference, so to speak, sets Columbus's New World
apart from Vespucci's as we shall see in greater detail in our next
chapter. As we have already seen, however, Columbus's is the old
New World either as the farthest East that is West of everything,

or as the New World long prophesied of old in venerable anticipation. Vespucci's, on the other hand, is a new continent that doubles the size of the known hemisphere. Copernicus, born a year after the prognostications of the Byzantine Patriarch Gennadius Scholarius and already twenty-eight years old at the time of Columbus's prophetic calculations, did see something new in the good news of Columbus and the newer news of Amerigo Vespucci. But there was, too, something old already even in the novel vision of the Polish astronomer, something that had been so terribly disconcerting to the orthodox and orthodoxy's cosmic order that it was gripped tightly between the jurisdictional parentheses of that order for a very long time, lest the drama's plot be altered and the expected final act thwarted. The notion that the earth was not the center of the cosmos and that the course of its providential history was not identical to the history of the cosmos was already advanced some 1,800 years before the similar claims of the ill-starred Copernicus. Heliocentric astronomy had already been proposed in the fourth century B.C. by Aristarchus of Samos.[18] And Aristarchus himself, by the way, was no slouch when it came to the computing tables of time, having added 1/1623rd part of a day that Callippus had left out of his calculation of a 365¼-day year. That indispensable leap addendum comes to 0.89 minutes, or 53.23 seconds. But even this fraction was more than the time of day Copernicus would be given by those who brokered the ideological futures of a futurity on which our New World would be founded. Copernicus's *De Revolutionibus* proved revolutionary, indeed; so much so that the tailspin into which it sent the Protestant Puritans' ideological forefathers kept the Catholic Church from condemning it officially from its first publication in 1543 until after the end of the sixteenth century. On the other hand, Giordano Bruno was eventually burned at the stake by the Inquisition for revealing the Polish astronomer's theory in his Ash Wednesday sermon of 1584. Bruno was thrown into a dungeon in Rome, where he was lured from Venice, in 1592, exactly one hundred years after our Columbian *annus mirabilis,* and was burned eight years later on the threshold of the seventeenth century. The Catholic Church did not admit the Co-

pernican recycling of Aristarchus's idea until 1820. The former
Augustinian monk Martin Luther, quicker than most, assessed
the significance of Copernicus's work in 1539, four years before
its publication: "There is mention of a new astrologer who en-
deavors to prove that the earth, not the firmament, moves and
revolves in circles. . . . This crackpot wants to disrupt the whole
art of astronomy. Nonetheless, as the Holy Scriptures indicate,
Joshua ordered the sun, and not the earth, to stay still." John
Calvin, even less inclined to disruptions of preordained order
than Luther, simply asked: "Who can dare place the authority of
Copernicus above that of the Holy Scriptures?" And the distinguished German Humanist Philip Melancthon felt terribly cha-
grined by the audacity of such talk: "A certain man, eager for
novelty," Melancthon wrote, obviously oblivious to Aristarchus,
"or wishing to make ostentation of his ingeniousness, has come
to the conclusion that the earth moves, and proclaims that the
sun and the heavenly spheres do not move. To assert such a thing
publicly is to be lacking in honesty and decency."[19]

The drama occupying center stage at the time was providential
history's and, clearly, Copernicus did not figure in its plot. The
novelty of the New World was absorbed as novel on wholly other
terms. And even when the novelty had already been novel for two
centuries and well beyond the apocalyptic end-year of 1656
prophesied by Columbus, its promise for other-worldly possibilities was being enthusiastically proclaimed. I cite from the New
England divine Samuel Sewall's *Phenomena quaedam Apocalyp-
tica, Or some few Lines towards a description of the New
Heaven As It Makes those who stand upon the New Earth*
(1697):

> For when once *Christopher Columbus* had added this *fourth* to the
> other *Three* parts of the foreknown World; they who sailed farther
> Westward, arriv'd but where they had been before. The Globe now
> failed offering anything New to the adventurous Travailer; Or, how-
> ever, it could not afford another new World. And probably, the
> consideration of *America's* being *The Beginning of the East, and the
> End of the West;* was that which moved Columbus to call some part
> of it by the Name of *Alpha* & *Omega*. Now if the *Last Adam* did give

Order for the engraving of his own Name upon this *Last Earth;* 'twill draw with it great Consequences; even as such will, in time, bring the poor Americans out of their Graves, and make them live. (p. 61)[20]

Sewall's Edenic optimism for a millennial dispensation in the only *new* New World, or *Last Earth,* possibly may be somewhat belated. It is, nonetheless, symptomatic of the momentum generated by the conviction that a literal millennial Sabbath in Puritan New England for God's new chosen people was imminently inevitable. The Puritans were fully convinced of their errand out of the hopelessly declined Old World toward a rendezvous with destiny in a New World whose novelty promised the Next World so persistently longed for through the centuries: "The Land Was as the Garden of Eden, or Paradise, Before them: and Behind Them a Desolate Wilderness," Sewall writes in his *Phenomena* (p. 57) in an obvious reversal of scripture and of Milton's closing stanza in *Paradise Lost.*

The most ardent enthusiast for the impending end-time among the Puritan settlers was the minister of the Massachusetts Bay Colony's covenantal theocracy, John Cotton, who was to be seconded and succeeded in the imminence of his expectation by his son-in-law Increase Mather. The *New World* had to come in the New World, obviously, and the Puritans, like the spiritual founding fathers of Iberian America of a century earlier, saw themselves singularly privileged by history, by geography, and by God's grace for the experience. In 1639, probing anxiously all signs and arithmetical tables, John Cotton calculated in his *An Exposition upon the Thirteenth Chapter of the Revelation* that the appointed time would be in the year 1655, an end-line sum that differs from Columbus's calculus by only one impatiently foreshortened year. We do not know whether it was fortunate or unfortunate for John Cotton that he did not live long enough to see his anxieties confirmed and his most fervent expectations disappointed. Nonetheless, in that would-be *annus mirabilis,* the Puritan apologists for the "New England Way" in London publish John Cotton's treatise, and his friend Thomas Goodwin postpones the appointment with the millennial advent until 1700.

Increase Mather, in his 1710 *A Sermon Shewing that the Present Dispensations of Providence Declare that Wonderful Revolutions in the World are Near at Hand* (clearly, no relation to Copernican revolutions), asserts with an optimism whose incremental conviction belies its own cheerfulness that 1716 has to be the year: "So that in the year 456, there were Ten distinct Kingdoms in the *Roman* Empire; consequently from that Year we are to date the Commencement of Antichrist's Reign: which is to continue from first to last but 1260 Years, which added to 456, brings us to the year 1716" (p. 23).[21] The year 456, according to Mather, marks the turning point in the purity of the church, and 1260 years are derived from scripture typologically, primarily from Daniel's apocalyptic book and from Revelation 11:2–3. The figure 1260 is significant, too, in the prophetic tradition associated with the Calabrian Abbot Joachim de Fiore and the Franciscan Spirituals so significant to Christopher Columbus's apocalyptic ledger.[22] Like the expectant faithful of the second century, the anxiety of New England's settlers was not over the possibility that the world would end, but over the obstinate tardiness with which the millennial end was delaying its advent. And, like the second century, the anxieties of the founding Puritans found a venue, a safety release, in the parenetic injunction of metaphor and *figural* transfiguration of the end that was *literally* anticipated in the beginning. The prophetic destiny of the founding fathers would become manifest in alternate ways, and the anxieties of that providential digression would become articulated in the contrite language of probation and the exhortation of the Jeremiad, a genre that would become naturalized in the New World with elaborate and stentorian resonances.

New Spain, we should remember, kept the founding Puritans of New England from being unique in this regard a century earlier. The prophetic vein and apocalyptic verve, as well as the attendant anxieties and contrite Jeremiads in Latinate America have been documented by the late John Leddy Phelan in his *The Millennial Kingdom of the Franciscans in the New World*,[23] to which the reader is referred for a more southerly version of this "ghost story."

Clearly, when Columbus named one of the capes on the island of Cuba *Alpha and Omega* on his first voyage, it is doubtful that he anticipated so many ends (and so many beginnings) for the New Earth he thought to have discovered and the New Earth he was convinced to have heralded.

Having begun with Hawthorne and Wallace Stevens, I should like to close this chapter with a few lines from the latter that might resound all too echoic by now. I cite from "The Comedian as the Letter C," where Christopher Columbus too is so preponderantly inscribed as prototype of peregrine *viatores* whose oceanic pilgrimage took them into the *plus ultra* of transworldly destinations. Stevens declaims:

> He was a man made vivid by the sea
> A man come out of luminous traversing,
> Much trumpeted, made desperately clear,
> Fresh from discoveries of tidal skies,
> To whom oracular rockings gave no rest.
> Into a savage color he went on. (p. 61)

CHAPTER III

New Worlds

Renovations, Restorations,
Transmigrations

History unfolds, in the prophetic tradition, by dint of a dialectical oscillation between becoming and overcoming, declension and regeneration, lapse and redemption, dis-grace and grace. The Elohist, or Jahwist, record moves from catastrophe and chastisement to antistrophe and hopeful expectation. This is the dialectical lurching that traces, as well, the progress of the New World's historical plot. "Any history written on Christian principles," R. G. Collingwood noted, "will be of necessity universal, providential, apocalyptic, and periodized."[1] The most hopeful soundings, it would appear, are taken at depths of bathos. The millenarian movements certainly bear out the crises-driven course of prophetically based strides. Historians and anthropologists as ideologically diverse as Norman Cohn and Peter Worsley concur on this point.[2]

The *renovatio mundi* about which Marselio Ficino wrote to his friend Paul of Middelburg in 1492 proclaiming the arrival of the Age of Gold has something inescapably suggestive in its timing for students of the American New World, though those resonances may well have been outside Ficino's Platonist humanism at the threshold of the Renaissance.[3] The Renaissance as a whole and not only Ficino's, of course, is yet another face of the irrepressible human impulse for cosmic regeneration. In this sense, the Renaissance, like the Reformation, is as much a culmination of Medieval Europe's apocalyptic drive toward a new dispensation as it is the product of Antiquity's rediscovery. The *plenitudo temporum* is certainly as real for Savonarola as it is for his fellow Florentine Ficino. And although Savonarola's dire Jeremiad echoes from the depths of prophetic anxiety and his contemporary Ficino's optimistic tidings proclaim the felicitous dawning of a Golden Age, both coincide in the annunciation of an imminent new era and a new world. The woeful apocalypticism of the eschatologist and the cheerful prognosis of the Platonist-Cabbalist are focused on the advent of a renewal and the redemption of a historical time whose nadir, or apotheosis, made the dawning of a new status inevitable.

Evangelical regeneration has had a clockwork periodicity in Christian history. Pauline theology, as we have seen in our previous discussion, programs self-overcoming, or movement beyond the individual and communal here-and-now, into the course of history's unfolding. Starting with the third century, reformation becomes a concomitant of renovation and the degree of zeal with which renovation is undertaken differentiates often the orthodox from the heretical. Renewal's enthusiasm may well be the most common element that binds heterodox impulses with the orthodox mainstream. It is the commonality that would bring, for example, Cardinal Ximénez de Cisneros, Spain's patron of the late fifteenth-, early sixteenth-century Catholic Reformation, face-to-face with such radical eschatologists as Charles de Bovalles. The cardinal and royal confessor—and zealous, some might say fanatical, crusader of Granada—of course, was also the avid promoter at court of Christopher Columbus, that other apocalyptic enthusiast who obsessively prophesied more than one kind of New World and Golden Age via the cosmogonic imagism of Pierre d'Ailly, the prophetic mirror of Joachim of Fiore, and the spiritual order this Calabrian's legacy spawned throughout the Middle Ages.

The prototypes of prophetic enthusiasm for *renovatio* were the third-century Novatians, also known by their Greek name of καθᾰρόι (katharoi), a name whose literal English translation,

"Puritans," would be derisively given to the most avid restorationists of the Protestant Reformation. Their pilgrimage would wend its way not only to a renewed world, but to a transoceanic New World. Europe's new-worlding tradition is of a continuous weave, tightly knit with skeins of prophetic apocalypticism that bind Novatian zeal, Joachimite arithmetic, orthodox eschatology, Reformationist enthusiasm, and Humanist expectation. The shape of this Humanist expectancy, of course, antedates Ficino's Renaissance Platonism. As we have seen in our first chapter, *renovatio* as eschatological necessity programmed by Providential history and its apocalyptic promise already subsumes Antiquity's periodic restoration of the cosmos by the third century. And by the time of Origen, Christian eschatology goes by the technical term ἀποκατάστασις, the Stoic's astral periodicity and cosmic *restoration*.

The hemisphere's western continent that woke up one morning in 1492 to a trinity of caravels at its shores would become the New World, an objective correlative of Europe's new-worlding zeal, an antitype to its typology, a realization of Europe's prophetic pilgrimage toward the ends of the End of its enthusiasms. The confounded inhabitants of the new-found world would ultimately end up in the Franciscans' and the Puritans' ledger as "the hidden, final, holy people" of a Golden Age whom the Latin poet Commodianus willed to the Kingdom of heaven on Earth in the fifth century.[4] We shall be examining this appropriative transformation further in due course. Suffice it to say, for now, that the conflated cyclicalism of pagan Antiquity and linear progressivism of prophetic, providential history yoke the renovation implicit in their temporal program to a spatial geographical movement that is analogously cyclical (circumnavigation of the globe by Hugo of St. Victor's westering pilgrimage already discussed) as well as progressive (the movement from a degenerated Old World toward a regenerative New World). This spacio-temporal convergence of the cyclical and the progressive becomes explicitly articulate in one of Renaissance England's most novelty-struck renovators and cosmogonic restorers, as the titles of his labor aver: *Instauratio Magna,* which includes his projected work as well as the two parts actually completed, the *De Augmentis Scientiarum* (1623, expanded version of *The Advancement of Learning*, 1605), and the *Novum Organum* (1620). In this Francis Bacon we read:

> For although they [the ancients] had knowledge of the antipodes . . . yet that mought be by demonstration, and not in fact; and if by travel, it requireth the voyage but of half the earth. But to circle the earth, as the heavenly bodies do, was not done nor enterprised till these later times: and therefore these times may justly bear in their word . . . *plus ultra* in precedence of the ancient *non ultra*. . . . And this proficience in navigation and discoveries may plant also an expectation of the further proficience and augmentation of all sciences, because it may seem that they are ordained by God to be coevals, that is, to meet in one age. For so the prophet Daniel, speaking of latter times foretelleth, *Plurimi pertransibut, et multiplex erit scientia*: as if the openness and through-passage of the world and the increase of knowledge were appointed to be in the same ages.[5]

The periodic, cyclical *renovatio* of the ancients becomes displaced, then, from its immutable circumscription of *non ultra* to a *plus ultra* of circumnavigation. Once the providentially ordained transit through the "openness and through-passage of the world" is negotiated in "these later times," as Bacon's prophet Daniel typologically adumbrates, new-worlding becomes tantamount to other-worlding. Francis Bacon, early precursor of our progressively unbounded scientific modernity, as sensibility of his historical moment, is also the belated child of the *devotio moderna* and *its* restorative innovation preparatory for the imminently anticipated other world of eschatology's *plus ultra*. What Bacon refers to as "these later times" are indeed times belated in multifarious senses. In one of these, Bacon emerges as the precocious and prescient augur of a cultural complex that will subsume the multiplicity of the *plurimi pertransibut et multiplex scientia* into its insatiable exuberance and rage: the Baroque of the seventeenth century. Yet, straddling as he does the centurial threshold, Bacon is also very much an epigone, a latecomer to what he calls "these later times," these being not only the apocalyptic end-times of prophecy's eschatology but also the epoch of a belated Renaissance in England that, as earlier in Italy, Spain, and other European countries, comprises multiple impulses that are at once anachronistically coeval and symbiotically antithetical. After all, the pagan Renaissance of classical Humanism is itself a discovery, albeit inadvertent, as is the wont of discoveries with greatest repercussion, a discovery precipitated, ironically, by orthodoxy's Christian zeal for the restorative conservancy of a disordered order. It was on 8 February 1438 that the Byzantine emperor and his numerous retinue arrived in Venice seeking the succor of the Roman West against the threatening Ottomans, bringing along the promissory tidings of a reunited Christendom divided since 1054. The Greek contingent was received by the Greek-named Roman pontiff Eugenius IV, himself and the papacy being under siege by a reformation-minded Council at Basel a hundred years before Luther. Eugenius IV, already declared "the Beast of the Apocalypse" by the Bishop of Prague and the leaders of the Hussite revolt, put the best face on his predicament to receive the Greeks at Ferrara. There, the plague of theological punditry, joined after eight months by the incurable and sempiternal plague itself that Thomas Mann would still be novelizing in our own era, forced the Council to accept Cosimo de Medici's invitation to Florence (1439). All the emperor's Trojans and all the pope's men, as history proved, could not put what was sundered together again. But more than one historian dates the birth of what is a rebirth, Latinately called the Renaissance, from that influx of learned Hellenism into the Medicis' Florence. And Marselio Ficino, himself possessed of a *multiplex scientia* that gleefully conjoined Plato, the Jewish Cabbala, and Hermes Trismegistus, would pun with renascent alacrity: "I have two fathers. The corporeal to whom I owe my birth [nascimento], and Cosimo de Medici, to whom I owe my rebirth [renascimento]." Ficino's quip would not escape Erasmus's perspicuity. Roterdam's reform-minded Latinist would rebaptize pagan Humanism's Renaissance by subsuming Ficino's born-again enthusiasm into that *Christi philosophia* that resonates so unmistakably, as Marcel Bataillon has so voluminously documented,[6] in Spain's Catholic Reformations and in England's Puritan restorations. Erasmus will query in his *Paraclesis:* "Quid autem aliud est *Christi philosophia,* quam ipse *renascentiam vocat,* quam instauratio bene condite naturae? [What is the *Christi philosophia* but a renaissance, a renovation of nature as it was created?]."[7] With one inquisitive stroke, Erasmus not only baptizes Ficino's Humanist Renaissance, but he also naturalizes it. The *renovatio mundi,* thus, passes as matter of course into the nature of things, as much inevitable and as intense a desideratum as the *renasci denuo* the perplexed Nicodemus hears from the lips of his Messiah (John 3:3–7).

If Cosimo de Medici opened the gates of Florence unto the *instauratio* of Classical Antiquity, his son, Lorenzo, endeavored to redeem his city from the invective of Florence's most famous and embattled native son, Dante. That fulmination occurs in the opening lines of the *Inferno*'s Canto XXVI. Suggestively for our purposes, this is the same canto in which Dante condemns Ulysses to the infernal flames for his daring transgression beyond the pillars of Hercules against the ancient admonition inscribed there: *Ne plus ultra,* a proscription whose violation Francis Bacon applauds in his magnifications and epistemological advancements. Canto XXVI concludes with Ulysses's ship in sight of the only land mass in the boundless sea of the southern hemisphere: the Mount of Purgatory, as history would indeed prove that hemisphere to be for its natives and for many of its conquerors, certainly so for Columbus, its "discoverer." Rather than intending to prophesy the Atlantic's future, however, Dante is cursing the Homeric hero and his ilk for their insatiable curiosity in pursuit of knowing, a curse that inadvertently also augurs the Hellenization of what was for Dante an already cursed Florence at the beginning of the fourteenth century. The Florentine who does prophesy Columbus, even as he seeks to redeem Ulysses in a palinode that might well have been directed at Dante is Luigi Pulci. Pulci's ironic wit and irreverent rendering of epic high seriousness into a romance epic of the people's vernacular as profane, though, perhaps, not as divine, as Dante's, seeks to undo Dante's curse upon Ulysses and those who would venture into the *plus ultra.* Writing in Laurentian Florence, Pulci works by a different light than Dante's; one could say by a diabolical, Luciferian light. I cite

from Canto XXV of Pulci's *Morgante Maggiore*. The demon
Astarotte, Lucifer's accomplice in rebellion and damnation, a duo
not unlike the double flame Ulysses and Diomedes in the incipit
of the *Inferno*'s Canto XXVI, addresses Rinaldo on the interdict
of *ne plus ultra*:

> Know that this theory is false; his bark
> The daring mariner shall urge far o'er
> The western wave, a smooth and level plain
> Albeit the earth is fashioned like a wheel
> Man was in ancient days of grosser mold,
> And Hercules might blush to learn how far
> Beyond the limits he had vainly set
> The dullest sea-boat soon shall wing her way,
> Men shall descry another hemisphere.
> Since to one common center all things tend,
> So earth, by curious mystery divine
> Well balanced, hangs amid the starry spheres.
> At our antipodes are cities, states,
> And thronged empires, ne'er divined of yore.
> But see, the Sun speeds on his western path
> To glad the nations with expected light.

Echoes of Hugo of St. Victor's westering pilgrimage resound
unmistakably Pulci's "glad" tidings for the unsuspecting world of
Europe's antipodes. Pulci completed his poem more than a decade before 1492. Columbus was then still off Guinea sounding
and charting Africa's Atlantic coast for King John II, his Portuguese patron to whom, some years earlier, in a letter of 25 June
1474, another Florentine, Paolo dal Pozzo Toscanelli, had already proposed a shorter way to the land of spices by a western
route "than that which you are making by Guinea."[8] Six years
after Columbus's successful return from his first voyage beyond
the pillars of Hercules, the *Morgante Maggiore* will figure among
the cursed objects Savonarola's Lenten youth brigades commit to
the pyre in the Piazza della Signoria on the final day of Carnival,
7 February 1498. Just over three months later, 23 May,
Savonarola himself will be consumed by flames in the same Piazza. His prophetic legacy and apocalyptic zeal will outdistance
Lorenzo's Humanism in the history of Florence and of Western

Europe. (Every year until 1703, on the morning of 23 May, the Piagnoni, Savonarola's party of lamentations, will scatter flowers in the spot of the fiery friar's immolation.) Lorenzo de Medici and Savonarola embody the antitheses not only of Florence, but of Renaissance Europe. It is strangely ironic that the secular Humanist should die in the year the eschatologist prophet prophesied that he would and that the year should be 1492. It is suggestive, too, that Lorenzo should have sought the last sacraments and his death-bed absolution from his uncompromising antagonist. Tradition varies as to whether Savonarola did or did not absolve the dying Lorenzo.

For any student of the New World, these vagaries of history are significant precisely because in the race among the multiple impulses of the Prophet Daniel's Baconian *plurimi pertransibut* that dashed toward the New World, Dante overtakes Pulci, Savonarola overtakes Lorenzo de Medici, and Luther's revolution outruns the revolutions of Copernicus. And, even though the prophetic and providentialist ethos endures all manner of chastisement in the experiential reality of its New World encounter, ultimately, the ideological scaffolding that sustains the edifice of explanation and self-sanction for the Old World's enterprise in the New is constructed with the lapidary and scriptural elements of Europe's prophetic tradition and Judeo-Christian mythology. And this is why the most significant manual that guides Columbus in his obsessive project is the spectral and imagistic *Imago Mundi* of the Cardinal Pierre d'Ailly. Columbus's personal copy contains 898 marginal notations in the Admiral's hand, a relatively preponderant referential base when we consider that the total number of postils Columbus made in all his books amount to 2,125.[9]

Clearly, something in the *Imago Mundi* compelled Columbus for it to become his fitting *vademecum* throughout his peregrinations. One suspects it might be because Pierre d'Ailly epitomizes that enchanted blend of Medieval mythos and scientific ethos that, eventually, would naturalize and appropriate the New World and, in doing so, legitimate its own enterprise *ad libitum et ad majorem Dei gloriam*. Willful righteousness conjures a potent alchemy, and d'Ailly operated with irrepressible energy in a

fourteenth-, fifteenth-century context that demanded as much
from a combination of wile and conviction as did Renaissance
Europe a half century later. Father Bartolomé de Las Casas, in the
second chapter of his *Historia de las Indias,* notes that d'Ailly,

> great theologian, philosopher, mathematician, astrologer, cosmo-
> grapher, . . . greatly influenced Columbus and *confirmed all the
> past* . . . I believe that among those of the past, this doctor moved
> Christopher Columbus the most towards his enterprise; the book
> [*Imago Mundi*] . . . was so familiar to Christopher Columbus, that all
> of it did he note and mark on the margins, writing there many things
> that he read and collected from others. This very old book many times
> did I have in my hands, taking from it a number of things written in
> Latin by the Admiral.[10]

As the sixteenth-century Dominican father notes, d'Ailly "confirms the past" for Columbus, a confirmation of the past the
mariner takes toward the future and the *plus ultra* of its New
Worlds.

Like the Medioaevum and the Renaissance that he straddled,
then, Columbus's innovative impulse derives its sanction and impetus from a "confirmation of the past." Reformation is in good
measure a confirmation and not just in the lexical semantics implied by the recursivity of the terms *renovatio* and *restauratio.*
Through Pierre d'Ailly, Columbus is the beneficiary of a *modernity* that consciously termed itself as such and that, like all programs and ethoi of modernisms, exhibits a progressive movement
whose vanguard is bound by an ineluctible continuity to the past.
I refer to the mid-fourteenth-century Ockhamist school of philosophy at Oxford that called itself the *via moderna,* after Abé-
lard's designation of the conceptualism he practiced three hundred years earlier, and to the *devotio moderna,* also of the mid- to
late fourteenth century, practiced by the Brethren of Common
Life at Windesheim and Deventer in the Netherlands. Though the
legendary razor William of Ockham took to theology in his
Centiloquium theologicum, doing Luther five theses better and a
century earlier, would find its nominalist tenets put into practice
by the *devotio moderna,* the most famous of the Brethren,
Thomas à Kempis, would react against philosophy's pernicious-

ness for the faith by writing his *Imitatio Christi*. Inadvertently, of course, Kempis was confirming that threatening differentiation the Franciscan William of Ockham aimed to reintroduce between philosophical and theological truths, between reason and faith.

D'Ailly journeyed to Deventer as papal legate to the Germanic people in 1413 and spoke in defense of the Brethren of the Common Life. His support and encouragement, in fact, led to the first written constitution of the *devotio moderna,* a constitution whose preamble acknowledges d'Ailly by name, inasmuch as the document "has been approved . . . and confirmed by Peter d'Ailly, cardinal of Cambray."[11] As for the Cardinal's Ockhamism, the opportunistic pragmatism that he practiced certainly attests to his command over contingency. It confirms his terminist harmonization with the contingent at the peril of the transcendent and the universal. His conciliar politics in an age wracked by papal schism found d'Ailly always ahead. And though he would have few friends in his ever-climbing career, he certainly influenced many people and maximized the return on the clericy of his diplomatic investments, at one point holding as many as fourteen benefices. Eschewing constancy for mutability, he denied papal infallibility and rejected, too, the immutable nature of conciliar judgments. Freed from theoretical imperatives of the universal, he translated nominalist philosophy into opportune practice of the particular. His own success is an articulate monument to the efficacy of the experiential. Able to transfer Ockham's razor from the slippery epistemologies of pure to the expedient empiricism of practical reason three centuries before Hobbes and Locke, d'Ailly emerged at once as equivocal and richly ambiguous embodiment of the nominalist *via moderna* and of the equally experiential *devotio moderna*. That the first aimed at the efficacious undoing of generality's universals, thus leading to a convivio with the complex and its unpredictable contingencies, and that the second, the *devotio moderna,* sought a return to primitive simplicity of an early and uncomplicated Christian ethos did not daunt the Cardinal. Nor did these contradictions prove daunting to his avid acolyte Christopher Columbus, who incarnated these ambivalences with willful conviction.

If dogma be what makes for self-righteousness, righteousness is the mechanism by which contradictions are dissolved and one's worldly actions find their justification; and self-justification, in turn, is the surest venue to legitimacy for one's faithful conviction. The circularity of this process did not deter the circumspect d'Ailly, nor would it discomfit Columbus or dispirit his conquering and colonizing progeny in the New World, whether Spiritual Franciscan or enthusiastic Puritan. Living as we are today in an age that we designate *postmodern,* either through the insight of lucidity or the mystification of delusion (or, more likely, both), we can discern that the cutting edge of nominalism's *via moderna* and the edgy zeal of a renascent primitive Christianity's *devotio moderna* comprise a double-edged ideological contrivance whose thrust would open up a New World for the world's irrepressible urge for *renovatio.* In this sense, our American New World is a congenitally *modernist* project whose impetus, *pace* our protestations and rhetorical postures, has yet to play itself out or abate into cultural or ideological exhaustion. The drive to "make it new" and the geographic possibilities of a *plus ultra* or manifest destiny may be circumscribed by the planetary horizon already overtaken. But the ideological, which is also to say rhetorical, space remains as vast and as righteously claimed as ever. The *via moderna,* transmigrated to a New World of its yearned-for experience, has become transmogrified into a new and expedient nominalism that views experience as terminist and as language, that is to say, as rhetorical figuration, and sees linguistic nomination as *de*terministic of experience. The *devotio moderna,* however, may no longer proffer the charity of its primitive simplicity sought after by the born-again puritanism of its early practitioners, but we certainly have no lack of what Valéry would call our *terribles simplificateurs* whose righteousness, libidinal and evangelical, sustains ideologies and rhetorics that justify political, economic, and territorial mastery, law and order, dictatorial left- and right-wing righteousness, and imperial hubris in hemispheric affairs. The New World, as the Old World's modernist legacy, then, seems inalienably linked to that providential history of prophetic and eschatological zeal that found and founded a transoceanic terrain to domesticate and bend to the willful and purposive ends of its progressivist pilgrimage. The *via moderna* and the *devotio moderna* would eventuate equally in Spain's Catholic renovation and in trans-Alpine Europe's Protestant Reformation. Both, in turn, would serve in conquering a geographical New World as objective correlative and confirmation of the righteous justification of each. The Catholic conquest would see the New World as compensatory terrain for the ground lost to the Ottoman expansion, whereas in Reformationist Europe, Protestant Puritanism would translate America into the theological, that is to say, ideological and rhetorical, concomitant of a *renovatio* that assured a worldly space for other-worldly ends. Columbus, of course, embodies both projects as primal precursor and wayward pilgrim.

The haunting ambivalence that bedevils Columbus's ends and means will resonate as damning ambiguity in the means and ends of Europe's project to conquer and save the New World. The Admiral's Christological devotion to the primitivist church tenets of the *devotio moderna* have been amply documented by Alain Milhou in his compendious *Colón y su mentalidad mesianica en el ambiente franciscanista español.*[12] His experiential, worldly pragmatism is virulently emphasized, not without some spleen, by Ramón Iglesias.[13] There is ample evidence in Columbus's acts and writings to sustain both Milhou and Iglesias and their respective modes of seeing enterprising Europe's primal entrepreneur in the New World. The reduction of this ambivalent precursor to one or other term of his complexity would border on intellectual penury. There is, indeed, something maniacal about Columbus and his drivenness. In this sense, he is prototype and epitome of the *renovatio mundi* that in the New World finds its terminist nomination as end-oriented modernism: an impetus driving and driven by ends that admit of no disorientation, even when, as in Columbus's case, the purported orient it has as its object proves to be an unprevisioned occident. One could read Columbus in this regard as our first line "Orientalist" of colonial empire after Marco Polo. The provisions made by Providential grace suffice in Columbus's case to countermand any empirical obstacle or contingency. Thus, even though Columbus is thoroughly infected, via d'Ailly, with the experiential pragmatism of the *via moderna*'s Ockhamist nominalism, its contagion does not suffice to disabuse him of the *devotio moderna*'s ideological determinations that suffuse his providentialist and eschatological enthusiasms. In this dual and duplicitous sense, Columbus is our prototypical New World modernist: he is suspicious but not self-suspecting. And in this regard, he is as much forefather to missionary conquerors of Catholic Iberia as he is to conquering missionaries of Puritan England. For the object of Columbus's suspicion is the "universalist" science of an old Scholasticism whose doxology, hardened into orthodoxy, proscribed any aperture to worlds beyond the syllogistic "realism" of its doctrinal ratiocinations. Acolyte of nominalist modernity, Columbus claims to trust, instead, in the simpler practicalities of experience. And, as inspired devotee of a simpler faith, he entrusts his project to a "spiritual intelligence" of divine election rather than to doctrinal erudition of the Salamanca "doctores" who kept him waiting, only to dismiss his proposed enterprise with scholarly indecision. In his mistrust of Platonist "realism" and doctrinal orthodoxy, Columbus prefigures, with expedient practicality, the conquering hordes his accomplishment would unleash onto the New World. In his simpler, devotional spirituality, he is in synchrony with the Spiritual Franciscans who often succored him and with the primitive Christianity of those latter-day Novatians, the Puritans, who would feel as elect in their vocation and New-World errand as Columbus himself. It is with an acute sense of vindication that Columbus writes to the Spanish sovereigns on 13 September 1501 a letter probably never sent, but included in the Admiral's *Book of Prophecies*, reminding Their Highnesses of the seven years, both real and symbolic, that he spent waiting the pleasure of the "authorities" only to be left suspended by endless deliberations that never did arrive at a final decision, thereby proving the professors' academic qualifications, as Daniel Boorstin knowingly puts it.[14] But God's will, Columbus notes, would not be denied, nor could what was prophesied in the scriptures of the prophets.[15] And a year later, in a letter of 2 June 1502, Columbus would remind the sovereigns of the primacy of "divine intelligence" and individual experience over the doctrines of doctoral science: "Allegamos más grande enseñanza de aquello que deprendemos por nuestra propia espirenzia [We derive greater knowledge from that which we learn by our own experience]."[16]

His own declarations notwithstanding, Columbus's nominalism was rendered nominal by an irrepressible realism that colored his vision and plagued his obsession.[17] And although he claimed to eschew learned abstractions and doctrinal universals in favor of experience and contingency, he would, in fact, be upstaged by the most contingent of coincidences (literally nominalist, in this case) that rendered his pilgrimage a symptom of the *via antiqua* rather than a venture to new horizons through a *via moderna*. In this peripety, his unsuspecting antagonist would be yet another Florentine, Amerigo Vespucci, and yet one more academic, Martin Waldseemüller, whose studies at the University of Freiburg perverted his geographical interests with poetic contagion and philological obsessions. I shall explain.

If the prophetic tradition rests on the visionary and on the insight of prophets into provisions made by Wonder-Working Providence for the purposive history of its chosen people, prophecy and prophesying ultimately derive from nomination, from what is said and the language of what is said. A prophet, then, is by etymology a "nominalist" in this sense, literally one who speaks before, a προ-φήτης (pro-phetes), as the Greek lexis would have it. But, beyond this etymological reduction, prophetic nomination parts ways with nominalism. For prophetic utterance emanates not from individual contingency but from universal necessity. As in Columbus's proclivities for providential explanations, the events and individuals of prophetic history are understood as necessary fragments of a universal schema and an inexorable unfolding toward a transcendent goal. And, in this sense, Columbus's declared adherence to empiricist, experiential practicalities of the *via moderna* is mitigated and outright compromised by his enthusiasm for the *devotio moderna*'s ineluctable necessity of historical occurrences. As in the John Donne I invoked early on, all occasions become for Columbus "emergent occasions" whose contingency is ruled by the necessity of divine determinations. And prophecy, of course, emerges as the indispensable instrument of necessary conveyance. This is why in his *Book of Prophecies* Columbus would pursue a compendium that gave his achievements the providential sanction of inevitability, attributing all his accomplishments thereby to prophetic injunction—"para la hesecución de la ynpresa de las Yndias ne me aprovechó rasón, ni matemática, ny mapamundos; llenamente se cunplió lo que diso Ysayas [in carrying out the enterprise of the Indies, I was served neither by reason, nor by mathematics, nor by world map; simply, what Isaiah said was fulfilled]."[18]

As I have intimated already, the true prize of nominalist contingency and of the peripeties of language would go not to Columbus but to Amerigo Vespucci; and the demiurge of that benefaction is the playful and plotting scrivener Martin Waldseemüller. If the universalist realism of necessity has its necessary and sufficient reason, happenstance contingency makes no less sense of the insensate turns fate visits on history. Unlike Vespucci, Columbus had an investment in a cosmological order whose ideological entailments proscribed the divestiture of received notions. Despite his claims in favor of individual, pragmatic experience, Columbus saw his own acts as prescribed by sacred prophecy and pagan augury alike. I have already noted that his compilation of a book of prophecies was precisely a way of assuring that this was the case, a reaching after a legitimacy grounded on scripture's and augury's venerable time, a time whose fullness had come and whose culmination is to be wrought by his own achievement. More of a Platonist, really more of a messiah, than an Aristotelian in this regard, Columbus never managed to move beyond cosmography and into geography. The cosmos he discerned was for him the one already graphed and ideologically charted. Whether in the Cathay or Cipangu of Medieval territoriality, or in the sacred terrain of the prophetic and eschatological New World, Columbus knew himself to be exploring the far and farthest shores of a cosmography already emplotted. The passage from cosmography into geography is brooked by Vespucci.

Unlike the Trinitarian and laic Tertiary Columbus, Vespucci could be called a "tertrarchist" because of his four voyages to

what he claimed, and so managed in his four letters to convince
the world, was a fourth and as yet unknown part of the geographical *orbis terrarum*. Though in his first letter (18 July 1500), believed to have been destined for Lorenzo di Pier Francesco de
Medici, son of Lorenzo the Magnificent who succeeded him in
1492, Amerigo Vespucci still speaks of his first voyage having
taken him "to a land which might be bounded by the eastern
parts of Asia,"[19] by his third letter (1502) to his Florentine patron, he writes unequivocally of his third voyage: "In effect, my
navigation extended to a fourth part of the world."[20] Shortly
after, in that most widely disseminated compendium of his four
voyages entitled *Mundus Novus,* Vespucci speaks with the self-
assurance of one who knows he has revolutionized the world. In
the meantime, Columbus, now in his fourth and final voyage, still
speaks of Cathay, of the "Indies," and of being only nineteen
days sailing from the River Ganges.[21] Imperial Spanish official-
dom, because it suited its colonial interests, was already well
under way in the institutionalization of such a nomenclature
through councils, houses of trade, and governing bodies, all of
which contained "Indies" in their titles.[22] Clearly, imperial and
colonial interests had very high stakes in mercantile expansion to
an already *known,* but as yet not accessed, Asiatic world. It is
revealing, in this regard, that by 1535 official historians such as
G. Fernández de Oviedo, Emperor Charles's official "Chronicler
of the Indies," would render the history of the New World in
such a way as to banish all claims by Columbus and his heirs to
any rights of discovery. What was "discovered," according to
Oviedo, were the Hesperides, ancient kingdom of the Hispanic
king Hésperos and, therefore, these were no new lands at all but
old Spanish territories recovered (*Historia general y natural de las
Indias,* Bk. II. chap. 3; Bk. XXIX. chap. 30). Hernando Colón,
Columbus's son, may have undertaken his history of his father in
part as a response to Oviedo and other official historians. In this
sense, too, one notes a strong coincidence between imperial goals
and orthodox ideology. The idea of as-yet-unknown parts of the
world was a subject of debate with which the Church fathers had
little patience. And, even though St. Augustine did grant the possi-

bility of the earth's sphericity, the existence of antipodes was deemed absurd, and the matter of their being inhabited was ruled out of the question (*De Civitate Dei*, bk. XVI, chap. 9). Amerigo Vespucci was not ignorant of that interdiction, a familiarity he knew himself to share with his fellow Florentine Dante, whom he cites on more than one occasion, most notably in his first letter. In his 1504 *Lettera* to Piero Soderini, Vespucci would recall, "If I remember rightly, I have read in some one that he held that the Ocean Sea was devoid of inhabitants, and of this opinion was Dante, our poet, in the twenty-sixth chapter of the *Inferno*, where he invents the death of Ulysses."[23] But, in the already mentioned and slightly earlier *Mundus Novus,* Vespucci writes with the adamancy of a man whose conviction is founded on experience:

> Those new regions which we found and explored, we might rightly call a new world. Because our ancestors had no knowledge of them, and it will be a matter wholly new to all those who hear about them. For this transcends the view held by our ancients, inasmuch as most of them hold that there is no continent to the south beyond the equator, but only the sea which they named the Atlantic; and if some of them did aver that a continent there was, they denied with abundant argument that it was a habitable land. But that this their opinion is false and utterly opposed to the truth, this my last voyage has made manifest; for in those southern parts I have found a continent more densely peopled and abounding in animals than our Europe or Asia or Africa.[24]

In this ternary enumeration, Vespucci leaves no doubt but that the *Mundus Novus* of his voyages is a non-Asiatic, non-Indic fourth continent of the world.

The debate on the authenticity of Amerigo Vespucci's voyages, on the truthfulness of his claims, and on the seemliness of his character is as voluminous as it is acrimonious. The controversy may antedate even Father Bartolomé de Las Casas who, already in the decade following Vespucci's death vilifies the Florentine for having usurped the rightful claims of the Genoese Columbus on the priority of discovery and on the nomination of the hemisphere. The good father's arguments still resonate in our time, having been assured their perpetuity by such distinguished scholars as Martín Fernández de Navarette (*Vajes* 3:322) and Alexander von Humboldt (*Géographie du Nouveau Continent* 4:267). Ralph Waldo Emerson's indictment is as splenetic, and as arguable, as Las Casas's acid garrulity on the subject:

> Strange . . . that broad America must wear the name of a thief. Amerigo Vespucci, the pickle-dealer at Seville . . . whose highest naval rank was boatswain's mate in an expedition that never sailed, managed in this lying world to supplant Columbus and baptize half the earth with his own dishonest name.[25]

The dispute lies beyond our purview, and I do not wish to venture into its particulars here. There is something compelling, something inescapably intriguing, however, in the very possibility that those who claim Vespucci was a fraud might be right. One is tempted to wish that it were, indeed, so, for the continent then would truly coincide in nominalist peripety with that "Ghostland" that Nathaniel Hawthorne descried in our earlier discussion as a phantom continent that *lies* "beyond the jurisdiction of veracity." Thus, we would be inhabiting a utopia more *u-topic* than the trope of Thomas More's wildest dreams, dreams whose contents were in large part conditioned by his reading of Amerigo Vespucci through Waldseemüller's *Cosmographia Introductio* and Peter Martyr's *De Orbe Novo,* and whose hero, Raphael Hythlodaeus, is portrayed as a mariner who sailed in three of Vespucci's four voyages. Tempting as that scenario may be, a more consensual version would have it that the terminist heterodoxies of a nominalism that at once attracted and bedeviled Columbus may have been responsible for giving linguistic and a continental name to his prophetic New World, thereby perverting its apocalyptic vocation and derailing its eschatological march toward the providential ends for which it was intended. Fraudulent or otherwise, Amerigo Vespucci becomes nominally contingent and unsuspectingly incidental in an impish game of philological boutades that a certain clergyman by the name of Waldseemüller set off and the cartographer Mercator completed some thirty years later. For the playful nomination the first tags onto the southern half of the newfound continent in 1507, the latter would casually extend to the northern half as well in 1538.

Amerigo Vespucci's first name extends back a number of generations on his genealogical family tree. It took a philological punster and his group of poetic revelers to appreciate the possibilities of the name within the context of geographical and cartographic punditry. This was the group of Saint Díe that the Duke of Lorraine, Renaud II of Vaudemon, gathered in his duchy at the turn of the sixteenth century. The canon of the little town in the Vosges Mountains, Martin Waldseemüller, and his poetic friends organized a learned society, the Gymnasium Vosgiensis, whose activities extended to the founding of a printing press in 1500, financed by the wealthy canon Walter Lud, for the publication of their cartographic and poetical works. A ludic crew they were, indeed, and somewhat prone to fascination with novelty. Engaged in the preparation of a new edition of Ptolemy that was to initiate their press, they chanced upon a printed copy of a French treatise with the title of "Four Voyages." Enchanted by their discovery, the Gymnasts of Saint Díe turned from Ptolemy to the compelling new world that threatened to undo their Ptolemaic charts. Their product is the *Cosmographia Introductio*, a 103-page recapitulation of received geographical wisdom, now galvanized by the stirring news of a *mundus novus* that captured their imagination: "We have thus been induced," they confess, "to compose, upon the subject of this region of a newly discovered world, *a little work not only poetic but geographical in its character.*"[26] I emphasize the final phrase of their statement, because this is perhaps the first and most overt instance in which the New World geography becomes conjugated not only with the prophetic but also with the poetic. And although "poetic" connoted "inventive," "novel," "ingenious" for their Renaissance diction, the imaginary would become hardened into reality, and nominalist contingency into inexorable universal nomination. No member of the group was as language-struck as Martin Waldseemüller who, cursed with a last name that hopelessly resisted Latinization into classical cognomen, he *forged* for himself the Greco-Latin name of *Hylacomylus* with which to sign his publications. The forged authorial name is a composite of the German etymons in Waldseemüller—wood, lake, mill— translated into Greek (the first and third terms), and Latin (the middle term), *Hy-laco-milus*. Anyone with Waldseemüller's philological penchant would clearly see the possibilities of the coincidence between the emergence of a New World and the etymological scansions that resonated in the name of who, for him, was its "discoverer." And resonate they did, for Waldseemüller notes on at least three occasions (chaps. 5, 7, and 9) in the *Cosmographia Introductio* that no name would be more appropriate for this "fourth part [of the earth which] has been discovered by Amerigo Vespucci" than the name of the discoverer: "Inasmuch as both Europe and Asia received their names from women, I see no reason why anyone should justly object to calling this part Amerige, i.e., the land of Amerigo, or America, after Amerigo, its discoverer, a man of great ability." I am translating from the 25 April 1507 edition (the second) of the *Cosmographia*'s chapter 9. Here is the key passage, often referred to, but seldom read, in full:

> Nunc vero et hae partes sunt latius lustrate, et alia quarta pars per Americum Vesputium (vt in sequentibus audietur) inuenta est, quam non video cur quis iure vetet ab Americo inuentore sagacis ingecnij viro Amerigen quasi Americi terram, sisve Americam dicendam: cum et Europa et Asia a mulieribus sua sortita sint nomina. Eius situm et gentis mores ex bis binis Americi nauigationibus quae sequuntur liquide intelligi datur.[27]

> [Now that these regions are truly and amply explored, and another fourth part has been discovered by Amerigo Vespucci (as will be heard later), I do not see why anyone can prohibit its being given the name of its discoverer Amerigo, wise man of genius, Amerigen, that is, land of Amerigo, in other words America, since Europe and Asia also took their names from women. Its location and customs of its people can be known easily in the account of Amerigo's four voyages that follow.]

No one could see any reason to reject Waldseemüller's proposal and, perchance, everyone did see the negative reasoning and ironic twist in his rhetorical poetics. Inasmuch as his nomina-

tive ratiocination is founded on gender, Waldseemüller's logic
had a problem, since Amerigo the Florentine macho mariner
would not seem to conform to the precedent in naming Europe
and Asia.[28] Declining the name into the genitive case, however,
had the simultaneous effect of feminizing the name's final syllable, thereby grounding Hylacomylus's reasoning on more solid
foundation. "Ge," after all, happens to be mother earth herself
whose telluric body is the very terrain on which any ge-
ographer's fancy inevitably lands. His work being "not only poetic but geographical," Waldseemüller, no doubt, descried, too,
the poetic possibilities of the geographical in the nomination. It is
in this spirit that I yoked earlier the poetic possibilities of Hawthorne's "Ghostland" and More's *u-topia* to the real imaginary
that Waldseemüller's gamesmanship implies. For *Amerige* indeed
scans as "Amerigo's land" in the genitive and it scans, as well, as
the "new land" that is "clear," "bright," "shining," "ever-
young," "ever-fair." The root of the Greek adjective ἀμέριγω
(amerigo) denotes all of these, and a number of historians have
been alert to these etymological implications.[29] However, to my
knowledge, no one has yet remarked what may have resonated in
the name most ironically for the obsessively etymologizing
Waldseemüller. That is the potential of the name to scan as *Nowhereland,* as *u-topia,* or *Numsquama.* If we take the first vowel
as privative "a," and the last syllable as genitive suffix and as the
word for land ("ge"), we are left with a two-syllable stem etymo-
logically rooted in *meros* (μέρος), an Aristotelian lexis that translates as "part," "portion," "lot," "share," but also as "place." It
is spellbinding to think that the "poetical" métier of
Waldseemüller's "geographical" enterprise ironically undermined the very ontology of the new and fourth part of the world
even as he was giving it linguistic and cosmographic substance by
putting the place on the map. And then, as through a double
enchantment that turns on itself, that very nominal inclusion as
"Nowhereland" takes on a worldly reality by the time of
Mercator, who now (1538) has a corroborated geography, a
hard-rock continental mass on whose bipartite land mass he projects the name of "no-place-land"—America.

I rehearse this onomastic peripety (this "most curious paranomasia," the rhetorician in Waldseemüller might quip) by
way of reminder that whether through poetic nomination or by
prophetic proclamation, the American New World is ultimately a
product of a rhetorical ideology, of a nominalist discourse, of
linguistic injunction. Anxious for the security of a *determinism*
that freed historical and imperial claims from the terminist ran-
domness and unpredictabilities of nominalism and its contingencies, the powers that named and claimed the New World as their
rightful inheritance by the grace of Providence naturally opted for
the discourse of necessity and the rhetoric of prophetic injunction. And, even though the *u-topic* name "America" would stick,
the Ghostland denoted by that nomination would become palpably realized in a transubstantiation with the Holy Ghost of its
conquerors' apocalyptic ideology. Thus, the language of eschatological desire and the desired New World that found in America
its ironically named object become consubstantial. In the authority of that (mis)deed, Europe's colonizing enterprise finds its justification and derives its sanction, as we shall see more fully in our
next chapter. The righteousness of Europe's actions in an appropriated New World taken as "promised land," then, will be
deemed as legitimate and as self-legitimating as its rhetoric. In so
much self-righteousness, any irony, nominal or otherwise, becomes occluded, submerged, though never eradicated. And, as a
result, though American history would cast a long and hard
shadow, it is, from the very nominal beginning, the shadow of a
poetic and a prophetic tall tale.

CHAPTER IV

Charting the Conquest

Estas tierras son muy fértiles . . . y todo deve de ser
cosa provechosa.

> Christopher Columbus. "Journal" of the
> first voyage, 4 November 1492.

To us they cannot come, our land is full; to them we
may go, their land is empty.

> Robert Cushman. "Reasons and
> Considerations," 1621.

CONQUERING CHARTS

Words themselves have histories. That is why I have undertaken
the etymological parsing of the name of America with which we
concluded our last chapter. Words are not simply history's innocent and lapidary components, and one needs suspect historiography's investment in the transparent instrumentality of language.
One needs suspect our capacity to make words consubstantial
with deeds, events, utterances, and even with the acts of record-
ing these as history. In other words (as always, inevitably), we
must be wary of rhetorical ideologies that are tantamount to such
consubstantiation.

Duly suspicious and self-suspecting, I choose to read, whenever
possible, the words of the historical personages themselves. And I
do so as I would any verbal concatenation concocted by the actors
to whose actions those words are meant to correspond. This is an
obviously interested usage of words, which is another way of saying that we are dealing with rhetoric and rhetorical constructs and,
inasmuch as these protagonists take their words to be identical
with their acts or as their actions' faithful echoes, we are dealing
with ideologies. Conversely, ideologies—philosophical, aesthetic,

political, economic—are forms of fiction insofar as they are ultimately rhetorical constructs. This is not to say that they do not
have all kinds of worldly "real" and practical entailments, tor-
sions, and repercussions. In fact, these are fictions that have
proven as consequential, and often as deadly, as what we are given
to privileging as "realities." In the case of the particular rhetorical
ideologies that interest us here, that is, those entailed in the illusion
that one's words and one's deeds are of a piece and are naturally
coincident or congruent, these are to be read as forms of fiction
precisely because of the problematic discrepancies that bedevil
such natural congruence and continuity. These are fictions that
history and historiography have compounded by multiplying or
repeating the "record" in a manner conditioned by the same presumptions of naturality and coincidence. That is why to read history's stories is to read multiples of fictionality, whereas to read the
stories of history and the stories of its elemental integers is to read
the words that *make* history, to read them even as they *unmake* the
monumentality and documentality of their scriptors or utterers.
What comes undone for us in such reading is the very nature of the
rhetorical, that is, the interested and self-interested usage, and the
presumption of ideology, that is, the realization of usage as actuality. And in that undoing, we glimpse (however opaquely, for our
own view and our own enablements are by no means pristine and
unpresuming) something of the conditioning assumptions and mo-
tivating factors that go into the making of history in the making.

If, as we have seen, America's name argues lexically against the
very ontology or existence of America, its foundations as a New
World belatedly founded rest on the equally antithetical and slippery grounds of remonstrance and protestation. In other words,
America, in addition to the antitheses in its name, is grounded in
a covenant of contention, a rhetoric of grievance, a clamoring
plaint, and prophetic pleading. From Columbus's epistles and
Father Las Casas's vitriolic dicta to John Smith's apologia and
William Bradford's purported plain style on Plymouth Plantation's Puritan provisions[1] and, yet again, from Father Gerónimo
de Mendieta's mendicant professions and Father Antonio de
Vieira's Sebastianist promptings to John Winthrop's modeling

charity and Roger Williams's protesting "bloudy tenents," America's foundations are poured against the grain, plied on the
adversative pinions of an anxious rhetoric. It is the rhetoric of
prophetic injunction which, whether desperate or parenetic in
register, takes the voice of Moses, when not of Jeremiah, as reso-
nant precursor. And it is less than ironic that the itinerary of
America's historical life as a project of Europe should begin simultaneously with yet another Exodus. Columbus's ships set sail as
Spain's tribe of Israel rides the same tide of river and ebbing
history to yet one more enforced wandering. Although Columbus
does not remark the coincidence, his subsequent writings are
steeped in the language and typological allegory of that simultaneity. As for the Puritan enterprise, of course, the tribal exodus
there is explicitly articulated in Mosaic terms and prophetic rhetoric. As successor nation of divine predilection, the new chosen
people will sanction their claims to a "virgin continent" in Testamental rhetoric and godly justification. From Pope Alexander's 4
May 1493 "donation" to Spain and Portugal of all lands discovered or to be discovered, and not already inhabited by Christians,
to Queen Elizabeth's first patents, granted almost a century later,
all lands not already duly baptized by Christian occupation are
taken as promised lands for aeons held in escrow for God's new
chosen people. Property and race and creed thus become reconfirmed as inalienable concomitants, as they still are by might and
main even in our own time, most notably in the biblical land that
begot the notion and willed its prophetic paradigm to America's
posterity.

Our historical canon invariably has it that the New World was
first "discovered" and that then it was "conquered," with the
latter action occluded behind the rhetoric of more benign synonyms such as "pacified" and "populated" in Iberian America or
"settled" and "planted" in the more northerly phase of the conquest. I should like to propose that the conquest of the New
World, in fact, antedates its discovery, and that the conquest was
already under way before any geographical encounter. Though
modest, this is not an original proposal. And we may have been
preempted in this regard by the very first reference to the New

World in a book to be printed in English, itself, more than likely, belated already. I refer to Sebastian Brant's *Shyp of folys,* in whose 1509 English version Alexandre Barclay, the translator, renders Brant's reference to a New World as "founde by maryners and crafty governours."[2] "Maryners and crafty governours" in this primal remark may be a plural allusion to the first "founder," made legion by those who followed his chartered privileges and patented crusade. The "maryners" could well be read as the multiply refracted "Admiral of the Ocean Sea" in supernumerary throngs streaming to virgin shores. And as for "crafty governours," the would-be "viceroy and governor" of the "Oceanic Yndies, discovered and to be discovered," spawned a myriad cavalcade after his own crafty example.

There is something undeniably arid in the matter-of-fact clauses of charters, patents, capitulations, and maritime contracts between European heads of state and enterprising visionaries, or visionary entrepreneurs of salvationist conviction. And yet, as I read these documents, starting with the Capitulaciones de Santa Fe (17 April 1492) that launched the Genoese mariner on the "enterprise of the Indies," I find a compelling series of remarkable presumptions that resist being remarked by a seeming inevitability in the ruse of their matter-of-factness. Matter-of-factness is, of course, a most repellent rhetorical shield against remarking the remarkable. Taking the matter at hand as fact and the facts as *pro forma* givens, matter-of-factness naturalizes the unthinkable into unthought assumption. Foregone suppositions, thus, take on an ordinariness that immunizes the questionable as much against afterthought as it was against forethought. This unassailable ground serves, of course, as the natural habit and habitat of ideology and its enfranchising charters. What is ideologically warranted thus lies on the safe side of any warrant's jurisdiction. The self-serving empowerment, in other words, not only need not be questioned, but it precludes the very idea of its being served a warrant by any logic or sense of justice other than the one that already sanctions its privilege on perfectly "natural grounds." From there on, one proceeds with any enterprise unproblematically; one fills one's sails and galleons as naturally as breathing. What is naturally *tenable* in mind's reason and in conviction's sanctity becomes *obtainable* in practice with unfettered naturalness. Galvanized by the righteousness of divine election and godly privilege, such unrestrained naturality overlooks any obstacle that might thwart its goals or mitigate its claims. Obliviousness to difficulty is an emphatic enablement, its force sufficient to vouchsafe the most extraordinary ventures. Columbus's brazenness in this regard is matched only by the righteous presumptions of the Western European royal courts. They are empowered by nothing less than the conviction that the rest of the world was their own solely by dint of exercise of their rightful claims. And should the world deem otherwise, institutionally sanctioned means empowered their agents to press those claims, naturally. A guileful perspicuity into the impertinence of such ideology may well be encoded in a work I've already mentioned: the satirist Sebastian Brant's 1494 German title that Albrecht Dürer illustrated and which in 1509 Alexandre Barclay rendered as *Shyp of folys*. In this sense, we can better appreciate the allusion to a New World as "founde by maryners and crafty governours." "Folys" or not, it is in the nature of ideologies not only to color reality but also to effect it, to *realize* the most improvident phantasmagoria as providential imperative and inexorable reality. So compelling are the linkages between ideological conviction and its worldly realization that in the case of Columbus certain historians of eminence have been persuaded that the Genoese mariner "discovered" the New World in 1492 for the second time, having already *realized* the undertaking he so relentlessly and, in the end, persuasively peddled to European royalty.[3]

The charter granted to Columbus on 17 April 1492 by Isabel of Castille and Ferdinand of Aragon is the literal prototype, the paradigm and *locus classicus* of its genre. Columbus, we might say, holds the patent on New World patents and licenses to conquer. The circumstances in that Andalusian spring are strangely consistent with the language, fundamental character, and ideological underpinnings that gird the primal charter. The place is a military camp. From there, Santa Fe de la Vega, the Catholic monarchs launched their final, and finally successful, assault on Moorish Granada, thus culminating the seven-hundred-year-long crusade of "reconquest." The "Infidel" capitulates on 2 January 1492. Their Highnesses have been waiting the preparation of secure and appropriate quarters for themselves in the Alhambra. The importunate Columbus has been waiting Their Majesties' royal pleasure since that legendary January evening when, at the end of his tether, he stamped off, headed for France with his proposal, but was overtaken by Isabel's emissary and convinced to return. Finally, now, two and a half months later, the monarchs and Columbus agree on the Capitulaciones de Santa Fe. They would be amplified and further formalized on 30 April. The site of what we could call the charter's "discursive formation" is a war camp of conquest under the banner of, and literally named after, the Holy Faith—Santa Fe de la Vega. The agreement was countersigned by the State Secretary of Aragon, Juan de Coloma. Eighteen days earlier, he had countersigned the order for the expulsion of the Jews. His own mother was Jewish.

Patently inscribed in the circumstances engendering the charter, then, is the unmistakable conjunction of two concomitant ideologies: the conquering or "missionary" imperatives of the Church Militant and the imperial dreams of the Universal Church, both ultimately invested with a prophetic narrative of the *ecclesia triumphans,* the Church Triumphant and its messianic eschatology. This providential conjunction was not lost on Pope Alexander VI who makes overt reference to the "Most Catholic Monarchs' " zeal and accomplishment in his "donation" of 4 May 1493 that granted them the Indies. Nor was the coincidence of the reconquest, expulsion, and discovery overlooked by Abraham Zacuto. The Jewish scientist's astronomical treatise, *Almanach Perpetuum,* would save Columbus's life in 1504 on the island of Jamaica when it enabled the shipwrecked Admiral at the mercy of the Indians to predict a lunar eclipse, thereby awing his "hosts." Zacuto notes the coincidences of 1492 in his *Sefer Yuhasin* (Book of Genealogies).[4] In the preamble to the journal of his first voyage, addressed to the Catholic monarchs, Columbus himself, a contemporary of Zacuto, also makes passing note of these coincidences, though he errs as far as dates are concerned.

I should state emphatically that I do not aim to invest religion, and Christian dogma in particular, as sole determinant or as overdetermining factor in the history of the New World's conquest. Instead of that reduction, I simply wish to maintain that Christianity and its providential rendering of human time and worldly events purvey the *ideological givens* that make *imperial taking* a natural right needing no further justification. In other words, prophetic history and its apocalyptic rhetoric serve as ideological shield for intricate and mixed motives for Europe's project in the New World, and in the rest of the world for that matter. This form of ideological self-empowerment, by the way, may not be unique to Western Europe and Christianity. But the fact is, as far as the New World is concerned, Western Europe with its dominant mythology is the particular agency involved in this historical context.

The text of the paradigmatic charter unmistakably falls into the category of "writing that conquers," writing that engages in the "production of places" that it takes as its object, to use Michel de Certeau's turn of phrase from a related context.[5] One could say, despite the risk of punning, that the Capitulaciones come about under heady circumstances. In the capitulation of the last "Infidel" stronghold, followed by the order of the expulsion of the Jews, the Catholic monarchs climax their Holy War. Now, universally Christian, Spain shifts the horizon of universality and the ends of its crusade from its Iberian frontiers toward *plus ultra*.

What becomes patently clear in the language, in the very grammatical structure of the Capitulaciones de Santa Fe is that the *plus ultra* shifts from a conjectural hypothesis to a future perfect of a subjunctive case, which in Spanish is identical to the imperative mode. The promissory inevitabilities of a "New World" imperatively enjoined resonate in the inventive and invocative discourse of official and juridical injunction. The charter makes patent the existence of "islands and main lands" in the generative formations of its language and, in doing so, assigns proprietary and jurisdictional authority for that terrain to its would-be, more accurately, its "will-have-been" discoverer and conqueror *as* "discoverer and conqueror." The 30 April 1492 amplified and formalized version of the Capitulaciones de Santa Fe is barely one folio in length, recto and verso. Within that textual economy, the most recurrent leitmotif consists of a dual-verb phrase: "descobrir y ganar," to discover and conquer. The construct occurs seven times, a symbolic redundancy for some numerologists, no doubt. In the first instance, the verbal binary occurs in the infinitive, undeclined: "Por quanto vos, Christoval Colon, vades por nuestro mandado a descobrir y ganar ... [Forasmuch as you, Christopher Columbus, are going by our command to discover and conquer ...]."[6] In the second instance, the verbal formation shifts to the future conditional subjunctive: "[E] se espera que, con la ayuda de Dios, se descubriran e ganaran algunas de las dichas yslas e tierra firme en la dicha mar Oçeana por vuestra mano e yndustria ... [And it is hoped that, with God's help, some of the said islands and mainland in the said Ocean sea should be discovered and conquered by your hand and labors ...]." The original infinitive, now having been conjugated into wishful injunction, passes in the third instance into the perfect tense of an implied future subsequent to an implicit consummation of the desired outcome: "[V]os, el dicho Christoval Colon, despues que ayades descubierto e ganado las dichas yslas e tierra firme en la dicha mar Oçeana o qualesquier dellas ... [You, Christopher Columbus, after having discovered and conquered said islands and mainland in said Ocean sea or, any of them ...]." The desired goals having been perfected in attainment and in grammar's perfect tense, the verbal scansion now passes into the sure inevitability of an apodictic future: "[Q]ue seades nuestro almirante de las dichas yslas e tierra firme que asi descubrierdes e ganardes, e seades nuestro almirante e viso-rrey e governador en ellas ... [You shall be [imperative] our admiral of said islands and mainland you shall thus discover and conquer, and you shall be our admiral and viceroy in them ...]." This particular conjugation occurs twice more, in the next instance,

and in the seventh and final one. The sixth occurrence takes the
discovery and conquest as a given, thus transforming the perfect
tense of the third instance into the pluperfect, rendering the other
world into passive participle, into object predicate already subjected to the project of discovery and conquest, already within the
grasp and mastery of both the grammatical and the imperial
subjects: "[S]eyendo por vos descubiertas e ganadas las dichas
islas e tierra firme en la dicha mar Oçeana . . . [Said islands and
mainland in said Ocean sea having been discovered and conquered by you . . .]."

Any Trinitarian numerologist, or any calculator of Genesis
(and doubtlessly s/he would be very much in the tradition of
Columbus), could compute this grammatical schema as the symmetry of a typological calculus whereby the third instance of the
perfect case subsumes and becomes transmogrified into the pluperfect of the sixth, and thereby deduce a divine arithmetic ruled
by a providential abacus. Who is to deny such wonder-working
reckoning on such "emergent occasions"? But I leave that task to
the subtlety of more devout hermeneutics. What I do wish to
remark through what, for some, may seem a tedious, grammatical parsing is the official creation of the New World on the
septenary scheme of this active verbal construct of "discover and
conquer," a creation animated as much in the official deed of the
charter as in the grammatical deeds of its language. As we see
repeatedly, the New World is a product of the collusion of deed
and language, of actions and rhetorical infrastructures, of praxes
and their ideological scaffoldings. In this primal charter for America, the grammatical case of the biverbal enterprise ("discover
and conquer"), beginning as it does in the indefiniteness of the
infinitive, and ending as it must in the inexorable surety of the
compelling (because prophetic) future, subtends the rhetorical
force of its statutory patent and purveys the ideological givens of
an appropriative presumption whose enablements are so authorized by conviction as to sanction their truth unquestionably. The
validity of the resultant claims thus not only become immune to
the charge of being (pre-)suppositious, but the truth of those
claims is rendered apodictic, that is, their legitimacy becomes

incontrovertibly granted. The grammatical, rhetorical, and logical enablement forms and performs the discursive ideology, the programmatic discourse that will easily translate the legitimacy of such granting of validity from the legitimacy of the juridical and statutory to the legitimacy of a territorial deed, that is, conquest. In other words, the passage from the authority of the charter grant to the deed of the land grant is already ideologically preconditioned, patently naturalized even before the discursively conceived and juridically engendered land is actually discovered. And the privileges granted to Columbus are unmistakably clear on what is meant by this process and its practical implications. Columbus may have been fully cognizant of the amazing nature of these implications. Their Catholic Majesties too quickly came to appreciate what all this entailed. That is why the Genoese mariner produced copy after copy and pressed for repeated reconfirmations of his chartered privileges. That is why, too, the Spanish monarchs and their successors saw fit to curtail, if not outright rescind, what was originally granted in the Capitulaciones. We can now begin to understand what Brant and the English translator of his *Shyp of folys* meant by "maryners and crafty governours." The Catholic monarchs granted Columbus, in exchange for "discovering and conquering" islands and mainland in the Ocean sea, the privileges of their realms' Admiralty and the viceroyalty and governorship of territories to be discovered and conquered. Clearly, then, the would-be New World already has a governor even before its discovery and conquest outside of the charter that engendered it. What Their Highnesses capitulate to Columbus is not merely a patent for exploratory activity, or even for a mercantile and exploitive venture, but a charter for the founding of an empire. Columbus's dismal failings as "viceroy and governor" and the monarchs' failure to take seriously the "maryners' " Admiralty gave a twist to the charted plot that furthered imperial goals all the more. And, in the final analysis, what becomes capitulated by the Capitulaciones is not the compensatory privilege bestowed upon Columbus but the territories "discovered and conquered" by him. At the end of the day, *to capitulate,* then, shifts in grammatical status and in worldly practice from an intransitive to a transitive verb. Thus recapitulated, the "enterprise of the Indies" renders the Oceanic territories into object predicate of the aptly, and now ironically, named charter that engendered them. Their capitulation was a foregone conclusion, and it was so written and charted that it should be. Columbus would invest his most assiduous energies in the time between his historic accomplishment and his death in an attempt to de-hypothesize, to actualize, the privileges granted him. The textual patent had made those privileges conditional upon the attainment of ends the text wrought as inexorable. Like the grammatical status of the document's titular verb ("capitulate"), the conditions of that hypothesis, paradoxically conditional and necessarily imperative at the same time, also shift. In that slide, the primary subject of the patent's sentence, Christopher Columbus, becomes elided, depersonalized into the diffuse and inescapably sticky web of imperial bureaucracy and state apparatus. Columbus, in this sense, set out as medieval knight-errant and premodern hero, only to return and be turned into instrumental agent of an elaborate imperial machine. His would-be Admiralty is significant in this regard and it is the one privilege that he most arduously fought to have reconfirmed, time and again, and the one that eluded him in substance if not in titular gesture and even, possibly, in royal jest. The privilege of Admiralty becomes capitulated, *de facto,* if not *de jure,* because its historical importance is empirically such that in its inclusiveness it subsumes even the office of "viceroy and governor."

In the title of Admiral, etymology and history, the history of a word and the words of history, collude once again, and the apperception of that collusion by human agency changes, if it does not set, the course of history. Our most immediate lesson in this plot consists of the unavoidable fact that the project of Columbus and the Spanish monarchs was, indeed, one of search and dominate, of discover and conquer, find and appropriate, and is not simply and innocuously a mission of exploration and discovery. The key term here is "Admiral," an Arabic term of war adopted into the Spanish language by Alfonso X, also called the Wise. Its root etymon lies in the verb *amara,* "he commanded," and in the noun *amir,* "commander," known to us by the more familiar and Hispanized spelling of *emir.* In his *Siete Partidas,* King Alfonso glosses the title of Admiral as pertaining to a "cabdiello de todos los que van en los navios para facer guerra sobre mar [Commander of all who go in ships to make war at sea]."[7] King Alfonso had created two Admiralties, one for the Mediterranean and one for the Atlantic. Spanish historians quibble on the matter of who first indisputably and identifiably held the title. Some claim it was Ruy López de Mendoza in 1254, others assign it to Ramón Bonifaz. The office does not become clearly defined until the fourteenth century with the Trastámara dynasty conferring the title on one of its family members, Alfonso Enríquez, in 1405. Although Columbus and the Catholic monarchs had a general idea of the prestige attached to the title, it is less than likely that either party had complete appreciation of the legal rights and the extent of statutory privileges it entailed. Simply put, it automatically gave Columbus civil and criminal jurisdiction over the entire sea-borne empire, to be discovered and conquered, over all ports and territories touched by the Ocean Sea; over the entire fleet system; over the value of one-third of all maritime cargo, one-third of all income from the fleet's activities, and one-third of the royal fifth accruing from private expeditions. In sum, Columbus's jurisdiction would extend over an empire larger than that of the monarchs, and his entitlements would amount to fifty-five and eight-tenths percent of the empire's maritime income.[8] Although he did not die poor, by comparison, of course, Columbus died destitute.

The charter of privileges granted to Columbus is more notorious in the breach than in the honoring of its terms. The Capitulaciones, nonetheless, did set the precedent for what became known, particularly in Elizabethan England nearly a century later, as the "proprietary charter." This, in turn, would serve as the foundational paradigm for colonial governance in the New World. I say "colonial governance" advisedly. Because, what is unmistakably clear in such documents, starting with the capitulatory prototype, is a policy of intended conquest, colonization, and governance. An appropriative design, more accurately, proprietary designs, then, prefigure the very "discoveries" in the language and declared ends of the charters and patents that produced the world to be appropriated. These charters, thus, are "proprietary" in the multiple senses of the term: they take the Roman praetorial precedent as model inasmuch as the privilege of governance is conferred upon the Imperial representative authorized by the charter; they grant the right of occupation, use, and capitalization of properties claimed to rightfully belong to the royal estate conferring the charter; finally, these charters are "proprietary" in the most literal and lexically self-sanctioning sense, that is, they precede, prefigure, and, in doing so, configure their putative object insofar as the Latin etymon *pro-priare* denotes a "going before." Thus, the appropriation of those charters' charted object and the realization of their proprietary designs are a *foregone* conclusion from the very beginning, from the graphic inception that writes a world to be claimed. And in this scribal project, scripture, of course, presides as ideological instrument and legitimating mechanism for the enterprise. Hence, the formulaic and, therefore, what passes us by as unquestionable and as unremarkable royal self-declaration that capitulates the Capitulaciones de Santa Fe, as it does all royal acts: "Ferdinand and Isabel by the Grace of God," and nearly a century later in England, "Elizabeth by the Grace of God." By the time of the Treaty of Tordesillas two years after the prototypical charter, when by papal blessing the world hemisphere is sliced into two parts, one for Spain and one for Portugal, propriety becomes a somewhat crowded family affair and the sanctioning invocation becomes reflective of a more elaborate menage and of the now concomitantly amplified exigencies of legitimation. Hence, the opening of the Treaty's second paragraph: "In the name of God Almighty, Father, Son, and Holy Ghost, three truly separate and distinct persons and only one divine essence. Be it manifest and known to all who shall see this public instrument that at the village of Tordesillas, on the seventh day of the month of June, in the year of the nativity of our Lord Jesus Christ, 1494 . . ."

Papal intercession in this instance is a conciliatory move designed to adjudicate conflicting imperial claims. It is also a reiterative intervention aimed to recapitulate papal privilege. In this recapitulation, we glimpse the fundamental presumptions, the ideological scaffoldings, if you will, that authorize Western Europe's proprietary claims upon the rest of the world, in this case the New World. Often, the most ingenuous question might unmask the most disingenuous strategy. We should ask then, by what authority did the royal houses of Western Europe confer upon the charter holders proprietary rights to the land, culture, history, and bodies of another people? Christian cosmology and its prophetic narrative underwrite that authorization rhetorically and ideologically. Papal privilege is a key in the process, at least initially, but even when the figure of the Pope recedes and papal authority is eroded, say, in Elizabethan and Jacobean England, the authorizing mechanisms, rhetorical and ideological, remain intact and continue to be operative, as evidenced by the language of the English proprietary charters, a sample of which we shall examine in due course.

Two seminal studies of Medieval and Renaissance jurisprudence offer a glimpse into the enabling conditions of European privilege vis-à-vis non-European cultures. The first is by the erudite specialist on Medieval canonical law Walter Ullmann and the second by the encyclopedic philosopher Silvio A. Zavala. Ullmann's *Medieval Papalism: The Political Theories of the Medieval Canonists*[9] and Zavala's *Las instituciones jurídicas en la Conquista de América*[10] disclose, respectively, the fundamental ideological presuppositions that rendered the authority to grant proprietary charters such as the Capitulaciones de Santa Fe beyond questioning, and the juridical and philosophical debates that followed once worldly real entailments began to test and exacerbate canonical precepts as a result of their exercise in the New World. Used in conjunction, Ullmann's and Zavala's now classic works divulge the significance of the New World experience to European jurisprudence. That fascinating subject is peripheral to our immediate task. Ours is the more modest concern with the actual enablements themselves as articulated and exercised rather than with the juridical implications of their metamorphoses.

On 17 April 1492 Isabel and Ferdinand grant Columbus the

privileges of "discovery and conquest" and a number of offices in
recognition of his projected achievements. One year later, on 4
May 1493, Pope Alexander VI, in an apostolic proclamation
commonly referred to as the "Bull of Donation," grants all islands and mainlands "discovered and to be discovered one hundred leagues to the West and South of the Azores toward India"
and already not occupied or held by any Christian king or prince
as of Christmas of 1492 to the Catholic monarchs Isabel of
Castille and Ferdinand of Aragon. How so? By what right? And,
for our purposes, how do these actions relate to the prophetic
tradition we have been tracing thus far and to the historical explanations this tradition makes possible? A glimpse into the ideological complex that underwrites and legitimates these actions is to
be had in the writings of the most virulent defender of the Indies
and the most garrulous challenger of European hegemony in the
sixteenth century. Father Bartolomé de Las Casas, notorious
apologist for the Indies, would be the last place one would expect
to find an apology or justification for the European enterprise in
the New World. And yet, in Proposition Seven of the Dominican
father's *Treinta proposiciones muy jurídicas* we encounter an
articulate and telling summary of the most significant authorizing
enablements for the enterprise that so often drew the good father's opprobrium and denunciation. Clearly, ideological and rhetorical determinants suffuse a culture's world view and practices
so thoroughly that those conditions are operative and determinant in corroborative as well as in dissenting actions of a society's
members. The grounds of contention and the grounds of collaboration, in other words, are patently and equally symptomatic of
the ideological constellation that makes conformity and dissent
possible. Here is the relevant passage from Father Las Casas's
seventh juridical proposition: "Wisely, diligently, and justly, the
Vicar of Christ by divine authority, in order to avoid confusion,
divided and can divide among Christian princes the kingdoms
and provinces of all infidels of whatever infidelity or sect they
may be. Commanding to them and committing them to the
spread of the holy faith, enlargement of the Universal Church and
Christian religion, conversion and health of their [the Infidels']

souls as ultimate end."[11] Lest any other Christian prince dispute this exclusive right in the New World granted by the Vicar of Christ to the Catholic monarchs in recognition of their Catholic exemplariness, noble deeds as conquerors of the Infidel and unifiers of Christendom in Spain, and for their initiative in supporting Columbus by rewarding him with the Admiralty of their kingdom, Proposition Sixteen reiterates the Holy See's apostolic authority to grant imperial monopolies and divide earthly jurisdictions: "With the same apostolic authority [divine authorization], the Holy See could prohibit all Christian kings under pain of excommunication, from going or sending to said Indies without license and authorization from the monarchs of Castille, and should they act to the contrary, they sin mortally and incur excommunication."[12]

Embedded in Father Las Casas's juridical propositions is a great deal of canon law, historical precedent, and sanctioning supposition that Walter Ullmann unpacks for us in his *Medieval Papalism*. Simply put: "The pope as the vicar of God commanded the world, as if it were a tool in his hands: the pope, supported by the canonists, considered the world as his property to be disposed according to his will" (Ullmann, pp. 16–17). Moreover, "[t]he medieval world monarchy, to use a strong, though appropriate word, arrogated to itself the powers to command and issue binding decrees to all nations. And since it was the pope who was to play the role of world monarch, his dominion was not therefore restricted to the confines of Christendom, but extended to all members of all nations, wherever they might be found and whatever creed they might embrace. This is the gist of the canonistic doctrine relating to a world ruler" (Ullmann, p. 115). Ullmann is summarizing the key precept of thirteenth-century canonical jurisprudence that, by extension, became all-important in determining the special privilege of the *Respublica Christiana* vis-à-vis the Gentile, non-Christian world. The pivotal notion of a world emperor, of course, is the linchpin that hinges the canonical and the prophetic together, both traditions having as common base John 10:16 to which we have already alluded in a previous chapter: "And I have other sheep, that are not of this fold; I must bring

them also, and they will heed my voice. So there shall be one
flock, one shepherd." This was certainly the key for the canonist
Pope Innocent IV "from whom the main ideas of papal world
government were derived," as Ullmann notes (pp. 119–120).
And, in her unmatched erudite compendium on the prophetic
tradition, Marjorie Reeves reminds us that "the reiterated motif
of 'unum ovile sub uno pastore' . . . runs like a continuum
through so many of the prophetic aspirations."[13] And prophecy,
which for Reeves never ceases to be "one of the bonds between
medieval and Renaissance thought" (p. 508), is ultimately focused on the ecumenical hope of *renovatio* and unity: "This
unites the medieval and Renaissance periods in an unexpected
way. Renaissance people changed neither their patterns nor their
expectations of history. Humanist hopes fastened eagerly on medieval symbols of the Golden Age and in a quite extraordinary way
the new discoveries, new learning, new printing, new religious
orders fell into the pattern as fulfillments of old expectations and
portents of the new age dawning. . . . The most universal of these
shared hopes—and to us, perhaps, the most poignant—was the
'unum ovile sub uno pastore' " (p. 507).

The poignancy felt by Reeves resides in the incongruity of a
persistent imperial hope of ecumenical unity and world monarchy (intensified by what we saw in our last chapter as the *plurimi
pertransibut et multiplex scientia* that Francis Bacon typologically descried in the Prophet Daniel for the Renaissance), at a
time when the very same advancements of discovery, learning,
printing, and religious intensities were leading to even further
atomization of European culture and of the *Respublica Christiana*. As we have noted already, imperial activity abroad may
well have proved a task of even greater urgency precisely because
of sectarian and schismatic fragmentation in Europe. And this
possibility of imperial expansion as compensatory gesture for an
internal loss of cohesion and mastery may well explain, at least
partially, the resurgence of papalist canonism and publicist fervor
at the end of the fifteenth and in the sixteenth centuries when
already the thirteenth-century reassertions of curialist claims and

prophetic fervor had betrayed a complex mixture of imperial hubris after the Crusades, and had evinced, too, a sense of disintegration, or certainly cracking, in the Universalist claims of a united Europe as a consequence of the "first Renaissance," as the thirteenth century is often called. What Reeves sees as "poignant" in a European context, in fact, proved fatal for non-European cultures of the New World that became the object of Western Europe's Universalist and monarchical dreams. Writing some twenty years earlier than Reeves in a Europe that had just endured the barbarous chastisements of a "universal dream" and a "final solution," Walter Ullmann did not fail to note, surely not without some poignancy, that "every political doctrine is prompted by actual circumstances or at least stimulated by the not too remote possibility of creating those circumstances which are favourable to the execution of the plan appearing under the cloak of an abstract theory" (p. 120). One need not be an initiate of dialectical materialist theory to perceive in the dubitative obliquity of Ullmann's observation an aptness for the New World project of Europe's enterprise of the Indies.

I would like to reiterate that I do not wish to reduce Western Europe's imperial expansion in the New World to a papalist plot underwritten by an ideological doctrine abetted in resurgent canonists and delirious prophets. As we have seen, and shall do so again, those who viewed papalism as symptomatic of Antichrist's reign, in fact, labored under the aegis of the same basic ideological sanction, even if in mirrored versions and rhetorical reversals. The fact is that the dominant "abstract theory" available to "cloak" imperial designs at the time of Europe's expansionist drive was the theory of Christian mythology and its prophetic narrative of world history. In this sense, just as Marjorie Reeves sees a continuity between Medieval and Renaissance expectations of history, Ullmann observes that the impetus that brought papalism and "world monarchy" to the fore in the thirteenth century extends beyond that beleaguered and ambitious time and well beyond the geographical and political frontiers that circumscribed its privilege and legitimacy:

The papalist claim to world monarchy was the direst result of the
stimulus afforded by the crusades.... It is true that the crusades
were primarily heralded as campaigns to take possession of land that
was of greatest emotional importance to Western Christianity....
But the crusades had only whetted the appetite of the curialist political thinkers and of the papacy itself. It was soon discovered that by a
logical elaboration of the ideas which first prompted the enterprise of
the crusades, papal powers and supremacy could be extended so that
it might, at least in theory, embrace the whole of what was known as
the universe. In other words, the crusades were considered only a
stepping stone in the direction of the eventual establishment of a fully
fledged world government. (Ullmann, pp. 120–21)

I shall go on to refer to the theoretical principles the canonists
educed to justify such a program in the context of the New
World. But, for now, I believe it might be instructive for us to
remember that, as I noted already, Christopher Columbus's "enterprise of the Indies" found its ideological baptism at the city
walls of Baza in 1489 when he witnessed the papal delegation
from the Holy City and, thereafter, became compulsive about
reaffirming his goal to devote the proceeds of his trans-Oceanic
venture to the reconquest of Jerusalem and the rebuilding of the
Temple on Mt. Zion. In other words, Christopher Columbus's
project is already invested with the ideological "cloak" of a crusade even before its royal authorization by the Catholic monarchs. We should remember, too, that for their part, the very
Catholic monarchs Isabel and Ferdinand chartered and patented
Columbus's enterprise in Their Highnesses' war camp and at the
heels of their own successful crusade, as noted by Pope Alexander
VI at the time of his "Donation" to them of the New World,
discovered and to be discovered, in his bull *Inter caetera* on 4
May 1493. Which returns us to our original question, the "cur ita
facies?"—an impossible query for it to have been entertained
with regard to papal actions since, for the canonists, God's vicar
could do no less than God ("papa est potest facere, quicquid
Deus potest"). The question of why what was being done was
being done at the time was not plausible, except in the perplexity
of those most immediately affected by those actions, that is, the
indigenous peoples of the New World,[14] or those who felt pre-

empted from the material returns that accrued to the worldly praxes of these ideological investments.

For the most part, of course, the indigenous peoples' reactions to what befell them are conveyed by those whose actions affected them. Despoiled of their history, they were also muted in their language. What we do know generally of their own response we know through those who spoke for them after having expropriated their language and appropriated their human fate. Thus it is that a certain *bachiller* Martín Fernández de Enciso, who held fervently to the curialist position of papal privilege, divine right, and world monarchy, and who accompanied one of the first expeditions to the mainland (that of Pedrarías Dávila to Darién) as official and primal *lector* of the *Requerimiento*, a proclamation of the conquerors' rights and the Indians' obligations, wrote in his *Suma Geografía* (Seville, 1519) of two chiefs and their response to the conquerors' dicta: "as to what it [the proclamation] was saying, that there was but one God that reigned in heaven and on earth, it seemed quite fine to them, and that's how it should be; but [they felt] that the Pope was giving away what was not his, and that the King who was requesting it and taking it must have been a madman, since he was demanding what belonged to others."[15] The merciless fate of the questioning chiefs is now history.

The English, particularly Elizabethan England, chafed implacably, and certainly made something of their exercised ambitions, as we shall see at greater length soon.[16] The French monarch Francis I, too, expressed his vexed qualms: "The sun shines for me as much as for anyone else. I would like to see gladly the clause in Adam's testament by which I am excluded from the partitioning of the Globe,"[17] a leading protestation that reinforces the ideological conditions that justify papal policy. For Francis I is not disputing the right of Christian Europe to appropriate the world. He questions rather his exclusion from the spoils of such a policy. The irked French king's reference to Adam's testament is not gratuitous, because the mythology of scripture is precisely the ground on which Western Europe's self-legitimation rests. In the juridical mind of the canonists, publicists, cosmographers, statesmen, and stateswomen (*tanto monta, monta tanto, Isabel como Fernando!*), proprietary claims on non-Christian cultures were naturally lawful claims and natural law was equivalent to divine law. Such rightful claims were only rightful if exercised under the aegis of the divinely sanctioned people, that is, people who were in the grace of God, the only creator and true lord of the world. Adam, the father of all mankind, the argument went, was created by God alone and Christ was his successor—"secundus Adam." The pope, as Christ's vicar, is "Adam's successor as the father of mankind." All mankind—for did not the Psalmist sign that "the earth is the Lord's and the fulness thereof, the world and those who dwell therein; for he has founded it upon the seas, and established it upon the rivers" (Psalms 24:1–2)? Indeed, intoned Pope Innocent IV, whose preponderant authority on world government Ullmann underscores: " 'All men,' said Pope Innocent IV from whom the main ideas of papal government were derived, 'faithful and infidel alike are through their creation the sheep of Christ' " (Ullmann, pp. 119–120), which brings us full circle to the pastoral powers of John 10:16 and the single flock with a single shepherd. But what of the rival claims of other creation myths and *their* divine laws and competing natural authority? The suggestively named Pope Innocent and those who followed his conviction saw no problem with them at all: "Non enim ad paria debemus nobiscum judicare, cum ipsi sunt in errore, et nos in via veritatis [We must not put ourselves on the same level as those people, because they are in error, and we walk in the path of truth]."[18]

Between David's Psalmist and John's pastoral, Innocent's *ex cathedra* proclamation presided (and in some quarters does still) steadfastly, *de jure* and *de facto*, over the Church Militant's campaign to move the world into conformity with the ideal and archetypal model prophetically pre-visioned as the Church Triumphant in all its heavenly promise for the faithful and the duly converted. A future with so much promise and authority so natural, ends so divine and means so righteous saw no reason to falter. And should the schoolmasters waver, there was always the Aristotle of the *Metaphysics,* book 12, and of the *Politics,* book 1, who in his reckoning, even before the true grace of divine light illumined his way, was able to discern, in typological anticipation, that government in the universe is always hierarchical, whether in nature or in military orders, with lower creatures ruled by the higher, and all of them by one.

The translator of Aristotle's *Politics* into Latin happens to have been Juan Ginés de Sepúlveda, whose treatise, *Democrates Alter*, on the just cause of war against the Indians proved too radical for the Spanish authorities to permit publication. Sepúlveda's virulence and influence, lack of publication notwithstanding, led to the famous Valladolid debate between himself and Bartolomé de Las Casas in 1550. Las Casas's line of argumentation coincided more with the officially articulated government policy on the status of the Indians. Nevertheless, it was Sepúlveda's unpublished premises that most often determined, or at least coincided, with actual practice rather than Las Casas's Christian charity or the royal decrees.[19]

Francis I's protestation, however, has a more ambiguous and a more subtle differentiation encoded in its reference, and it is a distinction that becomes more telling in the actual conquest and in the notion of "justified war" against the Indians. The query by the French king echoes Matthew 5:45—"so that you may be sons of your Father who is in heaven; for he makes his sun rise on the evil and on the good, and sends rain on the just and the unjust." Matthew's exhortation about loving one's enemies was invoked by Pope Innocent IV to moderate the bellicosity of the Christian crusaders against the infidels and was an attempt on Innocent's part to check the more belligerent view of Henricus of Segusia, more commonly known by the name of his bishopric, Ostia, as Hostienses. He would have succeeded to the papacy, like Innocent twenty years earlier, had it not been for his advanced age and infirmities. As acute a canonist as Innocent, and as influential a jurist, Hostienses would serve as precedent for the canonical justification of the conquest of the New World. He would be identified expressly as such by Bartolomé de las Casas. Hostienses's more radical extension of Innocent's decrees on curial privilege and the Church's natural (divine) right over non-Christian peoples would find its way into the language of the notorious

Requerimiento, which we shall discuss shortly. As Ullmann
notes, despite Innocent's moderation, founded on Matthew 5:45
that Francis I so cleverly and self-servingly invokes, Innocent's
final conclusion was unequivocal and, rather than moderate the
likes of Hostienses, furnished an authoritative precedent for juridical apologists of conquest and "just wars": "Sed bene tantum
credimus, quod papa, qui est vicarius Christi, potestam habet,
non tantum super Christianos, sed etiam super omnes infideles,
cum enim Christus habuerit super omnes potestatem [But we
believe nevertheless that the pope who is the vicar of Christ, has
power not only over Christians, but also over all infidels, since
Christ himself had power over everybody]."[20] From this conclusion, it seemed only natural to Hostienses to infer, and for Spanish apologists of the right to conquer to concur, that all infidels
ought to be subjected to the faithful ("Infidelis debent subjeci
fidelibus"), and that the rulers of infidel nations could be left
alone provided they recognize the dominance of the Church ("si
dominum ecclesiae recognoscunt").[21] These are the basic premises that underwrite the ideological assumptions of the conquest.
And Father Bartolomé de Las Casas, in his already cited *Historia
de las Indias,* chastises the likes of Palacios Rubios, author of the
just-mentioned *Requerimiento* to which we shall now turn, for
his fall "into the errors of Hostienses whose sectarian he was [en
los errores del Ostiense, cuyo secuaz fue]."[22]

Far from remaining, if ever they were, innocent word games of
canonical pundits and casuistical clerics, these crusading terms of
self-empowerment found their way, as ceremonial protocols or as
ritualistic war cries, into royal courts and battlefields, or into
both simultaneously when court and battle camp were one, as
with Santa Fe de la Vega where the Spanish Catholic monarchs
transited from one crusading front (Granada) to another ("islands and mainlands of the Ocean sea"). These enablements did
indeed launch Columbus with rights to "discover and conquer"
by way of juridical protocols termed Capitulaciones, charters, or
patents. Soon after, in Columbus's steps would follow the same
righteous enablements only now as ritualistic injunctions of war.
These would become legalized into standard juridical language,

lest the wars of conquest be deemed unjust or unrighteous. This is the language of the *Requerimiento,* a proclamation to be solemnly read to all indigenous populations, affording them the opportunity to conform to its terms, whether they understood its language, much less its rationale, or not. It is compelling to see how much canonical law actually becomes articulated in the ultimata of this proclamation. This should not be surprising. The *Requerimiento* was the work of a distinguished royal jurist, Juan López de Palacios Rubios who, in 1513, felt that conquests needed to be more orderly than they had been until then. The actual title of the proclamation reads: "Notificación y requerimiento que se ha de hacer a los moradores de las islas e Tierra Firme de mar Océano que aún no están sujetos a Nuestro Señor [Notification and requirement to be made of the inhabitants of islands and mainland of the Ocean Sea who are as yet not subject to Our Lord]."[23]

Like the Capitulaciones de Santa Fe of Columbus, the *Requerimiento* is a primal document. As such, it reveals the *a priori* suppositions of those who promulgate its terms. It discloses, too, the rhetorical strategies by which those convinced of the righteousness of their acts have come by their conviction. As sanctioning mechanism devised to legitimate motives, suppositions, practices, and claims, it becomes revelatory not only of its formative conditions but also betrays the expectations the instrument and its deployment are to yield. In other words, it reveals the presuppositious ends of its self-sanctioned means. It becomes telling of the ways and extent to which those carrying out this text's enablements presume on those to whom the "notification" is addressed and of whom its "requirement is made." I see, then, a direct continuity between the charter of the Capitulaciones that produced in its patent writing a world to be "discovered and conquered" and the *Requerimiento* as instrument that presided, as invocation, over the execution of the terms in Columbus's paradigmatic charter. The hypotheses of the Capitulaciones as proposal for a projected enterprise become actualized practice that transforms world-producing assumptions into self-reproducing presumptions. This self-reproduction resides in the fact that the world-object upon which those theses presume is made identical with the interests of the presumers who now see multiples of themselves. In this identification, the target world becomes the proprietary object to be subsumed, to be taken over and taken in to the world and mythology of those who narrate and serve its "notice" and impose its requirements. The two-part proclamation, then, like the double verbal action of Columbus's "discover and conquer," is a two-step instrument of conquest. Its unequivocating duality consists, first, in notifying the target peoples of the "true history" of the world (scripture's providential and prophetic history as understood by canonists like Palacios Rubios and the tradition of Hostienses, down to the papal donation of the New World to the Spanish sovereigns) and, second, in requiring their accession to the terms and version of that world history, a mandated admission that automatically incorporates them as subjects of that cosmological order. This incorporation, in turn, constitutes a validation of the mandated world order that automatically translates into the invalidation of the indigenous peoples' own history and historical narratives. Not to accept the version of cosmology as rendered by the "notification" constitutes "legitimate grounds" for war, persecution, capture, expropriation, and enslavement:

> Por ende, como mejor puedo vos ruego y requiero que entendáis bien ésto que os he dicho . . . y reconozcáis a la Iglesia por señora y superiora del universo mundo y al Sumo Pontífice llamado Papa, en su nombre, y al rey y a la reina nuestros señores, en su lugar, como superiores e señores y reyes desas Islas y Tierra Firme, por virtud de la dicha donación. . . . Si así lo hicierdes, haréis bien. . . . Si no lo hicierdes, o en ello dilación maliciosamente pusierdes, certificos que con la ayuda de Dios yo entraré poderosamente contra vosotros y vos haré guerra por todas las partes y maneras que yo pudiere, y vos sujetaré al yugo y obediencia de la Iglesia y de Sus Altezas, y tomaré vuestras personas y de vuestras mujeres e hijos y los haré esclavos . . . y protesto que las muertes y daños que de ello se recrecieren sean a vuestra culpa, y no de Su Alteza, ni mía, ni destos caballeros que conmigo vinieron . . .[24]

> [Thus, I beg and require you the best I can to understand what I have told you . . . and recognize the Church as mistress and superior of the

universe and the Holy Pontiff called Pope, in his own right, and the king and queen our lords, in his stead, as lords and masters and kings of these islands and mainland, by virtue of said donation . . . Should you do so, you will do well . . . Should you not, or should you maliciously delay, I assure you that with God's help I shall attack you forcefully and make war against you everywhere and every way I can, and I shall subjugate you to the yoke of obedience to the Church and their Highnesses, I shall capture you and your women and children and I shall enslave you . . . and I protest that the deaths and calamities that should ensue from this will be due to your own fault, and not His Highness's, or mine, or these gentlemen's who came with me . . .]

For the canonist Palacios Rubios, the Conquistador Pedrarías Dávila who first carried this proclamation on a conquering expedition to Darién, that most conquerable geography, as history continues to prove, that is the geographical umbilical cord of the Americas today called Panama, and for the *bachiller* Martín Fernández de Enciso, the first lector of the *Requerimiento* whose account of the Indian chiefs' reaction to the proclamation we cited earlier—for all of these Spaniards the choices offered by the dictum were perfectly clear and mutually exclusive. For the indigenous peoples it may have not been so, and history has proved that the options put to them were but the reversible coin of the same duplicitous face. The options, in fact, amounted to a choice between privation and deprivation, between being expropriated as a culture or being appropriated.

The Capitulaciones de Santa Fe produced a world to be "discovered and conquered." The *Requerimiento* actualized that hypothetical production by divulging its premises in their deployment as instrumentality, well beyond the heady, that is, capitulatory, symptoms of a mentality. If the Capitulaciones invented a world, to use a verb popularized by Edmundo O'Gorman and now much used,[25] the *Requerimiento* not only instrumentalized and unmasked the hypotheses subtending that invention, but it also superimposed a history upon the world born of the Capitulaciones. The period between 1492 and 1513, of course, was not a lethic limbo. Columbus's four voyages and the frenetic activity of the many who followed in his wake obviously attest otherwise, as Todorov's already-mentioned *The Conquest of America* and, more recently, Beatriz Pastor's fine treatise amply expatiate.[26] Silvio Zavala, in the augmented edition of his *Instituciones jurídicas* cited above, admits to the existence of a more rudimentary version of the *Requerimiento* proclaimed by Alonso de Ojeda in his 1509 expedition.[27] Nonetheless, the 1513 text by Palacios Rubios constitutes the most overt attempt to "order" the conquest and to lay out the terms of its legitimacy. In the process, the sanctioning suppositions of those terms are disclosed. The ideological cloak is revealed as a theological narrative whose representation of the cosmological order exhibits all the traits of the prophetic genre, from its imperious injunctions to its promised eschatology. As such, it expostulates not only a history that represents the past, but it narrates and decrees, as well, a history of the New World's inexorable future.

Like all injunctions dyed in the prophetic, the proclamations of the *Requerimiento* are *ex cathedra*. They evince the ineluctable urgency, imperative summons, and monitory exhortation of an ultimatum. Theoretically at any rate, the *Requerimiento* precedes and is intended to preclude action, provided those to whom it is directed accede to its terms. I say theoretically, because, poised as the deliverers of the proclamation were to carry out the sentence of noncompliance, their threat is nearly as aggressive as the threatened actions themselves. Less subtly, the delivery of the "notice and requirement" often followed the physical subjugation of the indigenous people instead of preceding it.[28] The point of this confusion of canonical theory in discourse and conquering acts in practice is that those animated by the theoretical premises of this particular mythology see nothing purely theoretical in it. The enabling discourse is strictly procedural, a blueprint, and those empowered by its terms simply proceed, most literally. The juridical-theological proclamation becomes, in fact, a mechanism for self-absolution, an instrument that shifts the responsibility for baneful actions of conquest from the perpetrators to the victims and their "obduracy," as the concluding lines of the passage cited above make clear. As a certain Dominican friar from San Juan, Puerto Rico put it in his complaint against abuses of the Indians, "mandó S. A. para la justificación de su real conciencia que ante todas cosas, antes que se hiciese le guerra a los indios, se les hiciese un requerimiento que acá ordenaron ciertos teólogos . . . [Your Highness, in order to justify your royal conscience before all things mandated that before war was made on the Indians, that a requirement be conveyed to them as ordered here by certain theologians]."[29] Clearly, in the eyes of the Dominican friar, the "royal conscience" too was in need of assuaging before the acts of conquest perpetrated in its name.

The clamoring against the abuses of conquest became correspondingly stentorian. In 1537, Pope Paul III would, finally, concede the Indians' humanity in his ironically titled bull *Sublimis Deus,* thereby unleashing all manner of protestation that, in the final analysis, mooted the Holy Sees' belated recognition of the Indians as human.[30] As the debates raged, the worldly and the other-worldly interests would move progressively to more polarized extremes, while official governmental efforts sought ways of breaching irreconcilable demands and vehement advocacies. The record of laws and decrees promulgated and periodically compiled is as long as they proved futile. For the most part, the official positions reflected the contending antitheses at large in the empire: laws and edicts echoed the humanitarian concerns of people like Las Casas; the actual execution of those regulations bent to accommodate the demands of curialist conservatives like Juan Ginés de Sepúlveda and of economic interests. As court policy tacked through such turbulent waters, royal rhetoricians struggled to find a discourse of circumlocution appropriate to the circuitous and ever-deviating circumstances of their empire and its providential course. The rhetorical strategies that became necessary for the accommodation of such meandering are quite intricate, albeit somewhat transparent in their disingenuous ploys. I cite as example from King Philip II's "Decree on Discoveries and Pacifications Dated July 13, 1573":

> Por justas causas y consideraciones conviene que en todas las capitulaciones que se hicieren para nuevos descubrimientos, se excuse esta palabra conquista, y en su lugar se use de las de pacificación y población, pues habiéndose de hacer con toda la paz y caridad, es

nuestra voluntad que aun este nombre, interpretado contra nuestra
intención no ocasione ni dé color a lo capitulado para que se pueda
hacer fuerza ni agravio a los Indios.[31]

[For just causes and considerations it is suitable that in all charters
contracted for new discoveries, this word "conquest" be dismissed
and, in its stead, "pacification" and "population" be used. As such
action should be carried out most peacefully and with utmost charity, it is our will that such a term [conquest] interpreted contrary to
our intentions, not occasion nor color the capitulated terms so as to
force or do harm to the Indians.]

While the rhetorical shift is toward a "kinder, gentler conquest,"
the ideological determinants do not change, though they do become complicated by the economic and jurisdictional interests of
all those who shipped out under that ideology's cloak. As for the
rhetorical ingenuity of the discourse masons at court, their clever
synonyms for conquest would resonate serviceably through the
centuries down to our own time. Certainly the euphemistic coin-
age of *populating* for conquest would become common coin in all
its ambiguous benignity in the "deserts" of New England's wilderness, and even in the postcolonial era of Romanticism and
nation-building in countries such as Argentina, the shibboleth for
holding barbarity at bay would become "civilizar es poblar." As
for pacification, the euphemism for countless acts of civilized
barbarity committed in its name become all too common for the
term not to prove as self-betraying as the word it replaced by
royal decree, so much so that in New England's New World the
verb would exchange its object predicate of populations for geographical terrain. Thus, the Godly Pilgrims and their progeny
would pacify territories instead of Indians, wherever the territories and whoever the Indians might be.

PATENT CONQUESTS

Pope Alexander's "bull of donation" (the *Inter caetera*) of 4 May
1493, whose monopoly Father Bartolomé de Las Casas defended
so categorically in his already cited "Propositions," was ambiva-
lently honored by English monarchs for nearly a century. Al-

though as early as 1497 John Cabot would obtain a charter for exploration in the New World, its terms were clearly circumscribed, expressly limited to territories "which before this time have been unknown to all Christians." By the third quarter of the sixteenth century, for an intricate constellation of reasons beyond our purview, England no longer felt constrained from challenging the Spanish monopoly in the New World. Following a number of reconnoitering missions in search of an elusive northwest passage (e.g., Martin Frobisher's between 1576 and 1578), Queen Elizabeth I granted a deliberately worded patent to Sir Humphrey Gilbert on 11 July 1578. Its authorization was to "discover, find, search out, and view such remote, heathen, and barbarous lands, countries, and territories, not actually possessed of any Christian prince or people."[32] How deliberately constructed and how precedent-setting this patent's language is will become clear as we proceed. Sir Humphrey did establish a colony in Newfoundland by 1573, but it was fated to perish, as did its founder who was lost at sea in the same year. Unfortunately for Spain, Sir Humphrey's half-brother, Walter Raleigh, would inherit the patent rights the following year.

I find a compelling continuity between Columbus's paradigmatic charter (that is obviously what makes it paradigmatic) and the charter-patents granted by English monarchs in the sixteenth and seventeenth centuries, a continuity that extends even to John Cabot's charter granted him by Henry VII on 5 March 1497. My observation may be tantamount to remarking the obvious for most historians who have come to view charters as a stock genre and dismiss this constancy as purely formulaic. Such is the case, for example, of as canonical and as broadly read a historian as A. L. Rowse, whose remark on the language of the Humphrey Gilbert patent does not go past the offhanded notice that "[t]hat was the regular formula."[33] Egregiously ethnocentric as this Cambridge historian is, he is not unexemplary of the historiographic canon in this regard. As I have noted already, consistencies that accede to the status of the formulaic or the obvious might be the most telling ground of sanctioning conditions and cloaked presumptions turned into enablements. Like most categories of stock

writing that become formulaic, particularly in bureaucratic contexts, charters are, indeed, patently generic. They are called patents because they dwell as form in the public domain. They are
literally "open letters," accessible to all, rather than private documents or privileged texts. Like patents, charters are a form of
"passport." And a charter is functionally the medium of "open
letters," since the Latin *chartula* by its etymology is the coin, the
common currency or "little papyrus leaf" that circulates as public
statement. Something so conventional and so pervasively
consensual is bound to be revealing of the general conditions that
give it currency. Beyond these lexical subtleties that we take for
granted or as patently obvious, however, when any historiographic canon or critical enterprise declares that letters patent or
charters are *generic,* this adjective of the commonplace should
connote two things at once, both reflective of their human and
historical contexts. First, we should understand that charters are
generic as typological instances, as species of a taxonomic genre.
Inasmuch as they are products of an identifiable kind of language, they are discursive generations or engenderments. Second,
and we have seen this aspect elaborately at work in the
Capitulaciones de Santa Fe, charters and letters patent are generic
because they are willfully generative and engendering. They engender a world that they then convert into their goal and take as
their object. This is what occurs, as we have noted, in the
Capitulaciones, where Columbus ostensibly did not know beforehand what the world of his charter was. In the event that he
might have known, as historians such as Juan Manzano
Manzano already cited claim, it becomes clear from later specimens of the genre that it would have made no difference. Elizabethan and Jacobean charters make this unmistakably clear. Spanish, Portuguese, Venetian, Florentine, and English mariners who
followed Columbus with charters in hand knew already of the
existence of a geography and a human world at the other end of
their oceanic crossing. No matter. Charters and patents, true to
their genre, did not cease to be generic in the dual sense stated
above, a duality that slips past certain historians with such stealth
and consistency that one might wonder whether, as common-

place writing, it does not turn into successful duplicity. As constructs that conceive and construe worlds, charters and patents are faithful to the proprietary presumptions and ideological enablements of their own rhetorical formations. They constitute a genre of discourse that neither accedes to nor wishes to recognize any world, existent or not, other than the world of its own design and of its designs. The object of that discourse, as desideratum, is a *tenable* object, one that is to be had, in every sense. Therefore, the conditions of that world-object must make it tenable. This explains, for example, the discrepancies between the world realities (whatever they might have been) Columbus was encountering and those he believed to be experiencing, disjunctions that have proved so perplexing to many scholars such as Todorov, as noted earlier. The conditions I speak of that make the object-world tenable are really preconditions that have to be met or conformed to before the object *could be had*. As charters and patents, these texts chart and patent a world of their own preconditions, irrespective of that world's modes of existence already. This is why these instruments are maps more accurately reflective of their own context and of their own conditions of production, the conditions that produced them as well as those they themselves produce. Once the projected world they engender is realized, that is, made or forged into a reality, then that world becomes, perforce, fair game, indisputably. Some who thus chart their worlds might even feel that at this stage they have a *natural* right (a generic right of parenthood), a moral obligation, a compelling duty, or a providentially commanded election to carry through with the patented enterprise they have capitulated. Certainly Columbus felt that way, and so did the planters who came to husband the "virgin terrain" of Virginia; nor did the brethren of the charter company of New England feel otherwise. Their Royal Highnesses the monarchs of Europe certainly felt duty-bound to aid and abet callings so noble and righteousness so patent.

The Capitulaciones de Santa Fe have revealed to us how certain grammatical and rhetorical scansions disclose a logic at work, a logic revelatory, in turn, of particular presuppositions that render

the world-object contemplated and the actions proposed in the
charter inevitable. We have, subsequently, traced the institutional
and ideological enablements, that is, the set of convictions and
modes of reasoning that sanction the genesis of the charter, authorize its terms, and legitimize the actions taken in compliance, or
pursuant to, if not always in compliance, with those terms. The
English charters and letters patent offer certain amplifications that
accrue to the variant light of a shifted perspective, albeit the end
results for the indigenous peoples are not substantially different.
The verbs in the Spanish and in the English charters are well-nigh
synonymous and functionally identical. For the Indian who read
no charters and knew neither language, these verbs translated into
the same actions. At the end of the day, *conquest,* as a cognitive
term rooted in the same lexis and economy for the Europeans, is
equally uprooting and equally ravaging in any language. It is very
important to recall that there is nary a reference to human beings in
the world "to be discovered and conquered" in the text of the
Capitulaciones de Santa Fe in terms other than hegemonic. The
object predicate of those repeated verbs consists of "islands and
mainlands." Hardly an oversight, and if so equally telling, this
eradication amounts to an unmitigated elision, a banishment of
any human factor from the landscape that might disconcert the
conquest plot charted by the Capitulaciones. The only reference to
human beings, as I said, in the "islands and mainlands to be discovered and conquered" renders them as already duly incorporated
into the dominion of Their Majesties' empire, as people in "our
kingdoms and dominions . . . you shall conquer and subdue . . .
our subjects and naturals now being, or that shall be for the time to
come."[34] This radical dehumanization that admits of no
"precolombian" humanity has interesting variants in the English
charters, though the desired ends, of course, are not appreciably
different. As for these stated ends that animate the enterprise, the
English charters tend to be more explicit, though by no means any
less mixed in motives. Ultimately, whether in Iberia's or in England's project, a rhetorical ideology and an ideological program
subtend the chartered voyages to the New World. And the modu-
lating principle of these European enterprises is a prophetic narra-

tive and its providential agency that make the whole project purposeful and give it a direction in both time and geography. A prophetic eschatology and an apocalyptic calling limn the determinacies and the musculature, as much of language for self-conviction as of the acts of the self-convinced.

Only a five-year period separates Columbus's Capitulaciones de Santa Fe from the "Letters Patents of Henry VII Granted to John Cabot." As in the Capitulaciones, a peculiar blend of indeterminacy and imperative determination makes up the document. Undetermined is the actual destination, at least ostensibly so: "[W]e have given and granted . . . full and free authority, leave, and power to sail to all parts, countries, and seas of the East, of the West, and of the North under our banners and ensigns with five ships . . ."[35] Obviously, this is too costly and all too tactically ambiguous an undertaking for so vague a "fishing expedition" to nowhere in particular. International politics modulate the indeterminacies, no doubt, and the triangulation of the stated cardinal points would indicate a precedent-setting expedition that spawned a lengthy lineage. Where East might meet West in the North is called a North Passage, and this geographical desideratum would become in time the history of an obsession. Equally undetermined is the geographical object of the expedition said to have been authorized "to seek, discover, and find whatsoever isles, countries, regions, or provinces," but with one qualification and a caveat: that the geography pertain to "heathen and infidels whatsoever they be," and, the circumscription, that these be "unknown to all Christians." The charge of the undertaking is quite explicit, its verbs forcefully determinate in their redundancy, whereas the predicates are all-inclusively vague: "We have granted to them . . . and have given them license to set up our banner and ensigns in every village, town, castle, isle, or mainland newly found by them, and that the aforesaid John and his sons, or their heirs and assigns, may subdue, occupy, and possess all such towns, cities, castles and isles found by them which they can subdue, occupy, and possess as our vassals and lieutenants getting unto us the rule, title, and jurisdiction of the same villages, towns, castles and firm land so found."

Clearly, the tenacious double-verb construction of Christopher
Columbus's "discover and conquer" is made triple in John
Cabot's letters patent. And the studied passage from the first set
of ternary verbs, "seek out, discover, and find," to the second set
of triple actions in the next sentence is not inarticulate. This
second verbal set reads "subdue, occupy, and possess," and its
repetition in the same clause should not be overlooked. The tri-
dentine verbal probe will point the way for Elizabethan policy
and the Virgin Queen's "doctrine of effective occupation," a
policy that will change the course of history and the virginal state
of many a terrain deemed as pristine as the self-convinced fiction
of the Queen's own virtue would have the world believe. More
on this shortly. For now, I believe it is important to pressure the
determination of these charted actions and the asymmetrical nature of their determinacy vis-à-vis that of their object predicates,
as already suggested.

In his admirably incisive reading of a number of colonial texts,
Peter Hulme recently points to a key discursive procedure in the
rhetorical symptoms of what I have been calling a "conquering
ideology." Hulme notes: "The strategies of colonial discourse
were directed in the first place at demonstrating a separation
between the desired land and its native inhabitants."[36] Hulme
proceeds to weave the libidinal metaphors ironically deployed in
the name of a "Virgin Queen," as suggested by Samuel Eliot
Morison,[37] and, as Hulme puts it, ignored by Henry Nash
Smith[38] and Annette Kolodny[39] who, despite the titles of their
respective treatises, "manage not to mention the native inhabitants at all."

Clearly, the rhetorical strategy of human elision still endures to
catch us unawares in a time well beyond the ideological suppositions that made that strategy indispensable. Peter Hulme makes
his observations in the context of his discussion of Captain John
Smith, Pocahontas, and the incipient Virginia plantations. The
force of what he notices in this earliest stage of European thrust
into North America becomes patent in its systematicity as overt
practice in Puritan New England a dozen or so years later. The
point I wish to press is that ideological determinants for what

Hulme notes (and a broad array of historiography already treats before Hulme) extend back to Columbus's *Capitulaciones de Santa Fe* and resonate sharply in the primal charter granted five years later by Henry VII to John Cabot. Our archeology of ideological forms that per-form the rhetorical constructs necessary to their ends, worldy and otherwise, indicate clearly that the "etymology" of conquering and colonizing policies is embedded in these charters. In this sense, these early texts are not only charters, they are the charts that rhetorically map and textually deploy the conquering ideology of Western Europe. Here, then, is how this rhetorical strategy operates 111 years before Captain John Smith's 1608 *A Trve Relation of such occurrences and accidents of noate as hath hapned in Virginia since the first planting of that collony* that Hulme is commenting.[40]

I noted that the two triple-verb sequences, those "trident probes," exude determination. The asymmetrically underdetermined object of those verbs ("all parts, countries, and seas of the East, of the West, and of the North . . . whatsoever isles, countries, regions, or provinces") afford an extraordinary determinative opportunity to the actions denoted. In other words, these verbs not only have the force of their denotative actions, they are also endowed with the productive capability to realize and define, to make and forge (and we do have instances of "forged" geographical realities starting with Columbus's log of his maiden voyage) their target world(s). This capability, of course, translates into an enablement that, as we noted already, is characteristic of the genre and that makes it possible for all ideological requirements to be met so that conquering actions may ensue. Philip II obviously recognized this strategy. He was called "the Prudent" because, I suspect, he knew how to read well, and he certainly did act as if he knew that paper realities can be more potent than actuated ones. After all, he did spend most of his life esconced in paper and memoranda he tirelessly wrote and avidly received. I impute such potency to Philip because his 13 July 1573 decree I cited earlier evinces the acuity of a reader with an insight into the powers of ideology and the rhetorical enablements it is capable of underwriting. That is why, I believe, he decreed the banishment of the word *conquest* from all capitulaciones and charters of discovery in favor of pacification and population. Prudence, more often than not, precludes originality, and certainly Philip was deserving of his epithet. What he knew well was the dogma and conviction of his orthodoxy, which, as far as conquests are concerned, was of a piece with the ideology of prophetic eschatology and the cosmological narrative that underwrote the missions and cloaked the commissions of Western Europe in the New World. Philip knew, of course, that it is easier to pacify territories and then to populate them. These are the tandem actions already at work in the human erasure of the Capitulaciones and in the population of deserts in "heathen and infidel lands." These are the actions that neutralize and discreate the human dimension starting with John Cabot's letters patent and extending through Smith's *Trve Relation*. The rhetorical turns this strategy takes in Anglo-America's primal charter is commonly referred to as *denominatio*. The procedure is allied with the figure we know as *paranomasia*, or misnaming, and the trope we call *metonymy*, or naming otherwise. Rhetorical strategies are by definition expedient mechanisms for realizing ideological ends through means otherwise. And certainly Western Europe's target in the New World is *the other* problematically, but expeditiously, maneuvered into domestication and, when not domesticable, into annihilation. Otherwise named and othered, or alienated, from itself in John Cabot's charter is the human component of his conquering acts' ("subdue, occupy, and possess") undefined object predicate. The humanity in this open-ended *carte blanche* is literally blanked out. The people are denominated into anomie, that is, into a separation or alienation from their very existence as human inhabitants, as "population." They become unmentionables under erasure, bracketed into topography or territorial locus, into mappable or chartable emplacements that can be "subdued, occupied, and possessed." In other words, they are subjected to what Elizabeth I's policy would promulgate in the next century as "effective occupation." Once brought under such proprietary control, the terrain had to be "populated." For the Spanish conquest of Isabel and Ferdinand,

this meant the legitimation of human habitats through the incorporation of their inhabitants—basically the process outlined by
the notice and requirement of the *Requerimiento,* that is, the
expunction of the Indians' accoutrements of humanity: history,
language, economy, religion, sovereignty, and the replacement of
these with the Spaniards' own. Columbus's Capitulaciones already referred to this process as "naturalization" when Isabel and
Ferdinand speak of "our subjects and naturals now being or shall
be for the time to come [nuestros subditos e naturales, que agora
son e seran de aqui adelante]."[41] For the English conquest, "effective occupation" begins, really, even if in the scriptive formulae of
textuality, with Henry VII and John Cabot's license to "subdue,
occupy, and possess," and is followed with what Philip II would
later encode as "population." The lesson of this early precedent
would not be lost on the Virginia "emplanters of civility," and
certainly not on the humanizing efforts of the Puritans who undertook the "inhabitation of desolate wilderness." In short, what
John Cabot's expedition is empowered to "subdue, occupy, and
possess" are peopleless "towns, cities, castles, and isles found by
them which they can subdue, occupy, and possess as our lieutenants getting unto us the rule, title, and jurisdiction of the same
villages, towns, castles, and firm land so found."[42] People, of
course, are nowhere and are nowhere mentioned. They are
"metonymically" displaced into annihilation. One can easily
imagine the relief and wonderment of the expeditioners and char-
terers at court when it was discovered that the masons of ideological discursivity and their rhetorical instruments did not have to
go to such lengths of lexical ingenuity because wonder-working
providence had already done their job of human eradication for
them. There were no "towns, cities, castles" to be subdued, occupied, and possessed after all. And the sundry nomads that pursued heathenish paths, furtively passing through "isles" and
"firm lands so found" would become "naturalized," after the
exemplary way of the Capitulaciones. However, since unlike the
Caribbean islanders and the Mexicans they could not be subdued
and incorporated due to their peripatetic and elusive ways, their
naturalization in New England (which in 1629 meant all of

North America "discovered and to be discovered," just as the
voracious reach of Virginia was all inclusive in her virgin time)
meant the automatic expropriation of any territorial rights to
their own territory. The year 1629 was that in which the New
England divine and founding father of what was, among other
things, the first real estate development company in Anglo-
America decreed the principle of *vacuum domicilium*.[43] Those
"domiciles" John Cabot's patent rhetorically vacated in depopu-
lating the geography of his charter's charts now become realized
as vacant outside of patent textuality and enacted as worldly
practice in territoriality. By Winthrop's reckoning, derived from
Purchas, *entre alii,* since the Indians did not "subdue" the land
(Queen Elizabeth's "doctrine of effective occupation"), they had
only "natural" but not "civil" rights to it.[44]

De facto possession was the Virgin Queen's most virginal
obsession, and the "doctrine of effective occupation," as noted,
has its genesis in the primal Elizabethan charter, the "Letters
Patent to Sir Humphrey Gilbert, June 11, 1578." Originally
designed to signal a departure from England's policy of acquiescence to canonist claims of papal supremacy and, hence, monar-
chic authority to "apportion the Globe," as Francis I put it in
his peeve, the key clause is modulated by two words, an adverb
and a participle: "actually possessed."[45] This minimal couplet
sets a new course for European empires and certainly *makes*
American history. Elizabeth elevated the genre of the charter
and letters patent to a shrewd art. The deliberate, deft, and
designing diplomatic moves necessary to a shifting policy find
their willfully mediate translation in the rhetorical formation of
the charters and patents. Beginning with the Humphrey Gilbert
letters patent, the charter becomes an intricate chart, a disingenuous map of action, its terms and clauses emplotted with calculation, the scripted moves consciously designed to maximize
worldly returns on the rhetorical investment. One cannot escape
the awareness that the charter has now become an instrument of
political discourse with a concomitant capability to be deployed
as a discourse of political posturing and imperial policy formation. Implicitly, of course, this has always been the case, starting

with the Capitulaciones de Santa Fe and its Medieval antecedents, as well as the language of the *Requerimiento*. These earlier instruments, however, evince a degree of naiveté, an unmediated self-conviction and an impregnable self-righteousness that makes their ideological overdetermination readily transparent. Such rhetorical primitivism and ideological "crudeness" resurfaces in the Jacobean charters of New England Puritans, as we shall see later in another chapter. The Elizabethan charter, on the other hand, has a subtlety that glosses over ideological determinations so that the charters read as matter-of-fact blueprints for a hegemonic policy of empire—discovery, conquest, settlement, incorporation, monopoly—without the audible clatter of ideology's sound and fury. Thus occluded, ideological determinations may actually become even more determinative by virtue of the greater versatility, expediency, and surreptitious pervasiveness their occlusion affords them. Ideology can operate in more insidious ways when it is not overt.[46] In this sense, the Elizabethan phase could be read as an interregnum between two heavy-handed and rather "artless" ideological epochs, the first being the late fifteenth-, early sixteenth-century Spanish conquest and the second corresponding to that ideologically "coherent beginning" that facilitates the ascription of "American Genesis" to Puritan New England for historians like Perry Miller. This Elizabethan intercession is slippery and its extension into the Stuarts' Virginian enterprise especially refractory. It does not mean, however, that this period is ideologically neutral or discontinuous. The overt and aggressive mercantile program of the Elizabethan era in fact has convinced some historians to generalize it to a point where an oversimplified contradistinction is made between the missionary and colonizing nature of Iberian conquest and the trading character of the English venture.[47] The fact is, the ideology of Christian mythology continues to be both serviceable, as we shall see in the case of the second Virginia charter in our next chapter, and reinforced, to the point where Puritan pilgrims can righteously deploy it with unthought impunity. What does happen during the Elizabethan phase of the conquest, it seems to me, is that the economic and hegemonic inter-

ests that were cloaked in the mythos of Christianity's cosmological narrative have themselves crystallized into social formations,
into a "consensual model" that exerts its own determinations
and makes its own ends into desiderata that motivate practices
and instrumentalize motives. As had been the case with Spain's
New World project for a century already, the two formations
will exchange roles as each other's cloak whenever expedient,
becoming mutually substitutable as enabling ideological structure to each other. That is why by the time of the Puritans the
other-worldly aspect of the New World becomes conflated with
the worldly interests of its conquerors, so that the earth and its
materiality, the real estate and its fruits, if you will, become
suffused with the mythos of the prophetic and the providential.
The territory, in other words, becomes spiritualized in ways that
make it easy and expedient for the chosen people to claim that
they have found and recognized, at last, their chosen land of
millenarian promise, and to press those claims on patently ideological grounds. The ground has in fact been cleared for them to
be able to do so by the wily and artful program charted in the
Elizabethan charters and carried out, albeit "incoherently," in
Virginia. Such ground clearing, as we have seen, begins with
Columbus's Capitulaciones, continues in John Cabot's charter,
and climaxes rhetorically and in practice, as we noted, in John
Winthrop's principle of *vacuum domicilium*.

The textual procedures of the Humphrey Gilbert patent, as one
could gather from the aforesaid, complicate the formula. The
charge is ostensibly the same, but subtly textured and conditioned in ways that enable the conquest to proceed systemati-
cally: discovery, conquest, settlement, colonization, expansion,
incorporation, monopoly. The verbs fall into formation: "to discover, find, search out, and view." Their object predicates, still
peopleless in the nomination, continue to be "remote, heathen,
and barbarous lands, countries, and territories." Indeed, the
prosopopeia or personification of the geography becomes patently formulaic. The screaming irony of this rhetorical turn is
that although the "lands, countries, and territories" are personi-
fied by adjectives such as "remote, heathen, and barbarous," they

are depersonalized, expunged of persons and inhabitants. Then follows the key phrase, "not actually possessed of any Christian prince or people." Here, finally, are some hypothetical people that might be inhabiting the land, but they only count if they are in actuality *not* inhabiting it. In other words, the non-presence of the "Christian prince or people" is more significant than the possible, though unmentionable, presence of human elements that heathenize and barbarize the terrain. The ternary enumeration of John Cabot's charter, "subdue, occupy, and possess" has its nominal and gerundial counterpart in "discovery, subduing, and possessing" of "all the soil of such lands, countries, territories . . . and of all cities, castles, towns, and villages," once again, unpeopled. Among the novelties introduced by this text, in addition to the libidinal "actually possessed" clause, figure a number of indications that, unlike John Cabot's undertaking, makes Sir Humphrey's expedition more than a *razzia*. For one thing, the letters patent granted to Humphrey Gilbert are for a six-year period. The charter speaks of the possibility of more than one voyage and of more than one kind, "habitative or possessive." In either case, the rights bestowed are proprietary, whether to "go and travel thither to inhabit or remain there, to build and fortify." The charter is elaborate on conditions of settlement, disposal of properties, payment of the royalty's royalty (the customary one-fifth), the exclusive monopoly, the incorporation of all "countries, lands, and territories so to be possessed and inhabited . . . within this our realm of England," the granting of citizenship to all inhabitants "born within our said realms of England and Ireland or within any other place within our allegiance" provided, of course, they be heirs of Sir Humphrey or those who journey with him. Granted, too, are the rights to devise and establish "statutes, laws, and ordinances [which] may be as near as conveniently may be agreeable to the form of the laws and policy of England; and also that they be not against the true Christian faith or religion now professed in the Church of England." Thus, the charter enjoins the grantee and "his heirs and assigns" to "have, hold, occupy, and enjoy" this as yet hypothetical and first projected outpost of the incipient British empire.

These letters patent shatter all curialist millenarian hopes for a
world monarchy and alter the prevailing narrative plot of "universal history," though not necessarily its prophetic itinerary or eschatological course. That pilgrimage would simply bifurcate, and
the redoubled intensity born of the contest between the two trajec-
tories would surely expedite Western Europe's conquest and expropriation of a World made new to its Old and a way station to
its prophetic Next World, as Columbus's providential oracle
made inevitable.

The imperial designs in Sir Humphrey's colonial project do
remain hypothetical following the failure of his Newfoundland
settlement and his own demise. Raleigh would be reissued his
half-brother's patent and his efforts would indeed eventuate in
the settlement of Virginia, and they would bring, as well, Western
Europe's bifurcated and contending colonization efforts into confrontation. Spain and England, the efforts of the Portuguese,
French, and Dutch notwithstanding, would emerge as the principal contestants, and their ideological mirroring would ever inten-
sify the vehemence of conquest. They would be spurred in their
drive for imperial hegemony in those mirrored reversals and reflective inversions of their face-off. Prophetic injunction and
providential election would be the exhortatory instruments of
both, and the stentorian invocations of godly duty and divine
predilection would resonate in echo from camp to camp. In that
din of rival self-exaltation, the New World would succumb to the
fractious fervor of self-righteousness, doubly justified in its redoubled zeal in the name of the same Divinity, now in the guise of
God, now as dis-guise of Mammon.

CHAPTER V

Salvaging the Salvages

Hec omnia habemus de uerbo ad uerbum in papiris.
Christopher Columbus, postille to d'Ailly's
Imago Mundi *folio 21 v.*

Vuestras Altezas se rieron y dixeron que les plazía.
Christopher Columbus, "Journal" of the
first voyage, 26 December 1492.

Though I confess it were more proper for mee, To be
doing what I say, then writing what I knowe.
Captain John Smith, A Description of New
England, *1616.*

Getting from here to there is more than a traversal; it figures a travesty. The Dante we already remarked knew it well—something he learned, no doubt, as adversarial Florentine, as wary exile, and wagering salvationist. That may well be why he condemns Ulysses to the infernal flame. Columbus came to know it too as he came and went, now on the wind, now in chains. And the other would-be "Admirall," Captain John Smith, made a vocation of this insight. To get there and back again, more than mere crossing, adds up to a double-crossing, even (especially) in eschatology's linear mathematics. A double-cross is the transom on which the voyager's epic yearning becomes crucified and where the godly pilgrim's zeal fixes its gaze on heaven's other world.

The treachery of chance looms most egregiously when history charts a most determined course. And when history's script is plotted by scripture's holy writ, happenstance betrayals are a divine curse. The vigilant faithful banish the hazards of fortuity, lest they feel abandoned by provident benefaction. In the sure course of prophetic history, then, the vicissitudes of the accidental become transmogrified into mystery and incomprehensible turns of divine intervention. The only betrayals are self-betrayals, despite which the slipping itinerant is held on steady course toward the appointed End. Thus, the master plot remains intact, its master narrative unsullied. And the faltering missteps taken become probationary opportunity for self-reconfirmation. As model for explaining and justifying history, this is an ideological formation unassailably at work. Its actual workings, however, cross themselves as actions and as language and, in that double-crossing, the impregnably symmetrical edifice of explanation and legitimacy founders. In the ensuing cracks and gaps one sees the scaffoldings that belie immaculate symmetries and paramount ideologies. History, then, becomes human history once more, which is to say an aggregation of untidy subplots whose itinerancy traces an unkempt path of lapses and relapses, irredeemable on any grounds other than mysterious. Mystery, of course, exacts a tremendous fascination when one invests in it, and to demur from doing so may keep one from partaking of its sublime dispensation. It was an avid student of the American sublime, the Transcendentalist Emerson, who saw in this privation a different kind of enablement as compensatory potential. The inescapable irony is that the Transcendentalist's insight points toward the "descendental," that is, toward the happenstance worldly rather than the impeccable orderliness of an other-worldly order. If the ironic could be resublimated into sublime mystery, America's New World history could then be writ as epic, with a plot as coherent and symmetrical as the plot of providential history that the prophetic ideology of its finders and founders idealized. Desirable as that plot may be for historians such as Perry Miller and Daniel Boorstin, and as sought after as they would wish to have it, that possibility of uniqueness was foreclosed when Christopher Columbus sailed and Christopher Guerra followed him. Captain John Smith and Virginia's second-charter publicists already corroborated the lesson of the Ecclesiastes. In human terms of history, the New World is a fiction as worldly novelty, and we can only be grateful to such historians for that fiction's perpetuation. Reality, of course, is more interesting than fiction more often than not, and America is doubly privileged with having fictionality as integral component of all things that make it real, starting with its very name, as we have seen already. But this unruly mesh of fiction and reality too is not a unique attribute, only more blatantly symptomatic because more often flaunted, now consciously, now unawares and with self-deluding righteousness. What makes the New World New are terms willfully declarative and not necessarily essential. What makes its history blatantly ironic, which is to say shrilly human, is the unbreachable gap between the declarations and the disheveled byways of the essentially "real" that waylays and undermines those declared terms. To seek a "coherence" like Perry Miller, a uniqueness like Daniel Boorstin, or an epic narrative tone like William H. Prescott in his histories of the Mexican and Peruvian conquests amounts to a willful, though not necessarily intended, perpetuation of America's fiction. For this reason, I am inclined to urge the wisdom and knowing wink of Alfonso Reyes, one of America's most lucid thinkers, against Prescott, Miller, and Boorstin. The Mexican philosopher, rhetorician, and philologist meditates with wakefulness on the question of "America, cradle of a new culture" in one of his better-known essays, "La posición de América" (1942). The proposition of America as "cradle of a new culture," Reyes notes, "should be protected and qualified by a question mark." Because, he continues, the question of America's position as cradle of a new culture

> does not belong to the order of statement which grammarians classify as the indicative mood, but to those which imply doubt and belief, insinuation and hope. Aristotle would have banned it from his *Dialectics* and have admitted it only in his *Rhetoric*. It refers to a principle of probability, not certainty. By reason of the spirit with which I approach it, I would venture to say that it belongs to a fanciful mood of grammar: the prophetic mood.[1]

Suggestively enough, the mood of grammar Reyes defines in this pithy observation is also the subjunctive, where "doubt and

belief" grammatically coexist, the "mood" that, as we have
noted already, is the unidentical twin of the imperative. Surely,
it is no accident that Columbus's writings and the Capitulaciones we parsed in our previous chapter should evince the
conjugation of "probability" and "certainty" with the imperative inevitability of ideological conviction. The result of that
crossing is precisely what Reyes calls the "prophetic mood,"
obviously a rhetorical dilation of grammar's jurisdiction so as to
embrace its rhetorical crossbreeds. The imperative injunction of
the "prophetic mood" is the fiction that bedevils the epic mode
with duplicitousness, a rhetorical/historical waylaying endemic
to irony's forked tongue. It is the fictionality that results when
the experiential crosses the predicative and the proclamatory—
in a most literal sense, a double crossing of what is declared or
claimed beforehand, which is another gloss for prophetic discourse and the rhetoric of its apocalyptic ideology. This is why,
I suspect, that elusive desideratum called "the great American
novel" is not to be found in our ironists, or limned against the
grain, but in the self-betraying irony of those epic voices whose
circumstances always and already speak one thing, whereas
their literary proclamations clamor otherwise. The spectrum of
such voices is large; it ranges from Herman Melville to Pablo
Neruda, the first a cultural pariah even as he sang, now sple-
netically, now in elegy, America's prophetic allegory; the second
a wanted fugitive in America while he intoned "the song of
ourselves," the epos of American history called *Canto general*.

Any self-characterization, and any self-determination much
more so, is a treacherous enterprise. Demurring to a determinative ideology of prophetic prevision and providential election may have been the surest way to beat the odds against waylaying contingency. Fortuity, however, has invariably proved imp-
ishly pertinacious, and the best-laid plans often went the way of
implacable reversals. Such was the fate of epic heroes, even when
they were viable. It took Ulysses a score of years to return to
Ithaca, only to be dispatched to irredeemable hell by Dante's
XXVIth Canto. Aristotle codified such fickleness of fate as a
peripeteia in the sixth chapter of his *Poetics*. Peripety takes on the

grimace of irony, in grotesque guffaw or sneer, when the waylaid stiffen into intractable formations. Predictably preprogrammed by unbending ideology's consensual determinacies, the itinerants of so straight a path now succumb to their self-duped determination, what otherwise could be called mystified tenacity. This, too, is a mighty enablement. And resolutely confronting fortuity with fortitude could result just as well in noble constancy as in incorrigible obduracy, depending on the outcome and on the side one happens to have been on. The "steadfast" always dictate the terms for the "incorrigible," and their dictation is writ as history, usually with righteousness and epic strokes of piety.

The question of when the dualities I have swiftly sketched turn into duplicities had to be countenanced in the New World beginning with Columbus. The mechanisms of self-subversion are a concomitant of any enterprise, and its seditionary correlatives gain a strength proportional to its driving force of conviction. No one could dispute Columbus's conviction in the pursuit of his undertaking. So decisively compelled and obsessively unrelenting was Columbus that, having watched him pass through thousands of pages and centuries of volumes, I have yet to see him smile or give himself to laughter. Other emotive manifestations are not alien to him and they range from the pathetic to the Job-like agonic. In the hundreds of letters, marginal notes, journal entries, testimonials, and sundry memoranda that flowed from his pen,[2] I have come across mention of laughter in the 25 December entry following his disaster (he is describing the sweet disposition of the Indians) and in the 26 December entry, as cited in the second epigraph at the head of this chapter. Both instances would prove treacherous. As with smiles of kings and clowns, it is well-nigh difficult to discern how much mirth this "laughter" of Their Highnesses actually contains. In the context of the occasion there is this ambivalence. But ambiguity is eradicated by certainty when one considers the peripeties that befell the proposal occasioning the royal smile. The fate of the proposed ends dictate ineluctably that the smile be read as smirk; whether as rictus or ridicule, that must remain ambiguous. As in everything touching Columbus, complete disambiguation is invariably elusive. The

Admiral writes these smiling words when providence smiles least upon him. It is 26 December. The previous morning of Christmas 1492 his flagship irreparably ran aground on the reefs of what he would not miss the opportunity to name Isla Navidad. On this hazard's occasion of Nativity and foundering, the first European settlement in the New World is founded. It will be a fort and it too will founder, thereby precipitating the Admiral's fortunes into embattled decline. Always predictable in his typological and providentialist reading of "emergent occasions," to use John Donne's phrase once more, this reversal of fortune would lead him to godly thoughts and divine designs: "All this says the Admiral. And he adds more to demonstrate that this was a great boom and determined will of God that the ships should founder so that he could leave people there [Todo esto dize el Almirante. Y añade más para mostrar que fue gran ventura y determinada voluntad de Dios que la nao encallase porque dexase allí gente]."[3] Parenthetically, we should remember that the narrative voice that speaks for the Admiral here, and throughout the journal of the first voyage, is that of Father Bartolomé de Las Casas who had a copy of the journal from which to paraphrase, the original having been lost to posterity. Yet one more inescapable twist would have the primal document on which America's history is founded reach us by way of paraphrase. Product of perverse peripety, that historiographical beginning would also be periphrastic. America's foundations, then, are not only anxious and founded on foundered intentions, but their narrative has to be grounded on the treacherous vicissitudes of an *histoire on-dit,* borne, that is, on the slippery terrain of circuitous hearsay. No doubt, this fate too resonates in that insight of Nathaniel Hawthorne, already cited in our second chapter, distilled by New England's supreme allegorist as a "Ghostland's" terrain that "lies beyond the jurisdiction of veracity." The predicate in Hawthorne's apothegm is no less treacherous in its homonymic equivocation. Does "lying" in a jurisdiction beyond veracity constitute a redoubled lie, a double-crossing that crucifies peripety's prevarication to salvage it as truth?

Digressive as our mounting parentheses may be, Columbus

saw nothing of parallaxes in his typological calculus. No shift, and no change in the line of sight. He remained tightly gripped in the pages of scripture ("uerbo uerborum in papiris"), in the prophetic parentheses of providential design, and every turn of happenstance was for him yet one more token that augured divine favor for predetermined ends. It is thus that he continues to reassure Their Majesties of his steadfast vocation and remind them of their royal smile:

> Y dize qu'espera en Dios que, a la buelta que él entendía hazer de Castilla, avía de hallar un tonel de oro, que avríam resgatado los que avía de dexar, y que avrían hallado la mina del oro y la espeçería, y aquello en tanta cantidad que los Reyes antes de tres años emprendiesen y adereçasen para ir a conquistar la Casa Sancta, "que así" dize él, "protesté a Vuestras Altezas que toda la ganançia d'esta mi empresa se gastase en la conquista de Hierusalem, y Vuestras Altezas se rieron y dixeron que les plazía, y que sin esto tenían aquella gana." Estas son palabras del Almirante.[4]

> [And he says that he hopes to God that upon the return trip he intended to make from Castille, he should find a cask of gold that those he would leave behind would have redeemed in barter, and they would have found the gold mine and spicery, and all this in such quantity that the King and Queen, within three years, should undertake and organize to go and conquer the Holy Sepulchre, "thus," he says, "I affirmed to Your Highnesses, that all the revenues from this my enterprise be spent on the conquest of Jerusalem, and Your Highnesses smiled and said it so pleased them, and even without it they wished to do so." These are the Admiral's words.]

Having observed in the opening of our third chapter that in the master narrative of the New World's prophetic history the most hopeful soundings are taken at the greatest depths of bathos, I should like for us to read Columbus's conjugation of his most obsessive and, in his own eyes, his loftiest and ultimate goal, with his most dire circumstances as symptomatic of that propensity. Carrying through with everything already scripted "uerbo ad uerbum," Columbus salvages the wreck as felicitous turn of divine dispensation. The eschatological ends of the End are thus maintained in tact and on course. His crusader's zeal for Zion's reconquest is a necessary and mediate step, a way station of providential history's ends imminently due as apocalyptic consummation. The calendar for that appointed end will have been set in the Admiral's arithmetic some seven years later, as we have seen already in our first and second chapters.

The ends Columbus articulates as the raison d'être of his enterprise clearly make the New World a means. And the "ends of the earth" that he will have willed to the Puritans are for him, as they will be for them in turn, a prefiguration of a posthistorical Other World. Thus hinged, America becomes pivotal typology, at once fulfillment and presage of eschatology's schema. Liminal geography, America will ever serve as threshold—New World to the Old, mediate end to the Next. In the sublime tenancy of this pivotal position, America's pilgrimage will not only twist and turn in peripety's chastisements, but it will also oscillate between a position of paragon in prophecy's "universal history" and a disposition of paradox in perverse fortune's flukes. Although adhering to the first role of this script, Columbus ends by playing the second and, in that travesty of fate, he becomes truly America's primal precursor. As one who saw himself in the role of providential agent with divine election, events past, present, and future are typologically figured for him in the sense of these terms discussed in our first chapter. What Columbus did not anticipate is the role he himself would prefigure. Surely, were he pressed, he would have not seen himself among the "maryners and crafty governours" of Brant's *Shyp of Folys*. His writings amply indicate that in his eyes he was more than mere "maryner," and in the ledger of history he undoubtedly proved much less than "crafty governour." The fate of the thirty-nine men and of the empire's founding outpost display in mirror's echo the prophetic aims of orthodoxy and the paradoxes of contingency's snare. In the hazards of this incipient step, America's subsequent history will have been prefigured.

Ravished by greed and libidinous rapacity, the natives of Columbus's inexorable colony would decimate, in turn, the internecine first settlers. The Christians' comportment in paradise proved damnable indeed. Colonization, or settlement as other than outpost of economic conquest, would fall from priority for a

number of years. In the meantime, the fundamental tenets of
Western Europe's enterprise would be established during the decade following Columbus's first sailing. These are interesting
terms inasmuch as they resonate in ways that betray ideological
velleities and their euphemistic screens. The verb *rescatar*, already
used by Columbus in the journal entry just cited, and its nominal
version *rescate* form the lexical precedent that frames the course
for worldly feats and sets the agenda of ecstasy for other-worldly
ends. The Latinate terms will find their English variants by and
by, and they will be no less echoic richocheting between mundane
interests and devotional vocations. The predicates *to ransom, to
redeem,* and *to salvage* will take as object-predicate their substan-
tive equivalents—ransom, redemption, and salvage, the latter
more often than not in the generalizable anonymity of its imper-
sonalized plural form. This self-betraying resonance is indeed the
lexical parting of an ideological veil, of that pervasive, consensual
forma mentis that would press its proprietary claims on what it
implacably believed to have been its rightful patrimony. One can
only *re-capture* (this is the meaning of the Latin etymon for the
Spanish *rescatar*) or re-deem, or ransom, or salvage what one
already had and lost through some mischance of fate. The official
symptom of this conviction will manifest itself in Gonzalo Fernández de Oviedo's *Historia general y natural de las Indias.*[5] As
already indicated in our third chapter, this official history by
Emperor Charles V's court chronicler renders the New World as
old Spanish territory finally recovered after centuries of relapse
and oblivion. For the curialist canons and their Puritan avatars,
of course, all unanointed terrain had to be redeemed from igno-
minious darkness. Oviedo's *Historia*, with its salvationist theory
and messianic zeal, dates from 1535, a third of a century after
Columbus and some three-quarters of a century before the redeeming planters of Virginia, who will manifest, as we shall see,
their own version of this conviction.

The Dominican Father Bartolomé de Las Casas often sees the
hand of providence and its divine retribution in the reversals of
fortune that befall the rapacious Spaniards. He seldom sees the
ironic peripeties that betray the symmetrical program of providen-

tialist ideology. Although he does acknowledge Columbus's fail-
ures, and ascribes them to divine justice, he spends a good quan-
tity of ink in his *Historia* (bk. 1, chap. 2) etymologizing the
Admiral's name and genealogy. He thus would have Columbus
be a redeeming colonizer by dint of natural necessity. The name
of Cristóbal Colón, as the Admiral is called in Spanish, becomes
emblematic and prophetically foreordained for the task divine
election has dictated for him. Cristóbal Colón's colonizing project, which begins with his Christmas shipwreck, does evince a
symmetry, but it would be the calamitous symmetry of a ruinous
ending that mirrors its beginning in catastrophe. Ruinous consequences are, of course, genesic dispensation for those who view
history as post-catastrophic plot, a plot that unfolds inexorably
toward the salvaging of a lapsarian world. If the *natural colony,*
that is, the *nascent Eden,* goes the way of its typological prototype in Genesis, the pilgrimage toward recovery must begin there
as natural commencement, as origination of history's march
through a redemptive odyssey toward deliverance. The pilgrim's
progress thus mirrors, analogically, the peregrination of the
Church Militant toward its destined rendezvous with the Church
Triumphant. Onward the savior soldiers march in step with the
script emplotted. The hazards of the happenstance, however, are
by no means foreclosed, especially for those who, despite requi-
site conscription, may find themselves out of step or out of the
parade. The march then translates for them into baneful maraud-
ing, and the bewildered natives of the New World can attest to its
consequences.

   If Father Las Casas sees a preordained vocation in Columbus's
name, the juxtaposition of Cristóbal Colón with Cristóbal Guerra
can be equally suggestive as an accurate, albeit perfidious, allegory for what befalls the enterprise of ransoming the fallen. The
Dominican father does not wax etymological when in book 1,
chapter 171 of his *Historia de las Indias* he relates Guerra's ex-
ploits, though he does pun on the name. His tone, rather, resonates with Jeremiah's, and he concludes his account by noting
that "God was not dozing when those sinners were committing
wars [*guerras*], principally Cristóbal Guerra, who must have been

the more merciless, or at least, who was leading the dance, because they did not enjoy the fruits of their impiety for long; divine
justice willed soon enough to wreck its retribution . . . for deeds
so perverse and nefarious. [N]o dormía D os [sic] cuando estas
injusticias, aquellos pecadores, guerras [sic] cometían, mayor-
mente Cristóbal Guerra, que debía ser el más sinpiedad, o al
menos, el que debía guiar la danza, porque no se fuesen mucho
gozando de tanta impiedad, quiso la divina justicia . . . obra tan
perversa y nefanda reprobar]." Father Las Casas's anathema attests to the righteous ire reserved for those who would travesty
the redemptive plot of providence. Guerra certainly displays the
human capacity to give divine terms a worldly twist. In this he,
too, like Columbus's thirty-nine settlers on Navidad, becomes
emblematic of human agency's inevitable proclivity to pervert
ideology's virtue, or, at least, to rend the veil of ideology. Having
amply succeeded in a first chartered *razzia* with Peralonso Nuñez
to prove the profitability of small trading expeditions (1499),
Cristóbal Guerra was granted a second charter on his own account in 1503 to return to the pearl beds that proved so fruitful on
his first voyage. Wishing to mix his pearls with gold and maximize his harvest, he would capture the trusting chief of territories
near Cartagena as hostage on his ship. The cacique's return alive
was contingent on the Indians' filling a grape-harvesting basket
thrown overboard with gold. After days of lamentation and scour-
ing the countryside, the Indians filled the basket, not before being
taunted with loss of their chief by Guerra who sailed away only to
make land again in different ports along the coast. Father Las
Casas narrates the episode with indignant pathos and makes the
telling observation that in their lamentable desperation the people
"called upon God, tacitly, even though they did not know him, to
do justice to their chief. [[D]aban gritos a Dios tácitamente,
aunque no lo cognocían, que le hiciese justicia . . .]."

   Cristóbal Guerra manages to twist terms so ideologically laden
with prophetic history's emotive force. The verb *rescatar*, the key
verb to his charter and charted enterprise, is stripped bare of all
the sublime connotations that shield its worldly ends. Terms such
as ransom, redeem, salvage, harvest, grapes, pearls, and gold are

shorn of all talismanic piety intended to make the venal venial. There is a supreme irony in this episode inasmuch as Guerra's second charter was granted him by Queen Isabel herself, independently of her husband Ferdinand of Aragon, whom many consider Machiavelli's paradigm of princely savvy. Isabel of Castille conferred the charter in terms urgently pious in the year before her death, stipulating expressly what she would reiterate in her last will and testament, that is, the good and godly treatment of the Indians, and sending along a few clerics in the event any of Guerra's crew should wish to stay and settle. They should thus be kept devout. In ambiguous terms whose subsequent use would make her look sadly ingenuous, Isabel indicates that "said X-val Guerra . . . can take Indians anywhere they be discovered for languages of those lands, as long as they not be made slaves or harmed and they be taken as much according to their will as possible, and," the text continues without interruption, "likewise he be allowed to take monsters and animals of whatever nature and quality they be . . . all of which shall properly belong to him, as stipulated, giving a fourth part of all to me [dicho X-val Guerra . . . que pueda tomar en qualesquier partes que descubrieren yndios e yndias para lenguas de aquellas tierras con tanto que no sean para escablos [sic, for esclavos] ny para les haser mal ny dapno [sic, for daño] e que los tomen los mas a su voluntad que ser pueda e que asy mysmo pueda tomar monstruos e anymales de qualquier natura e calidad que sean . . . lo qual todo sea suyo propio segund dicho es dando el quarto de todo ello a my]."[6]

Inasmuch as the sixth clause of the charter makes provisions for Indians brought by Guerra on his 1499 expedition to be taken along as interpreters, salaried and treated as free men, to facilitate his journey, the Queen's intent is clear with respect to "taking Indians for languages." The problem is, of course, that her own official language in the charter already speaks in tongues whose ambiguities would be exploited to the fullest and twisted to convenience by Guerra and his cohorts. He did not scruple about refinements of taking Indians "as much according to their [the Indians'] will as possible." Such terms had no need of disambiguation when all he was concerned with was fungible cargo, whether pearls, people, monsters, or animals of phenomenal nature. The textual composition of the charter itself allowed for not making any such differentiations. Cristóbal Guerra read the semantic charge of the verb *rescatar* most pharisaically. And, unmistakably, the prefix for him was not only an enabling redundant that allowed and authorized him to ransom from oblivion what the devil had lost, but he took the *re-* of *rescatar* as emphatic enablement that sanctioned him to capture with implacable vehemence. Thus, he turns the object of "ransom," "barter," and "redemption" into something to be ransomed not from the devil but from him. Queen Isabel, more than likely, did not intend it that way, but her charge made it possible and she did demand her rightful fourth, up from the conventional fifth, as her due royalty.

Cannibalism is an intricate phenomenon in the value-laden discourse on the New World.[7] Anthropophagy is not unique to Western Europe's Caribbean experience; but the displacement of the Greek term by its American equivalent is significant. Ideologically, "anthropophagy" served Greek hegemonic purposes for "othering" the barbarians into objects of legitimate war, conquest, and enslavement. Generalized from Greek antiquity to the rest of Europe, the term clearly lost its serviceable instrumentality. A cognate term became necessary for application to cultures outside a European context for the "barbarization" beyond what had already been for the Greeks, and hence Western Europeans, barbarian terrain. Having found a new geographical object, a commensurate new word became indispensable. The rest is etymological history, and any dictionary will refer one to the Caribbean origins of *cannibalism*. The word indeed displaced the European Greek term, and with that displacement, substituted not only a term founded on the cultural and geographical "other," but it also imputed an "othering" attribute as natural characteristic that makes that other culture fair game of conquest by virtue of that attribution. Although the canons and court jurists would debate the grounds of "just war" and enslavement, unanimity was to be had on cannibalism. Those who practiced it were unquestionably enslaveable. Considered irredeemably sinful, an egregiously sub-

human act against the laws of nature and God, its nefarious practice justified any act of war. In the charter texts, we find as early as
Cristóbal Guerra's 22 July 1503 charter the stricture against enslavement of the Indians. They can be captured "for languages"
but "according to their will as much as possible." In February of
the following year, the restriction would be reiterated in the charter granted to Juan de la Cosa. Only now, an exception to that
stricture is specified: "You are not to bring slaves except those
who by our command are declared as slaves, who are those on the
islands of St. Bernardo and Isla Fuerte and in the ports of Cajena
and in the isles of Baru who are called cannibals [[Q]ue no podays
traer esclavos salvo los que por nuestro mandado son
pronunciados por esclavos que son los que están en las yslas de
sant bernardo e ysla fuerte e en los puertos de cajena e en las yslas
de baru que se dicen canibales]."[8] The exception will be repeated
again in the notorious Pedrarías Dávila's 1514 charter to Darién.[9]

When chance consolidated Guerra's and Juan de la Cosa's
shipwrecked expeditions into one, between them they held over
six hundred Indians as slave cargo. Both expeditions would be
forced to beach their worm-eaten ships. Guerra would die at the
hands of the Indians he pillaged, as would Juan de la Cosa in
turn. Of the two hundred surviving crew members, less than fifty
would return from the voyage, but not before eating at least one
of their Indian prey. Cannibalizing the cannibals so literally
proves excessive even for the war-seasoned conquistador
Gonzalo Fernández de Oviedo. He has left us the most complete
account, as related to him by Juan Ledesma, the survived captain
of one of Juan de la Cosa's ships. Oviedo finds it necessary to
introduce the events he must narrate as a historian with apolo-
gies: "Because through no fault of mine I could not silence what
came to my attention of what each and everyone has distinctly
done in these parts. [Porque sin culpa mía no podría callar lo que
a mi noticia ha venido de lo que señaladamente ha hecho cada
uno en estas partes]."[10] As mystified as he was by the central plot
of prophetic history, Oviedo rarely shuns detail as a historian.
Having duly absolved himself for what his tale must tell, five
books later he comes to the account of the heinous act:

Pues llegados allí, como lo que hallaron que comer era poco, algunos destos cristianos, viéndose en extraña hambre, mataron un indio que tomaron, e asaron el asadura e la comieron; e pusieron a cocer mucha parte del indio en una gran olla para llevar qué comer en el batel donde iban los que esto hicieron.[11]

[Upon arriving there [the port of Zamba], since what they found to eat was so little, a few Christians, seeing themselves in extreme hunger, killed an Indian they had captured and roasted the entrails and ate them; and they put a goodly part of the Indian to stew in a large pot in order to have something to take along to eat in the ship's boat in which those who did this were travelling.]

By the end of Oviedo's chapter, the cannibal's anthropophagi have their just deserts, and the court chronicler sees divine justice in their death at the hands of the Indians. Captain Juan de la Cosa who spoils his cannibals' feast and chastises them, himself will meet an equally just end for his own plundering acts of barbarity against the barbarians. Oviedo, like Las Casas who shares his feelings on Cristóbal Guerra's end, wonders whether Juan de la Cosa's charter had authorized such assaults on the Indians (bk. 8, chap. 1). In fact, it did, as we have seen, though Juan de la Cosa's sense of equity is particularly ambivalent in discriminating among cannibals.[12]

As far as allegories of conquest go, admittedly Guerra's and Juan de la Cosa's are rather crude, perhaps as crude as the reality they capture. The more artful Captain John Smith would no doubt think so. But, then again, a hundred years of imperial experience did not elapse in vain. In the ongoing dialogue between Iberian and English versions of this tale, the English, of course, have the seasoned advantage of that experience, an advantage the Puritan divines will righteously relinquish, as we shall see shortly.

As peripeties of ideology, the allegories of reversal in Cristóbal Guerra's salvaging and in the cannibalism of Juan de la Cosa's shipwrecks function as inversions. They are mirrored transversals of cultural practices that belie their own ideological formations. Such predicaments are forms of self-double-crossing. They betray the self-serving and self-legitimating nature of enablements that authorize the transformation of another culture and its territory (figural and literal) into proprietary objects of conquest. Guerra and de la Cosa are crude examples of this travesty because they are purely instrumental and symptomatic of the ideological determinants that deploy them, these being, as often pointed out, enablements that issue from a prophetic and providentialist view of history that empower Western European peoples with the conviction and mission to salvage the "unregenerated world" believed lost to their ken. The ideological cloak cut from the fabric of this conviction is flouted by Guerra and Juan de la Cosa, as well as by other instruments of conquest whose conquering acts are to be shielded by it. Alternatively, the same cloak can be disingenuously flaunted as expedient cover, and even as sincere guise, as in the case of the propagandists for the Virginia Company to be examined shortly. Both alternative procedures—the flouting and the flaunting—can be self-betraying. Self-belying is a form of irony when those carrying it out are aware of its travesty. It becomes treacherous when those acting in all earnestness are duped by its treason. History is interesting, in part, because neither of these possibilities ever excludes the other, and because history as human institution is constituted by the hazardous peripeties of ingenuity that expose its subjects to such betrayals, even as they act with consummate perspicacity. Neither historiographers, nor cultural critics, of course, are immune to these hazards. And when a chronicler or publicist would also be the acting subject of historical events, as is the case with Columbus, Oviedo, John Smith, or John Winthrop, the risks become compounded. In this sense, the conquering entrepreneurs and divine redeemers of the Northern and of the Southern parts of the New World share not only an ideology, they also share a predicament.

As for predicaments, few men have had to negotiate as many as Captain John Smith, the mercenary turned explorer, turned imperial publicist and colonial propagandist. His predicaments span a geography that extends from Istanbul to Jamestown, and his activities range from murder to lexicography.[13] Our epigraph from Captain Smith's dedication of his *A Description of New England* "To the right Worshipfull Adventurers for the Country of New

England" betokens the fact that Smith has an awareness of the
treacherous terrain between what he knew, what he said, and
what he did. Many volumes and countless articles have been published attempting to make this threesome construe. An entire
genre and a publishing industry in English have been engendered
under the rubric of "literature of captivity" by a tenuous paragraph that, suggestively enough, does not exist in his *A True
Relation of Such Occurrences and Accidents of Noate as Hath
Hapned in Virginia* (1608), but which resonates wildly enough in
*The Generall Historie of Virginia, New-England, and the Sum-
mer Isles* (1624) to precipitate a myth and a national allegory. I
am referring to the paragraph in the latter work which relates
Smith's rescue by Pocahontas seventeen years earlier from the
clubs of Powhatan's chiefs, about to bash his head in: "but the
conclusion was, two great stones were brought before Powhatan:
then as many as could layd hands on him, dragged him to them,
and thereon laid his head, and being ready with their clubs, to
beate out his braines, Pocahontas the Kings dearest daughter,
when in intreaty could prevaile got his head in her armes, and laid
her owne upon his to save him from death."[14] Somewhere between the event ("beyond the jurisdiction of veracity" of *A True
Relation*, but within the specificity of *The Generall Historie*) and
its recollection in the Caesarian third-person narrative, lies another suggestive statement in *A Description of New England*. The
running synopses in the margins designate this section as "The
Authors conditions" and it figures on page thirty-seven of Smith's
original edition. The statement reads: "And if I abuse you with
my tongue, take my head for satisfaction."[15] Smith's rhetorical
constructs, the "discursive formations" of his elaborate corpus,
are as dizzying as the whirlwind of his itinerary. Many have
strayed hopelessly trying to trace his tracks. There is something
preferable, however, in allowing him his contradictions. Whether
we accede to his word, thereby conceding that his "tongue abuses
us not," or, like Pocahontas, choose to take his "head for satisfaction," thus legitimating the pivotal episode of his mythology, the
Captain and would-be Admirall has woven an intricate web that
would legitimate his enterprise whichever path we choose. Per-

haps we should not limit ourselves to any one venue to the exclusion of any of the others. If history be the exclusive ken of positiv-
ist cliometricians, then Captain Smith would be best read as a
nonhistorical figure, which, of course, does not preclude the historical significance of his persona(e), his writings, or the refracted
light his elusive figures may shed on less indomitable factors.
Thus considered, *A True Relation,* for example, reveals the dire
circumstances not only of the English colony at Jamestown but,
perhaps more significantly, the urgently pressing situation of
those who had a vested interest in salvaging their investment and
in assuring an English toehold, however precarious, in North
America. The text of *A True Relation* in this respect becomes
more symptomatic and revelatory of the historical context than of
Smith's veracity. The fact is, the desperate concern of those in
London who felt the critical need to save a bad situation is the
least disputable aspect of this text. Precisely because of those
pressures, an unbreachable gap yawns between the title and the
truth or authenticity of the document as it might have existed
prior to its publication. Philip Barbour notes in his editorial apparatus that this text is most corrupted, having been "ruthlessly
edited and hastily printed to an unusual degree." Because, Barbour points out, "the editing and the rush to press fitted the
Virginia Company's interests."[16] Smith's letter was what the Company needed just then. As the first account of the colony's first
year to reach London, it offered the Company the means to assuage doubts and disillusionment based on partial reports that
filtered back from Virginia. What sort of truth the *True Relation*
contains, then, is clearly mooted. What is not questionable, however, is the lengths to which the Company would go to assure
interest and continued investment.

I rehearse this episode and the key role of Captain John Smith
more for the significance they have for the colony's second charter and, eventually, for Puritan New England, than for rehashing
the anecdotal peripeties, still hazardous ground though thoroughly trod already. *A True Relation* as propaganda instrument
notwithstanding, the colonial project at Jamestown had to become privatized and rechartered accordingly. The new charter

was signed on 23 May 1609. This exacerbated the critical need to
"sell" the entire enterprise to the English public. In that urgency,
the Company will make recourse to the most venerable means
and most profoundly rooted ideological Ends: prophetic rhetoric
and the eschatological ideology of providential history. The desired goals would be achieved, although the colony would eventually be displaced northward by more persuasive, because ideologically purer, errands; and the Company would eventually be dissolved in 1624. Captain John Smith does indeed have a part in
that displacement also, his *A Description of New England* of
1616 having been instrumental in the formulation of the New
England colonial project. Ironically, perhaps with impish savvy,
in the same paragraph cited earlier from this work where Smith
would have us choose between believing his tongue or having his
head, prescient perhaps that his head would forever be shielded
by the legend of Pocahontas, he notes of New England's promise:
"[B]y the proofe of that wealth I hope yearly to return, if God
please to bless me from such accidents, as are beyond my power
in reason to prevent: For, I am not so simple, to thinke, that ever
any other motive than wealth, will ever erect there a Common-
weal."[17] Once again, Captain Smith may well be both right and
wrong. To reduce his multiple ambiguity to a monadic explanation, however, would be to impoverish not only the man but the
richness of history. One of Anglo-American historiography's
most singular lights would certainly have us do so, as he would
have us read the publicist campaign of the Virginia Company on
behalf of the second charter with the same unique coherence that
emanates from God's truth rather than from people's interested
improvisations, whether they be Spaniards, Virginians, Pilgrims,
or Puritans. In this vein, Perry Miller would have us take the
Virginia Company's campaign at face value. For in the pulpit
rhetoric of prophetic injunctions sponsored by the Company in
1609, Miller sees "a set of principles for guiding not a mercantile
investment but a medieval pilgrimage. The cosmos ex-
pounded . . . is one where the principal human concern is neither
the rate of interest nor the discovery of gold, but the will of
God."[18] Clearly, in certain instances, those who deployed the

ideology of conquest had greater immunity to mystification than those who inherited it.

If, as already noted, there is something crudely ingenuous in the betrayal of ideological formulations through acts of inversion and reversal of roles scripted in prophetic history's plot where Cristóbal Guerra and Juan de la Cosa are concerned, there is something ingenious in the Virginia Company's decision to deploy the most influential preachers of the day to shore up the Jamestown colony. Two historians chronicle the pulpit campaign for us, the first being Louis B. Wright in his *Religion and Empire*,[19] and the second, drawing heavily upon, but extending Wright's discussion, is John Parker.[20]

"From its foundation in 1606 until its dissolution in 1624," notes Louis B. Wright, "the Virginia Company employed preachers to deliver sermons before the shareholders on stated occasions. It printed these sermons at the expense of the Company and distributed them widely. It also rewarded preachers with payments in cash, and, in some instances, by giving them stock in the company. Dr. John Donne, dean of St. Paul's, was the most distinguished cleric in its pay, but there were many others almost as well known in their time."[21] The sermons excerpted by Wright from the Company's frantic campaign of 1609 make his point convincingly. John Donne, the poet, deacon, metaphysician, and typologist to whom we have alluded from the beginning of this study is a heavy-duty weapon to have had for one's cause.[22] The arguments educed by the preachers in favor of the Virginia enterprise are not unfamiliar. Nor do they differ considerably from the arguments we find in Spanish propagandists and chroniclers of a century earlier. The difference is, of course, that England has an earthly competitor, a political and imperial foe, not to say an ideological antagonist the English identify with Antichrist, though the ideology for both is essentially the same, only now more virulent by virtue of competition. The sanctification of English colonial projects begins in earnest with the second charter of the Virginia Company, as John Parker accurately observes.[23] That baptism begins concertedly on the occasion of Captain John Smith's *A True Relation*, quite likely a surprise to Smith himself, as must have been the case with the way his "News from Virginia" was deployed altogether. The introduction prefixed to Smith's text over the initials of "I.H."[24] is an encomium to Virginia and concludes with an invocation to "the mightie Johovah." The high note of the exhortation, however, enjoins the English nation to "the action most honourable, and the end to the high glory of God, to the erecting of true religion among Infidells, to the overthrow of superstition and idolatrie, to the winning of many thousands of wandering sheepe, unto Christs fold, who now, and till now, have strayed in the unknowne paths of Paganisme, Idolatrie, and superstition."[25] The second charter of the Virginia Company would certainly reflect this emphasis, and a comparison of this to the first charter (1606) does illustrate the refocusing of the Virginia project from a settlement colony with godly ways to nearly an outpost for a holy crusade, as the pulpit rhetoric would have it. The second charter is unequivocal on the priorities of the enterprise: "the principal effect which we can desire or expect of this action is the conversion and reduction of the people in those parts unto the true worship of God and christian religion."[26]

As early as Richard Hakluyt's exhortations to empire, citing Father Bartolomé de Las Casas became a commonplace among apologists for English expansion into the New World. Father Las Casas's humanitarian campaign on behalf of the Indians was translated to English in 1583 in a volume entitled *The Spanish Colonie*. It would become the basis for what came to be known as "the black legend." The "salvages" had to be salvaged from the ravages of Spanish tyranny and its atrocities as described by Las Casas. Although the Dominican friar is not absent from the sermons on behalf of the Virginia Company, the kind of "Christian religion" advocated and the methods prescribed for the English crusade are not those of the meek Christianity of Father Las Casas; nor are the rhetoric and actions it calls for the charitable process of the Dominican. Rather, what echoes from the pulpit and the presses of London at this time harkens more to the Old Testament Christianity and prophetic messianism of Las Casas's Spanish antagonists Ginés de Sepúlveda and Gonzalo Fernández de Oviedo. It is noteworthy that the texts of these English sermons are preponderantly based on Old Testament prophets and intertestamental typologies. In this sense, the refocusing of conquest's rhetoric from the mercantile venture to a legitimating discourse that is filtered through the lens of prophetic ideology becomes significant not just for Jamestown in 1609–1610. This rhetorical shift augurs the Puritan project of New England, even as it echoes the earlier Spanish enterprise. In this latter regard, the Virginia Company's campaign hinges the New England colonial conquest with the Spanish one to the south. We shall review that connection in more explicit terms by and by.

In terms of the ideological agenda of prophecy and eschatology detailed in our first chapter, it is not insignificant that for the first official sermon (25 April 1609) the promoters of the Company elected William Symonds. Two weeks later, his sermon was already entered for publication with the Company of Stationers. A preacher at Saviour's, Southwark, Symonds had achieved notoriety with a commentary (*Pisgah Evangelica*) he had published in 1605 on the Book of Revelation. Though his renown was founded on scripture's apocalyptic last book, his sermon for this occasion was based on the first—Genesis 12:1–3: "Now the Lord said to Abraham, 'Go from your Country and kindred and your father's house to the land that I will show you. And I will make you a great nation, and I will bless you, and make your name great, so that you will be a blessing. I will bless those who bless you, and him who curses you I will curse; and by you all the families of the earth shall bless themselves.' " For those, like Perry Miller and Sacvan Bercovitch,[27] interested in "American Genesis," Symond's Genesis-based sermon might have not been an unremarkable place to begin. Certainly the worldly circumstances and political context of this studied beginning in the beginning might have textured the coherent metaphysical (otherworldly) foundations they descry with more contingent and geophysical investments that never ceased to obtain in Western Europe's conquest of the New World. In this sermon, William Symonds strikes the precedent of typological procedure that will become the common coin of Puritan self-explanation in America. In the process, unbeknownst to him, his procedure echoes Colum-

bus's typological gambit in his *Libro de las profecías* (1501).
Symond's typological maneuver brooked no difficulty in equating
the English nation with Abraham. The relentless iteration of such
equations would render the New World in the minds of the English their natural and divine inheritance with a compelling obligation to press their claims. They did. And to the less convinced
who would quibble about the hegemonic appropriation of another people's country and home, Symonds replies: "[I]f these
obiecters had any braines in their head . . . they could easily finde
a difference betweene a bloudy inuasion, and the planting of a
peaceable Colony, in a waste country, where the people doe liue
but like Deere in heards."[28] Such objections, Symonds protests,
are "hatched of some popish egge"; he is willfully ignorant, obviously, that the course of action he advocates merely emulates that
already hatched and pursued by the "popish egge" he damns. The
notion of "a waste country where people doe liue but like Deere
in heards" is the leitmotif of English propaganda and harkens to
the desolation of the New World's terrain traceable to Columbus's and John Cabot's charters, as we have already seen. It also
augurs John Winthrop's principle of *vacuum domicilium* to
which we have referred and to which we shall return.

The vehemence with which objections to English incursions
into the New World were rebutted would indicate that there
were, indeed, those who questioned the morality and wisdom of
conquering another's territory, however vacant and distant that
territory and however alien and heathenish its culture. These
dissenters, however, clearly stood no chance against the prevailing ideological consensus and its stentorian rhetoric. Besides
which, economic and demographic pressures in England, as well
as political and doctrinal competition abroad, made it imperative
and inevitable that the ideology of conquest and expansion
should prevail. The sermons and tracts of 1609 are exhortatory
and admonitory in this respect. They enjoin the English nation to
action and admonish those who would dare dissent with what
they view as a divine calling and godly obligation. To the skeptics
who might have doubted the purity of motives in so ardently
enjoined an enterprise, Robert Johnson, an antipuritan chaplain

to the bishop of Lincoln, would address the issue of ulterior
motives and worldly ends thus: "[W]e must beware, that under
this pretence, that bitter root of greedy gaine be not so setled in
our harts." But, on a more pragmatically optimistic note, he
adds, "look it not be chiefe in our thoughts, God will give the
blessing,"[29] a promissory gladdening that echoes the Genesis text
William Symonds takes for his parenesis. Johnson's tract, *Nova
Britania. Offering most excellent fruits by planting in Virginia.
Exciting all such as well affected to further same* (London, 1609),
was dedicated to Sir Thomas Smith, treasurer of the Virginia
Company. Lest there be any doubts about the blessings that await
the diligent and righteous, the Reverend Robert Tyneley, fellow
of Magdalene College, Oxford, expands on Robert Johnson's
promise: "[W]ee may with Gods blessing assuredly expect the
fruits which vsually accompany such godly enterprises; as are the
name of his maiestie, whose name shall by this means be glorious
vnto the ends of the world, the enlarging and further strengthen-
ing of his Realmes and Dominions, the easing of this Land, which
euen groaneth vnder the burden and numbers of her inhabitants,
the plentiful enriching of our selues and our Country with such
commodities as she now laboureth with penury of them."[30] Of
course, avers Robert Johnson, the Indians have even more to gain
by such a holy enterprise: "Our intrusion into their possessions
shall tend to their great good . . . to bring them from their base
condition to a farre better: First in regard of God the Creator,
and of Jesus Christ their Redeemer, if they will believe in him:
and secondly, in respect to earthly blessings."[31]

The Reverend William Crashaw, preacher at the Inner Temple
and father of the better-known Richard Crashaw, the metaphysical poet, in a sermon of 21 February 1610 on the occasion of Lord
De La Waer's sailing for the colony, would amplify on Johnson's
"earthly blessings" to redound upon the Indians from the superi-
ority of the English not only in matters spiritual but in practical
matters as well: "For he that hath 1000 acres, and being a civill
and sociable man knowes how to use it, is richer than he that hath
2000 acres and being a savage cannot plow, till, plant or set. . . .

When they are civilized, and see what they have received from us, I dare say they will never make this objection against us."[32] Modern, modernist, and modernizing agencies for international development have never ceased to perpetuate William Crashaw's good sense around the globe. In the event any detractors from the noble goals of the special mission providence has reserved for England should wish to persist in their benighted objections, Robert Gray, rector of St. Benet Sherehog in Cheapwood and scholar of St. John's College, Cambridge, published an admonitory sermon in May of 1609 implying that such objections were contrary to God's designs, since He had made the adventurers of Virginia "instruments for the inlarging of his church militant heer upon earth" whose ultimate ends were to "to make you members of his Church triumphant in Heaven."[33] To dispel any ambiguities about the ordained militancy of the Church Militant, Gray invokes Joshua 17:14–18, in essence, a text that authorizes any conquest, and one that has had and continues to have an unrelenting career. Joshua's license to the children of Joseph to pursue their godly right and to take what is theirs by God's inheritance, casting out the unregenerate Canaanites in the process, is read, in effect, as a land deed signed by God Himself which hands over America to His chosen people for whom Mt. Ephraim (England in this case) has now proved all too narrow, literally. At the beginning of the seventeenth century, then, Robert Gray and his fellow preachers are invoking the thirteenth-century canonical and curialist rationale for "just war," not unlike the reasoning and justifications we have seen in our discussion of Hostienses and Pope Innocent IV. In essence, we witness a papalism with no Pope. Though the pulpit rhetoric would inveigh bitterly against the Pope, papalism, Constantine's Donation, and the Donation of the New World to Spain by Pope Alexander VI, the sustaining ideology and educed arguments for the English colonization of America are the same, albeit the material conditions these are called upon to assuage or propitiate may vary. If the Indians be "loving and gentle" and "desirous to imbrace a better condition," there would be no need to deploy the Old Testament justification for slaying idolators. Yet, "a Christian King may lawfullie make warre upon barbarous and Savage people," especially if "the holy name of God, should be dishonoured among the Infidels."[34]

The Virginia Company's campaign had the desired effect. Investments by stockholders increased sufficiently to launch a new phase and six hundred settlers joined the expedition headed for Jamestown. History would prove, however, that in many respects this effort was a dress rehearsal, even though the enterprise, in fact, was recapitulating the Medieval canonical tradition and the prophetic rhetoric that a providentialist understanding of history made possible. Splenetic denunciation of the Spanish conquest and its colonial enterprise notwithstanding, chroniclers, conquistadors, and apologists for conquest like Gonzalo Fernández de Oviedo harmonize exceedingly with the injunctions of the sermoners and their own justifications for conquest. Conquest's ideological blueprint varies very little, if at all, from Spain to England. It would be surprising were it to differ. After all, the precepts and formative master plot on which both projects are founded are the same. Certainly Robert Gray's arguments for "just war" echo faithfully the edicts of the *Requerimiento;* and the godly mission reserved for His Majestie King James and the English nation by the Reverend Robert Tyneley is not at all dissimilar from the role Oviedo seeks for his King and Holy Roman Emperor and for the Spanish people. Oviedo, of course, also was the royal official charged with having to certify the reading of the *Requerimiento* by Pedrarías Dávila's scribe at Darién in 1514, the debut of the official proclamation as composed by Palacios Rubios, the Spanish court's hierological canon.

The idea that in the divine dispensation that brought the New World to Europe's attention God was restoring lost lands and relapsed peoples to be salvaged by the righteous and redeemed for God's flock is argued by canons and conquistadors early in the sixteenth century. The notion would become a commonplace for Catholic missionaries and Puritan divines alike. The one to have overtly politicized this orthodoxy is the entrepreneur, political arriviste, conquistador, and court chronicler Gonzalo Fernández de Oviedo. I say "overtly politicized" because the idea itself al-

ways had political entailments and had certainly served expansionist purposes before Europe's encounter with the New World. The
efficient conditions for Oviedo's historical revisionism were the
ongoing litigations between Columbus's progeny and the Spanish
court over the privileges granted the Admiral in the Capitulaciones de Santa Fe and its amendments. The ultimate cause was,
among others, strategic reinforcement of the New World's papal
Donation by Alexander VI to Spain, a strategic move that rightly
anticipated assaults on the legitimacy of that act by other European nations, most notably the English. Oviedo's strategy is predicated on ancient wisdom and on Testamental doxology. Chapter
3, book 2 of Oviedo's *Historia* carries the telling title of "En que
se trata de la opinión que el auctor e cronista de esta *Natural e
General Historia de las Indias* tiene cerca de haberse sabido y
escripto por los antiguos dónde son estas Indias, e cómo e con
quién lo prueba. [Wherein is treated the opinion held by the author and chronicler of this *Natural and General History of the
Indies* that the ancients knew and wrote of these Indies' location
and how and with whom he proves it]." Oviedo's erudite demon-
stration is a melange of ancient wisdom, biblical legend, legendary history, and transparent casuistry. So transparent in fact, that
Fernando Colón, the Admiral's bibliophile, illegitimate son had
little difficulty in demolishing the "proofs" of Oviedo's visionary
revision.[35] Our concern is not with Oviedo's historical accuracy
here but with the status of his text as symptom of a particular
ideological formulation that conditioned historical understanding
and preconditioned policy and actions in the world. In this sense,
we are not reading Oviedo's *Historia,* at least in this instance, as
document but as monument that is articulate beyond its own
articulations. The long and the short of Oviedo's disputation is
that the Indies are the Hesperides, and they are so called because
they were Spanish territories named after Spain's legendary
twelfth king Hespero from Spain's legendary history. When
Oviedo winds his way home at the end of his chapter, his peroration is unmistakably providentialist, messianic, and celebratory of
the redemptive recuperation of a world that strayed into oblivion
for millennia:

Y porque al presente corren de su gloriosa Natividad mill e quinientos e treinta e cinco años, síguese que agora tres mill e ciento e noventa e tres años, España e su rey Hespero señoreaban estas islas o Indias Hespèrides; e así, con derecho tan antiquísimo, e por la forma que está dicha, o por lo que adelante se dirá en la prosecución de los viajes del almirante Cristóbal Colom, volvió Dios este señorio a España a cabo de tantos siglos. E paresçe que, como cosa que fué la suya, quiere la divina justiçia que lo haya tornado a ser e lo sea perpetuament, en ventura de los bienaventuardos e Católicos Reyes don Fernando e doña Isabel, que ganaron a Granada e Nápoles, etc., en cuyo tiempo e por cuyo mandado descubrió el almirante don Cristóbal Colom este Nuevo Mundo o parte tan grandísima dél, olvidada en el Universo; la cual, después, en tiempo de la Cesárea Majestad del Emperador Nuestro señor, más largamente se ha sabido e descubierto, para mayor amplitud de su monarquía. (Bk. II. chap. 3. p. 20)

[And because since His glorious Nativity it has been 1535 years, it follows that Spain and her king Hespero ruled these isles or Indies Hesperedes 3193 years ago; and thus, with so ancient a right, and as has been said, and as will be said further on in the prosecution of the Admiral Christopher Columbus's voyages, God returned this domain to Spain after so many centuries. And it would appear, as something which had belonged to her [Spain], divine justice wills that it should do so again and should be thus for perpetuity, as the good fortune of the fortunate Catholic Monarchs don Fernando and doña Isabel, who conquered Granada and Naples, etc., in whose time and by whose command the Admiral Christopher Columbus discovered this New World or such a large part of it, forgotten in the Universe; of which, afterwards, in the reign of the Caesarean Majesty of the Emperor our lord, more has been known and discovered, for the greater magnitude of his monarchy.]

Thus, in one stroke, Oviedo gives to God and Caesar their respective due. Columbus, in the process, is rendered a recoverer rather than a discoverer, and what is recovered is a form of restitution, by divine justice, of what was waylaid to its rightful owner. The sermons preached on behalf of the Virginia Company in 1609 and the tracts sponsored by the Company in that year are consonant with Oviedo's recuperative claims that would have the New World territories *not* conquered, captured, or invaded but justly redeemed from relapse into forgetfulness. The bases of this conviction, aside from Oviedo's nationalistic legend, are the biblical texts educed not only by the holy sermoners of London, but by the "unholy" Oviedo himself:

> E si desde nuestra Castilla se cultivó aca e transfirió la noticia del Sancto Evangelio en nuestros tiempos, no cesa por eso que, desde el tiempo de los apóstoles, no supiesen estas gentes salvajes de la redempción cristiana e sangre que nuestro Redemptor Jesuscristo vertió por el humano linaje; antes es de creer que ya estas generaciones e indios destas partes lo tenían olvidado; pues que *In omnem terram exivit sonus eorum, et in fines orbis terrae verba eorum.* Conforme a lo que es dicho del psalmista David, dice Sanct Gregorio, sobre el capítulo diez y seis de Job, estas palabras: la Sancta Iglesia ha ya predicado en todas las partes del mundo el misterio de nuestra Redempción. Así que estos indios ya tuvieron noticia de la verdad evangélica y no pueden pretender ignorancia en este caso. (Bk. I. chap. 7. p. 30)

> [And since the news of our Sacred Word was cultivated here in our Castille and transferred there in our time, it does not mean that from as long ago as the time of the apostles these savage people might not know of the Christian redemption and the blood that our Redeemer Jesus Christ sacrificed for the human race. Rather, it is to be believed that these races and Indians of these regions had forgotten it; because, *In omnem terram exivit sonus eorum, et in fines orbis terrae verba eorum.* [Ps. 19:4—Their voice goes out through all the earth and their words to the end of the world.] In keeping with what the psalmist David says, Saint Gregory says with regard to the sixteenth chapter of Job: the Holy Church has preached the mystery of our Redemption in all parts of the world. So that these Indians have had the tidings of the evangelical truth already and they can not pretend ignorance in this case.]

Indubitably, then, the Indians have an obligation "not to pretend ignorance" of the true Redemptive Universal history, especially once their lapsed memories are reawakened to the true condition of all humanity. In this unambiguous conclusion, Oviedo recapitulates the Medieval canonical tradition epitomized by the Bishop of Ostia, as discussed in the preceding chapter. He reiterates, too, the legal precepts of the *Requerimiento,* and he anticipates not only Sepúlveda and his mid-sixteenth century arguments against Las Casas, but Oviedo augurs as well the exhortations of

the Cambridge scholar and rector of St. Benet Sherehog on behalf
of the Virginia colony's second charter. Like Robert Gray's admonitory injunctions based on Old Testament prophets and their
overweening messianism, Oviedo had anointed the Spanish people and their monarch with the providentially ordained role for
salvaging this lapsed humanity and its territory from oblivion and
ransoming all of those souls from the devil. The New World,
then, is no happenstance phenomenon, but a miraculous event
and part of God's design for all nations in the world, among
whom the Spanish monarch and his people have a special election
and divinely appointed role:

> Y así nos enseña el tiempo, y vemos palpable, lo que nunca debajo
> del cielo se vido hasta agora en el poderío e alta majestad de algún
> príncipe cristiano. Y así se debe esperar que lo que está por adquirir y
> venir al colmo de la monarquía universal de nuestro César, lo
> veremos en breve tiempo debajo de su ceptro; y que no faltará reino,
> ni secta, ni género de falsa creencia, que no sea humillada y puesta
> debajo de su yugo y obediencia. Y no digo sólo esto por los infieles,
> pero ni de los que se llaman cristianos, si dejaren de reconoscer por
> superior (como deben y Dios tiene ordenado), a nuestro César. . . .
> Puede ser cosa más clara y visible, para verificación de lo que digo de
> su potencia y tesoros, que haberle dado sus capitanes y gente en la
> mar austral destas Indias, en un día solo, el año de mill e quinientos e
> treinta y tres, con la prisión del rey Atabaliba, cuatrocientos mill
> pesos de oro de valor, en oro e plata, de solo su quinto, e quedar un
> millón e seiscientos mill pesos de oro de valor, en solos estos metales
> para partir entre los pocos españoles que allí se hallaron? (Bk. VI.
> chap. 8. p. 157)

[Thus time teaches us, and we see palpably, what under the heavens
has never before been seen in the reign and high majesty of any
Christian prince. And thus should be expected what should come to
pass and climax from the Universal monarchy of our Caesar and we
shall see all under his scepter. And there shall be no kingdom, sect,
nor race of false belief that shall not be humiliated and subjugated to
his yoke and obedience. And I do not speak only of infidels, but even
those who call themselves Christians, if they should not recognize as
superior (as they ought and as God commands), our Caesar. Could
there be any clearer and more visible verification of what I say about
his power and treasures than his captains' and subjects' of the south-

ern sea of these Indies having given him, in just one day, in the year 1533, with the capture of king Atahualpa, gold and silver worth four hundred thousand pesos of gold as only his royal fifth, with a million six hundred thousand pesos of gold, in just these metals, remaining to be divided among the few Spaniards that were there?]

Oviedo's arithmetic is as indisputably precise as his rhetorical question is long. And if this be the proof of God's blessing, as the Reverend Robert Johnson put it in his *Nova Britania* almost a century later, certainly the caesarian claims of universal monarchy advanced for his king Emperor Charles V are incontrovertibly validated. With this precedent, of course, the Reverend Robert Tyneley of Oxford's Magdalene College knew all too well what expectations he, his English nation, and their monarch James were entitled to entertain in their godly mission: "[W]e may with God's blessing assuredly expect the fruits which usually accompany such godly enterprises; as the name of his Majestie, whose name shall by this means be glorious vnto the ends of the world."[36]

As the official notary and the crown's overseer on Pedrarías Dávila's expedition to Darién, Oviedo had responsibility for certifying that the *Requerimiento* initiated with this expedition was duly proclaimed. Oviedo saw little point to it, as he did not believe, rightfully, that the Indians could appreciate its noble and godly intentions. His suggestion that it would be best to cage the Indians before it were read and explained to them would draw the vitriolic denunciation of Father Bartolomé de Las Casas (*Historia*, Bk. III. chap. 58). Oviedo's most remunerative responsibility as royal secretary did indeed prove God's largess and blessing for his righteous enterprise, thereby confirming the holiness of his mission. As crown secretary, he was the official keeper of the branding iron for captured slaves (all cannibals, of course). For every Indian branded, the royal secretary received a just royalty. Oviedo became a very wealthy man, wealthy enough to validate the nobility he claimed for his pedigree.

The conquistador Pedrarías Dávila, one of the darkest figures of the Spanish conquest and the leader of Oviedo's expedition, could also be colorfully necromantic.[37] Implacable enemy of Oviedo, who as royal secretary had to function as the king's watchdog over the expedition, Pedrarías, too, was not remiss in demonstrating to the Indians their historical redemption through the Lord's crucifixion, resurrection, and the prophetic promise of a second coming and final dispensation and deliverance. It was Pedrarías's wont to always keep a coffin in his tent. It would appear that he was once declared dead and was being buried when he managed to stir as his coffin was being lowered into the tomb. Since that time, Pedrarías never lived or traveled without his coffin, including his conquering expedition to the ends of the earth. On the anniversary of his "resurrection," he would have the Requiem mass celebrated for himself as he lay in his coffin, after which he would rise, again. "In the New World," says Pérez de Tudela, "that emblem came to be entirely appropriate for him [En el Nuevo Mundo, aquella insignia vino a serle enteramente apropriada]."[38] The macabre travesty of sublimity's providentialist promise would also become entirely emblematic as allegory of the conquest and its tragic ironies.

CHAPTER VI

Divine Primitives

A visión profética se asemeja esto.
> *Christopher Columbus*. Lettera Rarissima,
> *7 July 1503*.

... these are the ten tribes which were led away from
their own land into captivity in the days of King Ho-
shea; whom Shalmeneser the king of the Assyrians led
captive; he took them across the river, and they were
taken into another land. But they formed this plan for
themselves, that they would leave the multitude of the
nations and go to a more distant region.
> *II Esdras (4 Ezra) 13: 40–41*.

PRIMITIVE DIVINES

The dual construct "civilization and barbarity" has had its most
productive laboratory in America's New World. It was given
greatest currency in the Latin American tradition by Argentina's
national schoolmaster at a time when a Romantic ethos of nascent nationhood wracked the continent with the rhetoric of birth
pangs. But the notion of "civilization and barbarity" predates
Sarmiento's usage by a few centuries.[1] Rather than construct of
alternatives with mutually exclusive terms, this binary figure
rings as the symptom of an ambivalence as early as Columbus.
The Admiral's wild oscillation, as recorded in the journal of the
first voyage, between seeing the Indians as the domitable Edenic
people of a Golden Age and seeing them as the devious cannibals
of a barbarous race, also becomes yet another paradigm of the
Europeans' ambivalent predicament before the New World.
Through the centuries, the rhetorical wordsmiths and cultural

diagnosticians of Europe's colonial discourse will lean enclitically now on one now on the other term of "civilization and barbarity." I say "enclitically" because, in either case, something of the world being characterized becomes elided, and not just by the disfiguring elisions that inevitably accrue to any exercise of representing the other. Rather, these discursive formations entail a willful subtraction in an arithmetic made to construe with an ideology of noble ends and imperious means. Thus, starting out as paradisal ancestor and as feral subhuman at once, the American native will forever be taken alternately as noble beast to beastly conquering nobles and as prehistoric anthropoid in rudimental stirrings toward civilization. French Enlightenment and Romanticism have been particularly productive in the rhetorical turns of this cultural trope and Jean Jacques Rousseau's name has become indelibly inscribed into the ambivalent and ambiguous notions of the noble savage. It was the Baronne Anne Louise Germaine Necker de Staël-Holstein (1766–1817), commonly known as Madame de Staël and universally recognized as enlightened Europe's most signaled culture broker, who would prophesy, not without a tinge of matronizing sufferance, the imminent future, so long prophesied, of the American New World. Upon meeting the New World's perennial fugitive Fray Servando Teresa de Mier, she would proclaim: "You come from a world that soon will exist."[2] Speaking in revolutionary France, she is, it would appear, proffering her sanctioning benediction on the parturient Latin American continent about to shatter into caesarean nationhoods inhabited by the crossbreed progeny of the noble savages. The attitude displayed by Madame de Staël has changed little since. But her pronouncement was tendered in a postenlightened time when the mythos of the supernatural was duly naturalized and the divine ethos found its human dimension, a process encoded by Thomas Carlyle's *Sartor Resartus* (1833–1834) as "Natural Supernaturalism." At the time Columbus is depicting his Jobean tribulations on his fourth voyage with the notation at the epigrammatic head of this chapter ("a visión profética se asemeja esto"), and when New England's Puritans, in their time, might have read themselves and the Indians in the verses cited from II Esdras (4 Ezra) as the wandering remnant, neither the mystery of the supernatural nor the injunctions of the divine had found such earthly redress. And the nobility of the noble savage may have had a pagan gilt in its Golden-Age filiation, but those ungodly linkages would be hermetically bracketed until a less pious age that corresponded to the European culture's French Madame and to Rousseau's sentimental time.[3] For the still venerable and seraphic epoch of Columbus and the New World divines, whether Franciscan or Puritan, the Indians perforce could still retain a primitive saintliness, one that affiliated them with the primitive divinity of those first Europeans in the New World. Commodianus, that Christian Latin poet himself too peripatetic a pilgrim through the Christian era's third to fifth centuries and through its Middle Eastern geography for scholars to pin him down, had prophesied that the lost tribes of Israel identified in II Esdras would be reunited in time with the rest of God's people. The Indians, as we shall see, become (super)naturalized just so. But first, I should like to rehearse the divine primitivism of Columbus and of those other primitive apostles of New Spain and New England who followed him to reunite God's sheepfold before the World's End. This is the epoch, as I suggested, when *Sartor Resartus*'s "Natural Supernaturalism" has yet to change vestments from a supernatural naturalism in which divinity still cloaks its numenous cosmic order.

By "divine primitivism" I wish us to understand foremost an immediacy. The immediate carries, by definition, the urgency of desire and the compelling gravity of dire predicament. It implies, too, the unmediated presence of what otherwise would require institutional, ceremonial, instrumental mediation. Such unfettered confrontation with divine presence I designate as primitive in a most literal, as opposed to a historical or developmental, sense. I do so because the encounter between the human and the divine occurs in the "first person," in a primal engagement rather than in one seconded by an intermediary agency. Within the mythological complex of the Judeo-Christian tradition, such immediate primacy corresponds to the role and privilege granted to visionaries and inspired prophets. Such inspiration or vision is possessed by those who would be possessed, in turn, by divine grace, the holy spirit, the godly effluence that takes the human subject as its elect agent. Under such conditions, human faculties of reason and deliberation become preempted by an intelligence of greater efficacy that transforms the human into its instrument for exalted ends beyond human comprehension. What I describe may echo a description of inspired states one might find in handbooks culled from scripture or hagiographies. If it should be so, it is not due to my diligence. Rather, it is because of Columbus's own, a diligence he clearly exercised to the point of identifying thoroughly with what he read and with what he took as paradigm for his own actions and self-apperception. For what I characterize here as divine primitivism is not an abstract category in human modes of existence but the concrete instance of Columbus as protagonist of his own script and in his own scripture.

Columbus's valuation of "spiritual intelligence" (*intelligentia spiritualis*) as his guiding light and his crediting of prophetic commandment as his enabling authority have been pointed out in our third chapter. Also discussed there is Columbus's devaluation of human reason, mathematics, and worldly maps as instruments that made his achievement possible.[4] He is making these assertions after his third voyage in the 1501 letter to the Spanish Sovereigns that serves as the preamble to his *Libro de las profecías*. At the end of the previous year, in a letter to Doña Juana de la Torre, governess of the fated Prince Don Juan, Columbus relates his first direct experience with divine revelation (on Christmas day 1499), the second such experience dating from his trying fourth voyage at a moment of greatest tribulation. The latter experience is related in a letter to the king and queen from this his final voyage dated 7 July 1503. All of these key proclamations and experiences postdate his third voyage (May 1498–October 1500). This particular voyage is pivotal in understanding Columbus's self-conception as divine instrument in the eschatological plot of providential history. It might be useful to our scansion of the Admiral's mystical experiences and prophetic writings to recall that the third voyage may have been an even more godly pilgrimage to the prophetic tradition's "ends of the earth" and its apocalyptic New World than the first voyage. After two years' preparations and a day's delay to avoid the French marauders that lay in wait off Cape St. Vincent, Columbus sailed from Sanlúcar on Wednesday the thirtieth of May 1498. On July thirty-one, the first New World land formation would come into view, three hills on an island he would baptize Trinidad. The next day what would eventually be discerned as the continental mainland of South America was sighted. At first Columbus called the peninsula Graceland ("tierra de Gracia"); the natives told him it was called Paria. On August second, he sailed through what he called the Serpent's Mouth ("Boca del Sierpe"), and on the twelfth he entered the Dragon's Mouth ("Boca del Drago"), exiting the next day, now almost blind, to sight Assumption Island ("Asunción"), so called because of the Virgin's Assumption (August fourteen), today called Grenada. On the day of the Virgin's Assumption, Columbus writes of having discovered "another world" ("otro mundo"), of having arrived at the end of the Orient ("fin de Oriente") where East and West meet, an alpha and omega. He educes ancient wisdom and scriptural insight to conclude that he has arrived in the region of the Earthly Paradise. From that godly promontory, the Earth's nearest point to Heaven ("más alta parte en el mundo y más propinqua al cielo"), Columbus's trajectory will take a bathetic and pathetic dive, literally for him, figuratively in the ledger of history. The sad tale of his administrative troubles on Española, his tribulations on the contentious ground between overweening colonial mutineers and Indian "recalcitrance" that would lead, on Christmas day 1499, to his putting to sea alone in a light caravelle there to be joined by God's own voice, and his eventual degradation and shackling in October 1500 that has him returned from his holiest of voyages in chains, are all too familiar. Upon his arrival in Spain, he would don the Franciscans' garb of apostolic poverty on his way to Granada, where he is received by Their Catholic Majesties on the seventeenth of December 1500, thus closing another peregrine circle by arriving back where his duly chartered pilgrimage began eight years and seven months earlier to the day.

I review these details from the historical record not for their

anecdotal significance necessarily, but in order to sketch the skele-
tal scaffolding on and by which Columbus builds the rhetorical
and prophetic edifice that monumentalizes his divine primitivism
and millenarian conviction. Three particular documents suffice to
illustrate the case. These are the Admiral's relation of his third
voyage, composed shortly after his arrival in Santo Domingo on
31 August 1498 and, therefore, covering only the outward leg of
the voyage and the events prior to his being deposed and put in
irons; his letter to the governess of Prince Don Juan, written after
his humiliating return to Spain; and the letter to the Spanish
monarchs dated 7 July 1503 from his fourth voyage, a letter
deemed so remarkable by its Italian printer that he entitled it
Lettera Rarissima, a designation most often used since to refer to
the document.

Columbus may not have belonged to the Order of Tertiary
Franciscans, as John Phelan cautiously notes,[5] though he did take
the garb of the Third Order on his way to Granada at the end of
his third voyage, as noted, and on his deathbed, not an uncom-
mon practice among pious laymen. Nevertheless, the metaphorical language and commanding arithmetic of Columbus's third
voyage is unmistakably trinitarian. To say "metaphorical language," as I do here, could be misleading. For Columbus, metaphor was not merely a figure of speech. His language is figural,
but it figures a worldly reality and literal correspondence between
that reality as named and as it is envisioned. As with visionaries
in general, Columbus finds the filiation of vision, world, and
language inalienably continuous and purposively significant, certainly portentous. The world, thus, is read as a book, a book
whose script and plot correspond ineluctably to the purposeful
masterplot of scripture. And so it is that the world becomes a
mirror, a sentient presence, or a *speculum* as the Medieval tradition had it, of the divine blueprint.

Columbus undertakes his voyages in the name and under the
auspices of the Holy Trinity. He certainly declares as much with
regard to the first, "partí en nombre de la Sancta Trinidad, y
bolví muy presto con la experiencia de todo cuanto yo avía dicho
en mano. [I set out in the name of the Holy Trinity and soon

returned with the experience of all that I claimed in hand]."[6] He asserts the same with regard to his fourth and final voyage in a letter to the Bank of Saint George in Genoa that survives in Columbus's own hand in Genoa's Palazzo Municipale: "Yo buelvo a las Indias en nombre de la Santa Trinidad para tornar luego. [I go back to the Indies in the name of the Holy Trinity, after which I shall return]."[7] Two days later, 4 April 1502, he likewise informs his spiritual mentor and collaborator on the *Libro de las profecías,* Fr. Gaspar Gorritio. The letter to the Genoese Bank of Saint George is particularly interesting. In effect it constitutes an improvised form of life insurance policy. Columbus stipulates that the bank is to retain in perpetuity one-tenth of all income from his estate. In turn, it is to assure the welfare of his descendants, "because," he says, as he sets out on his final voyage, "I am mortal [porque yo soy mortal]." During the preparation of his previous and third voyage, Columbus stipulated a guarantee of another, but related sort with the same bank. In his will and testament dated 22 February 1498, Columbus included a clause that would have a portion of the annual income from his estate deposited in the Bank of Saint George as a revolving fund destined for financing the crusade for the liberation of the Holy Sepulcher in Jerusalem.[8] The clause does not figure in the final will of 25 August 1505.[9]

But the third voyage, of course, is the most blatantly triadic, one could say tautologically so. Like the journal of his first voyage, Columbus's original letter relating his third voyage to the Spanish sovereigns has not survived. Father Bartolomé de Las Casas did have an original copy that he cites extensively and paraphrases in his *Historia* (Bk. I. chap. 154). From that extract, the Admiral's own account is constituted. Unmistakable in this report is Columbus's sense of his own apostolic mission and providential election. The Holy Spirit that Columbus hispanizises as "inteligencia espiritual" has its triune and one personification for him in the figure of the Trinity. As Columbus renders it, the Holy Trinity is more Jahwist (Exodus 31:3) than Johannine (John 14–16) inasmuch as the enabling divine afflatus is more the plenipotentiary presence of the "Spirit of the Lord" than the

auxilary counselorship of the Paraclete. This is the Spirit of the
Lord that comes upon and seizes certain individuals elected for
special tasks—"And I have filled him of the Spirit of God, with
ability and intelligence, with knowledge and all craftsmanship"
(Exodus 31:3). In the letter to the Sovereigns on his third voyage,
Columbus sees not only himself, but also the Spanish monarchs
as possessed by a spiritual intelligence and assigned to the divine
task by the instrumentality of the Holy Trinity. Accordingly, his
missive begins: "La sancta Trinidad movió Vuestras Altezas a
esta empresa de las Indias y por su infinita bondad hizo a mi
mensajero d'ello [The Holy Trinity moved Your Highnesses to
the enterprise of the Indies and by its infinite goodness made me
its messenger]."[10] Commissioned thus, Columbus takes his ministry to the "ends of the earth [in finis orbis terrae], to the gates of
the Earthly Paradise, and to an other world, literally in his calculus, figuratively in its language. And so it is that the integers of
Columbus's arithmetic are preponderantly triune, with the topography of the New World in full collaboration. The first land mass
to be sighted are three hills on an island dubbed Trinidad; the
terrain covered in the first voyage, now recovered in memory's
recollection, is three hundred and thirty-three leagues—
"descubrí por virtud divinal trezientas y treinta y tres leguas de la
tierra firme, fin de Oriente [I discovered by divine virtue three
hundred and thirty-three leagues of mainland, end of the
East]."[11] This discovery comes, of course, after a voyage of thirty-
three days, the duration of the first crossing, during which, the
Admiral tells us, his eyes did not shut a wink, despite which he
did not endure the hardship that leaves him well-nigh blind on
this, his third voyage, "que bien qu'el viaje que yo fui a descubrir
la tierra firme estoviese treinta y tres días sin conçebir sueño y
estoviese tanto tiempo sin vista, non se me dañaron los ojos ni se
me rompieron de sangre y con tantos dolores como agora
[though on the voyage on which I went to discover the mainland I
was with no sleep for thirty-three days and I was for that length
of time with nothing in sight, my eyes suffered no damage nor did
they become bloodshot with so much pain as now]."[12] The mainland, or "tierra firme," Columbus refers to is not the *terra firma*

of the continental land mass that now blinds him, but the island of Cuba that his cosmography and wide-eyed clairvoyance on his first voyage dictated had to be the mainland of the Grand Khan.

More visionary than ever, and as close as he comes to the blind Tiresias as seer, Columbus declares his erudite conclusion that he is, in fact, at the gates of the *hortus conclusus,* the Terrestrial Paradise where, according to the biblical tradition he knew so well, the prophets Enoch and Elias dwell in anxious anticipation of the end of the world so that they could raise their prophetic voices against the Antichrist. Columbus pulls back from the gates of that sacred terrain and from the brink of heretical enthusiasm, demurring just in time "because, there, I believe, is the Terrestrial Paradise where no one can go lest it be by God's will [porque creo que allí es el Paraíso Terrenal, adonde no puede llegar nadie salvo por voluntad divina]."[13] Nonetheless, all the scientific sources he educes—Aristotle, Ptolemy, Pliny, Comestor, Averroes, Pierre d'Ailly—concur with the divine Church fathers, such as Saint Augustine, Saint Ambrose, and the sacred scriptures he so often invokes—Genesis, II Esdras—as well as their glosses by exegetes such as Nicholas of Lyra. They all concur to convince Columbus that he could be nowhere but East *and* West of everywhere at once, what "I call the end of the East where end all land and islands [llamo yo fin de Oriente adonde acaba toda la tierra e islas]."[14] This geographical land's end is indubitably the eschatological and apocalyptic time's end as well, as far as Columbus is concerned. And, in his mind, it is no accident that he should be the one to have led the world to the world's ends since his divine commission as providential minister imbued with the Spirit of the Lord and His Holy Trinity dictates that it should be so: "[B]ecause, it is true that everything passes but not the word of God, and everything He said shall be fulfilled, what he so clearly spoke about these lands through the mouth of Isaiah in so many places of His scripture, affirming that his holy name would go abroad from Spain [porqu'es verdad que todo pasará y no la palabra de Dios, y se complirá todo lo que dixo, El cual tan claro habló d'estas tierras por la boca de Isaías en tantos lugares de su escriptura, afirmando que de España les sería divulgado su sancto nombre]."[15] Isaiah is the prophet most often cited in Columbus's *Libro de las profecías*. Isaiah's prophecy of "new heavens and a new earth" (65:17) is a source Columbus cites repeatedly. We find it in his letter to Doña Juana de la Torre and in the preamble letter to his book of prophecies. In both instances he joins John the Divine to Isaiah as prophets of his own mission and New World enterprise. The connection he forges between those prophetic voices and his project is clearly typological and figurative and his procedure is in keeping with the hermeneutic procedures of the medieval tradition. We have an idea of how licit such connections are, and how pervasive the ideological force authorizing them, from the fact that Father Bartolomé de Las Casas, commenting on Columbus's invocation of Isaiah in his letter on the third voyage, states simply that since Isaiah was a prophet he could have well been prophesying the discovery of the New World (*Historia,* Bk. I. chap. 127). Columbus was clearly laboring under the aegis of perfectly licit and canonically legitimate criteria. The Admiral's most frequently educed sanction for such a messianic self-conception are the verses of Psalm 19:4 which, as already noted in our second chapter, Columbus invokes no less than five times in his *Book of Prophecies*.[16] Convinced that in his apostolic election he has taken the Lord's Word to the ends of the world, the ends of the world scheduled to ensue from that prophetic fulfillment cannot be far behind. Columbus is writing his letter on the third voyage in 1498. Three years later, as we have seen already, he will have calculated that inexorable cosmic peroration with eschatological precision, a proleptic enthusiasm that augurs the apocalyptic arithmetic of New England divines.

Before leaving the letter of the third voyage, I should like to accord even passing mention to the toponymic impulse, the rhetoric of place naming, that runs with such consistent sublimity through the language of the inspired Columbus. Being so close to Paradise, serpents and dragons could not be far at all. Indeed, as already noted, the names Columbus gives to the tidal waves and eddies that buffet his ships and threaten to devour his fleet evoke the eschatological imagery of John's Apocalypse (Revelation 12:9; 20:2–3) and the Old Testament sea monster that threatens God's creation (Psalms 74:13–14; Isaiah 51:9; 27:1; Job 7:12). Along with Graceland ("tierra de Gracia"), Trinidad, and the *locus amoenus* where he was pleasantly entertained by gold-clad natives and which he dubbed Jardines (Gardens) "porque así conforman con el nombre [because they conform thus with the name]," Columbus's Adamic nominalism betrays his prophetic consistency in the face of adversity as well. On entering the Gulf of Paria, Columbus's ships encounter the furious currents of the Orinoco River that come rushing, in four streams, into the Atlantic Ocean. The four branches of the estuary corroborate Columbus's conviction that these are the four rivers of Genesis that must flow, according to tradition, from their source in the Terrestrial Paradise. The fury of the eddies provokes monstrous associations in Columbus's exulted mind. He dubs the tempestuous passage between Trinidad's Punta Arenal (Icacos Point) and the eastern shore of Isla Gracia (Paria Peninsula) "Boca del Sierpe" (the Serpent's Mouth), and a high wave on 4 August 1498 that floats his ships to frightful heights like insignificant jetsam in the Serpent's Mouth produces visions of Leviathan, the *tannin*, or sea-monster of Isaiah (27:1). On August twelve and thirteen he enters and exits what tidal treachery leads him to call "Boca del Drago" (Dragon's Mouth). Clearly, a divine mission like his to land's and time's ends could not countenance adversarial contests except with foe and tribulation matchingly supernatural and fittingly apocalyptic. Having vanquished such adversity, like the divine agon of Isaiah and Revelation, Columbus is confirmed in his divine role and elect agency. His subsequent writings and personae assumed from their rhetorical delivery will reflect faithfully the spirited experience of this reconfirmation.

In this, as in many other respects, Columbus is a compelling character of his own ideological drama. He is most fascinating as interstitial character, constantly verging on the brink of one or another orthodoxy, without quite managing to free himself from the diverse traditions that exert their claims on him, traditions that range from the prophetic primitivism of the Hebraic patri-

archs to the apocalyptic end-time of Christian millenarianism. An
ancient spiritualist, he is also a medieval enthusiast and a Renaissance cosmologist. It is not that he oscillates from one of these
poles to another, if these indeed be poles rather than continuities,
but that these constellations coexist in him in simultaneity. In this
sense he may well be the paradigmatic Renaissance man, if by this
designation we understand the personification of multifarious
impulses Francis Bacon would encode as the *multiplex scientia*
referred to in our fourth chapter. This is not to say that this
diversity harmonizes into stillness in Columbus's persona. There
is no such harmony, and Columbus displays the embattled character of the ideological ground he occupies and the grounds that
occupy him. The transitions entailed in the passage from the
letter of relation on the third voyage to the letter of late 1500 to
Doña Juana de la Torre, governess of the crown prince, serve as
instructive indices to what Bacon referred to as *plurimi per
transibut,* and those multiplicities in transit swirl and eddy in
Columbus's restless and agonic itinerary. The dominant ideological formation that informs the letter we just examined is Jewish
paradisal messianism. Having traced it in our third chapter, we
have seen that the passage from this messianic paradise to apocalyptic millenarianism is a natural progression. Columbus has plotted his role as providentially elect and prophetically anticipated
messenger whose pilgrimage has found its destined way East of
Eden and to the Ends of the Earth. He in effect has descried his
role, scripted in Isaiah's and David's psalms, as one that typologically prefigures his own apostolic and apocalyptic antitype. In
other words, passing from one letter to another, we see that
Columbus has emplotted his role as the fulfillment of his own
prefiguration. From Old Testament messianic divine, he passes
on to New Testament millenarian apostle, the first having made
the second role inevitable in typological adumbration. But, for
Columbus, this is too linear a trajectory, too reductive a plot.
Because, having crossed from one to the other, Columbus crosses
himself again, and if the letter to Doña Juana figures as juncture
where Isaiah and John the Divine meet, Columbus complicates
that intertestamental crossing, making it resonate with the pro-

phetic injunctions of calamitous tribulation and exhortatory deliverance in the Mosaic and Jobean text of the *Lettera Rarissima*. Let us look at the letter to the Governess first.

The letter in question serves as articulate symptom of the irreducible nature of Columbus as protagonist. He is, in his own eyes, Old Testament messiah, New Testament apostle; but he also depicts himself, as we shall see, as Medieval knight-errant and as Renaissance hero of the romance epic. It is useful to remember that Columbus is writing his letter to Doña Juana de la Torre shortly after his return to Spain in irons, his charter privileges trampled, his writings confiscated, and his position as governor under threat from a bureaucratic inquest. For one who had just come from the gates of the Earthly Paradise and from the earth's closest point to Heaven, his predicament is abject indeed. Under such circumstances, Columbus's own stated criteria by which he should be judged are telling. What these reveal most is the complexity of cultural formations he embodies. The letter opens with the lament of one chastened by the world, and with the affirmations of faith's invincible strength. Rhetorically, this is a masterfully constructed document. The preamble anticipates the letter's narrative with a suggestive prolepsis, a distillation of the author's argument into a terse adumbration of what the tale will tell. It is a tale of woe and vicissitude, as the trying conditions of its composition dictate that it be so. But it is also a tale of divine deliverance through the steadfastness of faith and, in this sense, it is a declaration of perseverance braced by the conviction of sure vindication. The godly victory and deliverance in the tale of the letter become a harbinger and an allegory for the vindication that surely awaits the outcome of the circumstances that necessitated the writing of the letter. The compelling thing is that the hero of the tale in the letter and protagonist of these circumstances now writing the letter are one and the same Christopher Columbus. In this way, Columbus has prefigured himself as his own antecedent, a typological prefiguration, one is tempted to say, to be fulfilled beyond the epistolary narrative in the world of the epistle. This is in part why I began the first chapter of this study by referring to Columbus as a Hermetic character. He is his

own messenger inasmuch as he is the message, the apostolic link
and providential instrument that connects this world to the other,
the Old World to the New, the New World to the Next, and the
Next World to his mission. Accordingly the epistolary tale in the
letter's narrative takes place in the New World, the composition
of the letter occurs in the Old World, and the animating ideology,
the *intelligentia spiritualis* that enables and validates its process
of composition emanates from the powers of the Next World.

The letter begins in the writing. It ends there too. In between
these two moments of the writer engaged in the writing is the
epistolary narrative whose tale conforms to the plot of a different
order of writing, the master script of scripture, whose divine
Scriptor has dispensed through His Grace the tribulations and
deliverance that have led to the writing of the letter. As I said, this is
a tale of woe and of exultation. Thus, the writing frame conforms
to that duality. It begins with woe and ends with imperative injunction, a beginning and ending proleptically mirrored in the letter's
preludial sentences. Columbus's skill as a writer may well match
his sailor's uncanny ability at dead reckoning. And many a sea-
wise adept, including Admiral Samuel Eliot Morison, has waxed
hyperbolic on Columbus's seamanship. Here is the letter's
proemial paragraph that so suggestively mirrors the letter to issue
from it:

> Muy virtuosa Señora: Si mi quexa del mundo es nueva, su uso de
> maltratar es de antiguo. Mill combates me ha dado y a todos resistí
> fasta agora, que no me aprovechó armas ni avisos. Con crueldad me
> tiene echado al fondo. La esperança de Aquel que crió a todos me
> sostiene; su socorro fue siempre muy presto. Otra vez y no de lexos,
> estando yo más baxo, me levantó con su braço derecho, diziendo: "O
> hombre de poca fe, levántate, que yo soy, no ayas miedo."[17]

> [Most virtuous Lady: If my plaint against the world be new, the
> world's wont to abuse is ancient. A thousand combats has it given me
> and, till now, I have resisted them all, and without advantage of arms
> or of intelligence. It has plunged me cruelly to great depths. The hope
> in Him who created all sustains me; His succor has always been
> prompt. Once, and not so long ago, finding myself most abject, He
> raised me with His right arm, saying, "Oh, man of little faith, stand
> up, it is I, have no fear.]

The time "not so long ago" when God raised Columbus "with His right arm" and His divine proclamation is the pivotal event in the rest of the letter that follows. That was on Christmas day 1499, the previous year, when events in Española took the hopeless turn that would eventuate in the "abject depths" from which the letter is written. Surely, then, deliverance by the Grace of divine intervention could mean nothing less than that now; and to propitiate the outcome of that portent Columbus closes his letter with an admonitory jeremiad that invokes divine judgment, decrying most bitterly of all the loss of his writings at the hands of the court officials dispatched to bring him down. Thus, if he is writing this letter to court (the Governess Doña Juana is quite likely a conduit to Queen Isabel) in order to exonerate himself, he is doing so by virtue of necessity, and the letter being written is a compensatory gesture for those writings that would serve his cause most, but of which he has been deprived:

> De mis scripturas tengo yo mayor quexa, que así me las aya tomado que jamás se le pudo sacar una, y aquellas que más me abían de aprovechar en mi disculpa, esas tenía más ocultas. Ved qué justo y honesto pesguisidor. Cosa de cuantas él aya hecho me dizen que aya seído con término de justicia, salvo absolutamente Dios Nuestro Señor está con sus fuerças, como solía, y castiga en todo cabo en especial la ingratitud de injurias.[18]

> [My writings I lament most, for he [Bobadilla, the court official] has taken them from me without relinquishing any, and those that would serve me most in my exoneration, those he had most hidden. See what honest and just inspector! Whatever he has done, I am told, has been in the name of justice, but only God Our Lord is absolutely so empowered, as is His wont, and punishes most forcefully especially ingratitude and wrongdoing.]

Inveighing against the Comendador Bobadilla in a letter to Doña Juana de la Torre, Columbus's target of remonstrance and intended epistolary addressee, it seems to me, is really neither. Columbus is aiming, through the scheming functionary and the benign Governess, at Queen Isabel and King Ferdinand, especially the first whom Columbus has always considered a helpmate in divine inspiration, instruments both of the Lord's *intelligentia spiritualis,* as he noted in the opening of his letter on the third voyage, and reiterates now in the letter to the Governess. I believe it is because of the putative readers he intends for his lament and protest that in two consecutive passages toward the end of the letter Columbus dictates the terms on which he *should be* judged, as opposed to the "justice" to which he has been subjected. Here, then, is Columbus adjudicating the terms of Columbus's judgment, betraying in the process an ideal of self-portraiture:

> Yo debo de ser juzgado como capitán que fue d'España a conquistar fasta las Indias a gente belicosa y mucha y de costumbres y secta muy contraria, donde por voluntad divina, e puesto so el señorío del Rey e de la Reina, Nuestros Señores, otro mundo, y por donde la España que era dicha pobre es la más rica.

> Yo devo [sic] de ser juzgado como capitán que tanto tiempo fasta hoy trae las armas a cuestas, sin las dexar una hora, y de cavalleros de conquistas y del uso y no de letras, salvo si fuesen griegos o de romanos o de otros modernos, de que ay tanto[s] y tan nobles en España.[19]

> [I ought to be judged as a captain who set out from Spain to the Indies to conquer many belligerent peoples of contrary creed and customs, where by divine will I have placed under the sovereignty of the King and Queen, Our Lords, another world, by which Spain, who was called poor, is now the richest.

> I ought to be judged as a captain who for such a long time until today wears his armour on his back, without leaving it for an hour, and as one from among real knights of conquest not from those of literature, save these be from Greeks or Romans, or others who are modern, of whom there are many and so noble in Spain.]

Columbus's anaphoric emphases, reiteratively enjoining terms of judgment other than bureaucratic, are a poignant reminder of what I noted earlier (in chapter 4) when discussing the Capitulaciones de Santa Fe; that is, that Columbus's knight errantry is overtaken by the sticky web of the Renaissance state and its officious apparatus. Although the terms and privileges patented by his charter still have legitimacy (restitution of Columbus's losses was made by the monarchs, except for his governorship), Columbus has come to realize through harsh experience that what makes state actions licit are terms and grounds different from those he thought operative when he contracted his charter and sallied "to conquer strange lands and peoples of contrary sects." On that precarious and shifting ground, more treacherous for the chivalric hero than the strange terrain of his conquests, Columbus steadies his course by steadfast adherence to the jurisdiction of ultimate authority. He seeks his sanction, then, in the divine will that ordains all and serves as ultimate arbiter for subjects, states, governors, and princes alike. This is the same divine will that governs as principle in his epistolary narrative. Its godly dispensation determines historical events and its divine grace takes Columbus and the Spanish sovereigns as its anointed instruments. And if the Holy Spirit of the Trinity, as Columbus says, moved Their Highnesses and made him its messenger to the ends of the earth, the scriptural citation that animates the letter to Doña Juana indicates a switch. Between the letter on the third voyage and the letter to the Governess, the focus of Columbus's apocalyptics shifts from paradisal geography to temporal eschatology. What animates Columbus now is the millennium prophesied by John's Apocalypse and by Isaiah, and their prophetic revelations are finally on the verge of fulfillment through the long-foretold instrumentality of the Spanish monarchs and Columbus, as the latter would have it:

> Yo vine con amor tan entrañable a servir a estos Príncipes, y e servido de servicio de que jamás se oyó ni vido. Del nuevo cielo y tierra que dezía Nuestro Señor por San Juan en el Apocalipsi, después de dicho por boca de Isaías, me hizo mensajero y amostro aquella parte. En todos ovo incredulidad, y a la Reina, mi Señora, dio d'ello el espíritu de intelligençia y esfuerzo grande y lo hizo de todo heredera.[20]

> [I came to serve this King and Queen with profound affection, and I have rendered service never before seen or spoken of. God made me the messenger of the new heaven and the new earth of which He spoke through Saint John in the Apocalypse, after having spoken of it through Isaiah, and He showed me to that location. There was disbelief in everyone, and Spiritual Intelligence gave to the Queen my

Lady Its inspiration and great power and made her the beneficiary of everything.]

With the intercession of the *intelligentia spiritualis,* Columbus's enterprise has its providential ally, and what their errand portends is unmistakably proclaimed in the "new heaven and the new earth" God provides through John of Ephesus at Patmos: "Then I saw a new heaven and a new earth; for the first heaven and the first earth had passed away, and the sea was no more. And I saw a holy city, new Jerusalem, coming down out of heaven from God" (Revelation 21:1–2). The realization of God's promised new heaven and new earth in John's apocalypsis has been taken by the millenarian tradition as its own. The vision, as Columbus notes, has its typological harbinger in the words of Isaiah so often invoked by the Admiral: "For behold, I create new heavens and a new earth; and the former things shall not be remembered or come into mind" (65:17). Isaiah's and John's "new world," as already mentioned, had served to animate the millenarian expectations of steadfast believers for centuries before Columbus. Teachings such as the twentieth book of the *De Civitate Dei,* where St. Augustine seeks to dampen expectancy's fervor by declaring that the millennium is already subsumed in the history of the Church, did not assuage the yearning for a paradisal dispensation in historical time and this side of the day of reckoning. Columbus was clearly an adherent of this millenarian tradition, as traced in our second chapter.

But Columbus's abiding rapport with the other-worldly and with divine intercession did not always have recourse to prophetic mediation and scriptural summons. The *Lettera Rarissima* of 1503 is the most elaborate instance of Columbus's unmediated communing with the Lord after the uplifting voice and divine "right arm" (cf. Revelation 1:17) that miraculously succored him on Christmas day of 1499. Here is his account of that earlier revelation as recounted in the letter to Doña Juana de la Torre:

Día de Navidad, estando yo muy afligido guerreado de los malos christianos y de indios, en término de dexar todo y escapar, si pudiese, la vida, me consoló Nuestro Señor milagrosamente y dixo:

"Esfuerça, no temas. Yo proveeré en todos: los siete años de término del oro no son passados, y en ellos y en lo otro te dará remedio." Esse día supe que avía ochenta leguas de tierra y en todas, cabo ellas, minas. El parecer agora es que sea toda una. Algunos an cogido ciento y veinte castellanos en un día y otros noventa, y se han cogido fasta dozientos cincuenta.[21]

[Christmas day, greatly afflicted by Indians and bad Christians, wishing to leave everything behind and escape, if I could, from life, I was comforted miraculously by Our Lord who said to me: "Have strength. Do not fear. I shall provide for all: the seven years of gold are not over, and in that as in the other there will be remedy." On that day, I discovered that there were eighty leagues of land and in all of it, end to end, mines. It seems now it is all one mine. Some have gathered 120 castellanos worth in one day, and up to 250 castellanos worth have been gathered.]

Teetering between the figurative gold of the seven sacraments and the apostasy of the Golden Calf, Columbus finds godly solace "in the one as in the other." Thus christologically anointed in gilded dispensation, Columbus can justly claim to be the divine "messenger to the new heaven and the new earth," as he writes to Doña Juana in the passage already cited. And Isaiah, once more, furnishes the augural precedent: "The Spirit of the Lord God is upon me, because the Lord has anointed me to bring good tidings to the afflicted; he has sent me to bind up the brokenhearted, to proclaim liberty to the captives, and the opening of the prison to those who are bound; to proclaim the year of the Lord's fervor" (Isaiah 61:1). Indeed, Columbus takes Isaiah's words to heart, and although millenarian enthusiasts such as the Patriarch of Byzantium, Gennadius Scholarius, discussed in our second chapter, would take the year 1492 as "the year of the Lord's fervor," Columbus's arithmetic would remove the inevitability of the *annus mirabilis* to 1665. This does not preclude the possibility of divine intervention, where God's anointed messenger is concerned, before the year of eschatology's plentitude and the end of time, as Columbus's experience on his fourth voyage recorded in the *Lettera Rarissima* reiterates.

The *Lettera Rarissima* is the letter of a shipwreck without a bottle. No need for that proverbial vessel in which to seal his

message and commit it to the hazard of the waves. At hazard's
most extenuating hyperbole, Columbus turns from the dire to
the divine. The record of that encounter on Columbus's final
and most desperate voyage spells a recapitulation. Only now,
the capitulating parties are not the starry-eyed mariner and the
reticent monarchs of a decade and a world earlier. The Capitulaciones de Santa Fe now take on a more literal meaning. No
longer a juridical patent and a place-name, Columbus's inaugu-
ral charter becomes recapitulated into augural and portentous
covenant, now an apocalyptic letter-patent between a clamoring prophet and his vigilant God attending to His helmsman's
distress.

The covenantal nature of Columbus's relation to God is so
archetypal that students of Columbus such as Salvador de
Madariaga use the *Lettera Rarissima* as evidence of Columbus's
Jewish origins.[22] One is hard-pressed to dispute Madariaga's
claims on ideological grounds. As for the question of race, the
issue is moot. By Columbus's time, race and ethnicity, or genealogical tribe and cultural identity, are a murky proposition that
usually falls to the obsessions of Inquisitors and deluded
eugenists. That is not to say that such distinctions are not made.
The year 1492 is, after all, the year of the exodus for Spanish
Jews. But to say that Columbus is ideologically a Jew is to speak a
tautology. His figurative language, his sense of history, his cosmology, and a good deal of his scientific knowledge are necessarily Jewish inasmuch as they are governed by views, ideas, metaphors, and self-sanctioning notions that are scriptural, intertestamental, and prophetic. His reactions in the face of adversity, the element most constant in his life, are biblically preconditioned, as are his reflections on his perseverance and overcoming.
So that, when Columbus records the voice of God addressing him
in his most trying hour, his testimonial resonates with the timbre
and turn of phrase that Hebrew prophets willed to their scriptural progeny. If one were to insist on differentiating attributes of
the "New Covenant" from the Old, Columbus would still echo as
Hebrew prophet in his covenantal relation to the divinity, but not
necessarily to the exclusion of his Christian ethos. Because, al-

though Columbus's "covenant" is an unmediated relation between himself and the divinity whose voice speaks to him, and
whereas the references of his testimony are Old Testament figures, Columbus's experience is still an apocalyptic revelation of
sacrifice and forgiveness with a Pauline glimpse of glory (2 Corinthians 3: 14–18; here Paul distinguishes between the Old and
New Covenants). Most important, however, although the voice
heard by Columbus is a divine voice, it speaks of God though it
be God speaking. In other words, there is, after all, a level of
mediation in that intercession of the Spirit, be it rhetorical or
christological, unlike the Lord of Moses who speaks to His people in the first person as in Exodus 20: 1–20. But the theological
edges are not really central to our discussion. The point to be
made is that Columbus is indeed suffused by the biblical tradition
and, as such, the conditions that make the production of his
testimonial narrative possible are inevitably Hebraic inasmuch as
they are part and parcel of Columbus's culture.

Here, then, is the key passage of the *Lettera Rarissima* that
carries a dateline of Jamaica, 7 July 1503. By the time Columbus
reached Jamaica, all four ships of his fleet had to be beached,
having become so worm-eaten as to no longer be seaworthy.
Columbus and his crew of shipwrecks are to be stranded on
Jamaica for a year and five days (25 June 1503 to 29 June 1504).
The passage in question follows a long and dramatic description
of a storm with endless rains and "boiling seas" that threaten the
ships now barely afloat. In the midst of the storm, of a fever, and
loss of all hope ("la esperança de escapar era muerta"), Columbus raises his voice to the thundering skies, yelling frightfully into
the four winds, all to no avail. He suddenly passes into a different
state of consciousness, a hypnagogic swoon, when a voice speaks
to him:

> Cansado me adormeçí gimiendo. Una voz muy piadosa oí diciendo:
> "O estulto y tardo a creer y a servir a tu Dios, Dios de todos, ¿qué
> hizo El más por Moises o por David, su siervo? Desque naçiste,
> siempre El tuvo de ti muy grande cargo. Cuando te vido en edad de
> que El fue contento, maravillosamente hizo sonar tu nombre en la
> tierra. Las Indias, que son parte del mundo tan ricas, te las dio por

tuyas; tú las repartiste adonde te plugo, y te dio poder para ello. De
los atamientos de la mar Occéana, que estavan cerrados con cadenas
tan fuertes, te dio las llaves; y fuiste ovedescido en tantas tierras y de
los cristianos cobraste tanta honrada fama. ¿Qué hizo El más al tu
pueblo de Israel, cuando le sacó de Egipto, ni por David, que de
pastor hizo Rey en Judea? Tórnate a El y conoçe ya tu yerro: su
misericordia es infinita. Tu bejez no impedirá a toda cosa grande.
Muchas heredades tiene El grandíssimas. Abraam pasava de çien
años cuando engendró a Isaac, ni Sara era moça. Tú llamas por
socorro. Inçierto, responde: ¿quién te ha afligido tanto y tantas
vezes: Dios o el mundo? Los privilegios y promesas que da Dios no
las quebranta, ni dice, después de aver recibido el serviçio , que su
intención no era esta y que se entiende de otra manera, ni da
martirios por da color a la fuerza. El va al pie de la letra; todo lo que
El promete cumple con acrescentamiento. Esto es su uso. Dicho
tengo lo que tu Criador ha fecho por ti y hace con todos. Ahora," me
dixo, "muestra el galardón d'estos afanes y peligros que as pasado
sirviendo a otros." Yo, assi amortecido, oí todo, mas no tuve yo
respuesta a palabras tan ciertas, salvo llorar por mis yerros. Acabó El
de fablar, quienquiera que fueses, diciendo: "No temas, confía: todas
estas tribulaciones están escritas en piedra mármol y no sin causa."[23]

[Weary, I dozed, moaning. I heard a very pious voice say: "Oh,
foolish man, slow to believe and serve your God, the God of all.
What more has He done for Moses or for David His servant? Since
your birth, He has always cared for you greatly. When He saw you at
an age He thought fit, as a marvel He made your name resound
throughout the Earth. The Indies, so rich a part of the earth, He gave
to you as your own. You disbursed them as you pleased by the power
He vested in you. To the mysteries of the Ocean Sea, bound in chains,
He gave you the keys; and you were obeyed in so many lands and
honored in fame by so many Christians. What more has He done for
your nation of Israel when He led it out of Egypt, or for David who,
from a shepherd, He made King of Judea? Turn to Him and admit
your error, His mercy is infinite. Your age will not keep you from
anything of greatness. Great is His inheritance. Abraham was over a
hundred when he engendered Isaac, nor was Sara a girl. You call for
help. Doubter, answer: Who has caused you so many afflictions so
often, God or the world? The promises and privileges granted by
God are not forgotten, nor does He say, after services rendered to
Him, that He had other intentions to be understood otherwise, nor
does He dispense punishments for the display of power. He goes by
the letter. He fulfills every promise with a boon. This is His wont. I

have said what your Creator has done for you as with everyone. Now," He said to me, "show the reward of all these trials and dangers you have endured serving others." I, mortified, heard everything. I had no answer to words so sure, but wept for my errors. He finished speaking, whoever He might have been, saying, "Do not fear, trust: all of these tribulations are written on marble stone and not without reason."]

Alain Milhou has painstakingly correlated every key sentence of this passage with its biblical referent or source.[24] No need to duplicate that conscientious effort here. One important precedent Milhou might have added with relevance to this passage, as well as to Columbus's earlier revelation and divine succor on Christmas day 1499, discussed above, is the second chapter, first and second verses of Ezekiel, whom Columbus cites extensively in his *Libro de las profecías:* "And he said to me, 'Son of man, stand upon your feet, and I will speak with you.' And when he spoke to me, the spirit entered into me and set me upon my feet; and I heard him speaking to me."

There is, obviously, a strong quotient of contractual bonding in the cited passage. This venerable institution of the covenant functions in Columbus's *Lettera* on various planes simultaneously. Once more, Columbus aims to achieve a number of ends through the rhetorical formulae of his prophetic testimony. Certainly this is the testimonial narrative of a moving religious experience in which the covenanted parties, God and Columbus, inventory their commitment and service to each other. It is, too, a figural narrative of a mystical experience as tale of trial and overcoming through faith. But it is an allegorical form of discourse also, by whose venue Columbus recapitulates his debits and credits not only with God, but with Caesar as well. One learns not to make any of these possibilities mutually exclusive in Columbus, though some historians have opted to give emphasis to one or another purpose that motivates the Admiral in the rhetorical formulation of this episode.[25] For someone like Columbus, for whom the worldly and the other-worldly are so inextricably enmeshed, the privileging of the mystic or of the clever impresario does not hold much promise for understanding the multifari-

ous and ambivalent personae he embodies. In his divine primitivism, godly justification and ulterior motives coexist inalienably.
The efficient cause for all is tantamount, immediately and most
fundamentally, to the Ultimate Cause which, as he Mosaically
notes at the end of the cited passage, is "written on marble
stone." This is the lapidary contract of a prophetic forerunner
who, in his relation to God, echoes the Patriarchs of Mount Sinai
and of Mount Horeb (Exodus 20:22–23, 33; Jeremiah 31:31–
34). His legacy will resonate, in turn, in the convenantal divines
of New Spain's apostolic missions and in New England's enthusiastic Puritans.

Within the apocalyptically revealed terms of this compact, the
New World of the Indies figures as God's bequest. Like the lands
of the Old Testament that become sanctified as God's blessing for
his elect people, the New World real estate forms part of God's
inheritance bestowed upon Columbus as covenanting party so
that he may disburse it "as you please by the power He vested in
you." Lands so sanctified in this Columbian precedent would
naturally be claimed as the rightful inheritance by the same God's
chosen people when covenantal compacts proliferate, as do the
tribal remnants that wander off to stake their claims in blessed
territory. Thus, the charters granted to Pilgrims and Puritans
alike will also function as blessed corporate compacts between
God's worldly representative and his royal subjects, at least as
initially intended by the state apparatus and until "compact" and
"covenant" become a direct channel between New England divines and their Godly benefactor, thereby foregoing the venue of
kingly and state mediation. It did not take very long, in fact, for
the introduction of this covenantal emendation that linked divine
pilgrims with God's jurisdiction directly, the improvised "Mayflower Compact," for one, being an augural turn in that direction
even before New England's godly remnant reached New World
shores.

Land becomes the most immediate emolument promised to
settlers under the *corporate charter,* as the charters of both the
Plymouth and Massachusetts Bay colonies were called. Under the
proprietary charter already discussed in our fourth chapter, land

was held in "royal desmesne," an institution founded by William I, the Conqueror, in 1066 that gave the king ownership of all the land. Now, under the corporate charter, land could be "alienated" from that "desmesne" by those holding the charter and offered, unencumbered with any feudal restrictions, as inducement to potential colonists who, in turn, could sell it freely. This is what I meant earlier when I referred to John Winthrop, in chapter 4, as the founder of one of the first real estate development companies in the New World. But the charter that put Winthrop in business, of course, was preceded by the charter granted to the Plymouth colony on 3 November 1620, and its terms had already blessed such real estate transactions with divine grace and covenantal sanction:

> And forasmuch as We have been certainly given to understand by divers of our good Subjects . . . that there is noe other the Subjects of any Christian King or State, by any Authority from their Sovereignes, Lords or Princes, actually in Possession of any of the said Lands or Precincts, whereby any Right, Claime, Interest or. Title, may, might, or ought by that Means accrue, belong, or appertaine unto them, or any of them. And also for that We have been further given certainly to knowe, that within these late Years there hath by God's Visitation raigned a wonderfull Plague, together with many horrible Slaughters, and Murthers, committed amongst the Savages and brutish People there, heretofore inhabiting, in a Manner to the utter Destruction, Deuastacion, and Depopulacion of that whole Territorye, so that there is not left for many Leagues together in a Manner, any that doe claime or challenge any Kind of Interests therein, nor any other Superior Lord or Souveraigne to make Claime thereonto, whereby We in our Judgement are persuaded and satisfied that the appointed Time is come in which Almighty God in his great Goodness and Bountie towards Us and our People, hath thought fitt and determined, that those large and goodly Territoryes, deserted as it were by their naturall Inhabitants, should be possessed and enjoyed by such of our Subjects and People as heretofore have and hereafter shall by his Mercie and Favour, and by his Powerfull Arme, be directed and conducted thither. In Contemplacion and serious Consideracion whereof, Wee have thought it fitt according to our Kingly Duty . . . to second and followe God's sacred Will, rendering reverend Thanks to his Divine Majestie for his gracious favour in laying open and revealing the same unto us, before any other Christian Prince or

State, by which Means without Offence, and as we trust to his Glory, Wee may with Boldness goe on to the settling of soe hopefull a work, which tendeth to the reducing and Conversion of such Sauages as remain wandering in Desolacion and Distress, to Civil Societie and Christian Religion, to the Inlargement of our own Dominions, and Aduancement of the Fortunes of such of our good subjects as shall willingly interesse themselves in the said Imployment, to whom We cannot but give singular commendations for their so worthy Intention and Enterprize.[26]

One clearly recognizes here the juridical precedents of the Elizabethan charters discussed in our fourth chapter. The principle of "effective occupation" by Christian princes, the "vacancy" of the targeted lands, and the "duty" to incorporate the "Saueges" to human civility and to godly ways are the stock components of charter protocols. But there is something novel also in this charter of the Plymouth Company for New England. This is God's complicity and express will manifested in such acts as the "wonderfull Plague," by which is meant "miraculous plague," and the internecine slaughter that leaves the land desolate, and in God's "gracious favour in laying open and revealing the same unto us." By this dispensation, God has created a necessity that compels the English king "to seconde and follow God's sacred Will." And having shown His mercy and grace to the English people, they are obliged now to carry out His divine intention. The conquest and occupation of the New World, thus, becomes a covenantal imperative. Between Sir Humphrey Gilbert's letters patent and this charter, we have the Virginia Company's divine mission and its sanctification by the pulpit campaign of 1609. Clearly, in the decade since that campaign God has worked His will in the duty-bound conscience of the English and in the unbounded desolation of the territories crying for deliverance. No exegete could be more articulate on the underlying suppositions of the Plymouth Company's charter than the Pilgrims' able and persuasive apologist Robert Cushman. His diligent advocacy made the enterprise possible. His *Reasons and Considerations Touching the Lawfulness of Removing out of England into the Parts of America* (1622) reads as suggestive synthesis of Columbus's testamental epistles and the Virginia Company's publicist sermons of 1609. Cushman, himself a member of the Pilgrim church that removed itself to Leyden in that same godly year of 1609, actively participated in making the financial arrangements for the migration. Having organized the party that sailed on the *Mayflower,* he himself boarded the ironically named other ship, the *Speedwell,* whose unseaworthy condition, or its shipmaster's guile, forced it back to port.[27] He would sail with a second group he actively recruited in 1621 on the more auspiciously named ship the *Fortune,* though its return voyage gives the lie to its name since it was pirated by French marauders and stripped of its cargo. Cushman would return to England after a three-week stay in the New World, a sojourn that enabled him to speak with even greater authority and surer persuasion on behalf of the Pilgrims' godly enterprise.

Cushman's *Reasons and Considerations* could be read justly as apologia for colonization and empire. Certainly the title itself suggests as much. Nevertheless, there is something more compelling and equally urgent in this tract, something in its rationale that textures Columbus's divine primitivism. It elicits readings of Columbus through which, as I suggested already, one could find multiple levels of readability in the Admiral's texts. In this respect, Cushman is as suggestive as some of the Puritans of the Massachusetts Bay Colony, though more repercussive in his writing than the text of the Plymouth Company's charter which he helped secure. According to Cushman, the whole project of "such removals and plantations," as he euphemized "invasion and conquest," aims to "give content to the world."[28] His *Reasons and Considerations,* analogously, purveys a reasoned content. It displays, in considered words, the ideological presumptions that condition the production of the New World as world in need of content. That determinate formulation extends Columbus from the incipient sixteenth century into the seventeenth. In doing so, however, Cushman explicitly bares what Columbus's visions, arithmetic, and rhetorical formulations take as données. As presumption, these givens were assumed to be generally understood because of their unquestionable status as ultimate condition for all that occurred. This animating end is the eschatological climax

toward which providential history and its elect agents, such as
Columbus himself, are making their way. Columbus's too is a
pilgrim age and its teleology crystallizes as the enterprise of the
enterprise, the project to ensue from "the enterprise of the Indies": the crusade for Jerusalem, the recovery of the Holy Sepulcher, the rebuilding of the temple, the return to/of Zion. We have
seen the millennialist framework subtend Columbus's visionary
and ultimate goal that becomes articulated at key junctures in his
itinerary. We have traced the tradition and scriptural corpus on
which these conditioning presumptions of Columbus rest in our
first and second chapters.[29] In his *Reasons and Considerations,*
Robert Cushman calls up this apocalyptic eschatology but, in
doing so, his vision shifts from the divine primitivism of Columbus as Patriarchal prophet and focuses on the final dispensation,
the consummation and fulfillment of the New Covenant. Unlike
Columbus who communes with his God as Moses or Job in the
wilderness of trial and by the fire of vicissitude, even as his sight is
set on the promise of the end-time, Cushman owns to a belatedness in eschatological time and convenantal grace that points
beyond the past and its present, beyond the world and geography
of the Old Testament and its typological realization in the world
of the New, toward an other world, less metaphorical than Columbus's "otro mundo," that renders the American New World a
transitory way station, a divinely foreordained stopover. In this
sense, as with Columbus, the New World of the Indies becomes
incidental, a necessary, though expedient, instrumentality on the
way to Jerusalem for Columbus the crusader and millenarian,
straight to the anagogic, heavenly Jerusalem for Cushman.

Inasmuch as the New World for Columbus becomes a source,
or mine, for the means necessary to bring about the millennium
by facilitating the mediate step of reconquering the Holy Sepulcher and Mt. Zion, the *sine qua non* of the Medieval apocalyptic
tradition, the New World has a metaphorical value as the new
heaven and the new earth of Isaiah and John the Divine. But, for
Columbus's prophetic ethos, the New World is also the Old Testament's sacred geography, as we have seen in studying his writ-

ings. There is no inconsistency in this simultaneity. Columbus's typological understanding of history and geography makes this coexistence of the old and the new dispensations continuous. Thus, just as the Old Testament and its world are a typological adumbration of the New Testament and its New Covenant, the New World of the Indies is the typological prefiguration that augurs and engenders the apocalyptic and millennial New World of the prophetic tradition. The neat, sequential delineation, or analogical parallel, is not always so clear since Columbus conflates the multiple worlds he inhabits into immediate simultaneity. The same will be the case to some extent with the more enthusiastic Puritans, because this sort of immediacy and simultaneity are the mark of divine enthusiasm. But with Cushman, the pilgrimage is a straight path, the way stations well laid out, the covenant's terms clear. Columbus, not unlike a number of Puritan enthusiasts of his legacy, inevitably mixed, in the calculus of his cartography and on the abacus of his calendar, visions and divinations. Robert Cushman's arithmetic aims to do its figuring through "Reasons and Considerations," though, of course, these be reckoned by equally urgent promptings of godly ends and heavenly blessings. Even though, according to Cushman, these promptings originate in "examples and precepts of Scriptures," these must now be "reasonably and rightly understood and applied," *they* "must be the voice and the word, that must call us, press us, and direct us." Because, "God . . . now . . . speaks in another manner."[30] And just as "extraordinary revelations" have given way to "ordinary examples," the compact between God and His people as binding covenant has a new form. It is the form of a promissory contract pointing to deliverance, but it is also an interim deed until that Last Day dawns:

> Neither is there any land or possession now, like unto the possession which the Jews had in Canaan, being legally holy and appropriated unto a holy people, the seed of Abraham, in which they dwelt securely, and had their days prolonged, it being by an immediate voice said, that he (the Lord) gave it them as a land of rest after their weary travels, and a type of eternal rest in heaven. But now there is no land

of that sanctimony, no land so appropriated, none typical; much less any that can be said to be given of God to any nation, as was Canaan. . . . But now we are all, in all places, strangers and pilgrims, travellers and sojourners, most properly having no dwelling but in this earthen tabernacle; our dwelling is but a wandering, and our abiding but as a fleeting, and in a word our home is nowhere but in the heavens.[31]

The dividends anticipated by Cushman's covenantal invest-ment are clearly other-worldly and postapocalyptic. But, of course, being a pilgrim he cannot stay at home and wait, for home too "is but a wandering." And since the sojourn to that end-time must abide by its errand, God's mysterious and gracious Will has determined, "in his great Goodness and Bountie towards Us and our People," that the faithful make their journey through the "Destruction, Deuastacion and Depopulacion of that whole Terrytorye," as the Plymouth Company's charter has it, that beg to be "possessed and enjoyed by such of our Subjects and People as heretofore have and hereafter shall by his Mercie and Favour, and by his Powerfull Arme, be directed and conducted thither." The ends of the Ends of the Earth compel vigorous means, and if the "barbarous heathens" had any inkling of what those ends entailed, "they would even pluck the kingdom of heaven by vio-lence, and take it, as it were, by force."[32] Having more than a mere glimpse of Zion's awaiting glory, Robert Cushman is wont to exercise these hypothetical exertions he would impute to the heathen. His *Reasons and Considerations,* then, is a forceful ex-hortation to action, and the "reasons" that legitimate the orderly enterprise of the enlightened righteous in the wilderness of the blind are consonant with the sustaining ideology that underwrites every charter since Sir Humphrey Gilbert's, including the charter secured by Cushman's reasoning advocacy for the Plymouth Com-pany. Cushman sums up his reasons thus:

It being then, first, a vast and empty chaos; secondly, acknowledged the right of our sovereign king;[33] thirdly, by peaceable composition in part possessed of divers of his loving subjects, I see not who can doubt or call in question the lawfulness of inhabiting or dwelling there. . . . Yea, and as the enterprise is weighty and difficult, so the honor is more worthy, to plant to rude wilderness, to enlarge the honor and fame of our dread sovereign, but chiefly to display the efficacy and power of the Gospel, both in zealous preaching, professing, and wise walking under it, before the faces of these poor blind infidels.[34]

But these, of course, are the mediate and efficient "reasons," what John Donne referred to as "secondary causes" and John Winthrop called "second causes," as we shall see presently. In Cushman's exhortatory injunctions, there are weightier and ultimate considerations that enjoin Cushman and his countrymen to such actions, and these considerations are, as in Columbus's case, both primal and ultimate at once, resting as they do, simultaneously, on the prehistory of prophetic adumbration and on the posthistory of millennial fulfillment. We have remarked the imminence of the latter in Cushman. As for the first, the justifications advanced simply move those godly warrants from Genesis educed by the Reverend William Symonds on behalf of the Virginia Company in his 25 April 1609 sermon just one chapter ahead. Instead of Genesis 12: 1–3, Cushman invokes Genesis 13: 6, with the self-sanctioning gloss that "as the ancient patriarchs, therefore, removed from straiter places into more roomy where the land lay idle and waste, and none used it, though there dwelt inhabitants of them, as Gen. XIII.6 . . . so is it lawful now to take a land which none useth, and make use of it."[35] Although such divine precedent justifies taking the land, the ultimate justification is the redemption of the territory from ignominy and the salvaging of the heathens from iniquity, because time is running short for the world's worldly sojourn. Like Columbus, then, Cushman, in the final analysis, sees the enterprise of the Indies as the pressing duty of God's apostolic elect.

If Robert Cushman be the most articulate advocate of the Plymouth Company's Puritan pilgrims, the Puritans of the Massachusetts Bay Colony have their divine apologist in their seven-time governor John Winthrop. Like Cushman, Winthrop adheres to the compact of a New Covenant, a primitive apostolic dispensation that derives its ideological sanction from "ordinary examples" rather than "extraordinary revelations." Yet, this investment in the "ordinary" has no less an expectation of extraordinary, other-worldly, and divine returns: "Though miracles be now ceased, yet men may expecte a more than ordinarie blessing from God upon all lawfull meanes where the worke is the Lords and he is sought in it according to his will, for it is usual with him to increase or weaken the strength of the meanes as he is pleased or displeased with the Instruments and the action; else we must conclude that God hath lefte the government of the world and committed all power to the Creature, that the successe of all things should wholely depend upon second causes."[36] Like the spokesman of the pilgrim Puritans, Winthrop deliberated and proclaimed at length on behalf of his own Puritan remnant's errand. His deliberations, in which our citation above originates, carry the title of "Reasons to be considered for iustifieing the undertakeres of the intended Plantation in New England, and for incouraginge such whose hartes God shall move to ioyne with them in it." The second part of this exhortation consists of responses to "Diverse obiections which have been made against this Plantation, with their answears & Resolutions." In its cursory, enumerative form, this treatise may well be the most succinct justification of the Puritan enterprise in the New World and, as such, the most overtly revealing with regard to ideological enablements that make the enterprise not only possible but also imperative. Like Columbus, Winthrop is convinced that his and his company's work is "a worke of God." And, as he puts it in the passage cited above, "[t]hough miracles be now ceased . . . the worke is the Lords" and His will is what moves His "Instruments and the action." Necessarily so, lest we be deluded that "God hath . . . committed all power to the Creature, [and] that the successe of all thinges should wholely depend upon second causes." What Winthrop calls "second causes" is explainable in contradistinction to God's will, in other words, human intentions, reason, learning, and actions. These are the faculties and instruments that, as we have seen, Columbus himself confessed did not serve him a wit, crediting, instead, the guidance of divine grace, the *intelligentia spiritualis* he hispanized as "inteligençia espiritual," and Winthrop refers to as "more than ordinarie blessing from God." This coincidence, obviously, does not make Columbus a Puritan, nor does it turn Winthrop into what he and Robert Cushman referred to as visionaries of "extraordinary revelations" and "miracles" of the Patriarchal prophets. But these Puritans clearly do have something undeniably powerful in common with Columbus, and this is the inclination to forego the mediating role of human and ecclesiastical institutions in carrying out God's work that has made them its elect instruments. Such commonality is not accidental. The Reformation that energizes the nonconformist enterprise and fundamentalist convictions of the Puritans does have as antecedents the "primitivism" of the millenarian movements and prophetic impetus of such traditions as the "simplicity" of the Franciscan Spirituals and their most visible precursor, Joachim de Fiore. Columbus's direct connection to these traditions has been amply documented, most notably by Alain Milhou, often referred to and cited in our study. Such scholars as Marjorie Reeves, already cited, and Morton Bloomfield have documented the repercussions of these medieval traditions in northern Europe and in England.[37] The divine primitivism that Columbus shares with Cushman and Winthrop is the apostolic zeal and evangelical simplicity of the early Christian Church. But although Columbus does cast himself, as we have seen, in the role of Old Testament prophet in unmediated commerce with God, an immediacy of revelation and miracle the Puritans disclaim, the precedent invoked by both Cushman and Winthrop is the authority of the same Hebrew texts and prophetic experience of the Old Testament patriarchs so crucial to Columbus. We have already noted this invocation in Cushman. Winthrop's *Reasons to be considered,* likewise, founds its "reasons and considerations" on the same premises. The most fundamental premise in Winthrop, as in Columbus, is the conviction of divine election, a special relationship compacted with God for the fulfillment of providential ends. For Columbus, this relationship is in large measure personal and individualistic. For Winthrop, it is congregational and collective. He sees his company and "tribe" as God's preferred remnant chosen from an otherwise corrupt and irredeemable humanity. In this sense, Winthrop sees his com-

pany as typological analogue of ancient Israel, the chosen people
on a holy mission and the righteous path: "All other churches of
Europe are brought to desolation," he notes, "but that God hath
provided this place to be a refuge for many whome he meanes to
save out of the generall callamity, and seeing the Church hath noe
place lefte to flie but the wildernesse, what better worke can there
be, then to goe and provide tabernacles of foode for her against
she comes thither."[38] The New World, then, is sacred terrain for
the sacred people of the Lord's predilection, provisions both for
the fullness of time and the plentitude of eschatology. In this
sense, there is indeed something messianic and patriarchal in the
covenant Winthrop attests to between his people and the Lord's
design. And, though he, like Cushman, would eschew miraculous
revelations and prophetic visions, Winthrop is not sanguine
about proclaiming the righteousness and special privilege ac-
corded to himself and his company as beneficiaries of God's won-
drous blessing and unequaled dispensation:

> It appears to be a worke of God for the good of his Church, in that he
> hath disposed the hartes of soe many of his wise and faithfull ser-
> vants, both ministers and others, not only to approve of the enter-
> prise but to interest themselves in it . . . Amos 3: the Lord revealeth
> his secret to his servants the prophetts, it is likely he hath some great
> worke in hand which he hath stirred up to encourage his servants to
> this Plantation, for he doth not use to seduce his people by his owne
> prophetts, but committe that office to the ministrie of false prophetts
> and lieing spiritts.[39]

Clearly, Winthrop does "expecte a more than ordinarie blessing from God," though as Cushman put it, "God . . . now speaks
in another manner." Winthrop's invocation of Amos 3:7 would
still have prophecy as an indispensable part of God's wonder-
working on behalf of His people. And, of course, there is no
question in Winthrop's mind as to who are God's people and
who His rightful prophets in the enterprise of New England's
Plantation. As for the rights to "the wilderness" that remains the
final refuge for the faithful remnant, Winthrop invokes the same
reasons as Cushman and his company's charter, in essence, the
same reasons that justified Hostienses and Pope Innocent IV in

the thirteenth century, that is, Genesis: All of the earth is God's dispensation to humanity and all humanity forms part of God's fold. Surely, those closest to His divine grace cannot be denied any part of His domain: "The whole earth is the Lord's garden," says Winthrop, "and he hath given it to the Sonnes of men with a general Commission: Gen. 1:28 increase and multiplie, and re-plenish the earth and subdue it, which was againe renewed to Noah: the end is double and naturall, that man might enjoy the fruits of the earth, and God might have his due glory from the creature: why then should we stand striving here for places of habitation . . . and in the meane time suffer a whole Continent as fruitfull and convenient for the use of man to lie waste without any improvement?"[40] Why, indeed? And to assuage any possible objections to such self-evident reasoning, Winthrop introduces a distinction between "naturall" and "civil right," the latter accru-ing to those who would cultivate and improve the land for assur-ing the greater glory of God. And those who do no such thing, such as the "Natives in New England, they inclose noe Land, neither have any setled habytation, nor any tame Cattle to im-prove the Land by, and soe have no other but a Naturall Right to those Countries. Soe as if we leave them sufficient for their use, we may lawfully take the rest, there being more than enough for them and us."[41] There should be no problem in such accommoda-tion since the lands are well-nigh vacant by God's graces and munificence since "God hath consumed the Natives with a great Plague in those parts, soe as there be few Inhabitants lefte."[42] As for those who are left, "they have of us that which will yeeld more benefight [sic], then all that Land which we have from them."

Lest this godly enterprise of the righteous remnant be confused with the adventurers of the Virginia Company, especially since so much in Winthrop's "Reasons to be considered" echoes unmistak-ably the pulpit rhetoric of twenty years earlier on behalf of the Virginia Company's second charter, the Patriarch of the Massa-chusetts Bay Company hastens to differentiate this Puritan under-taking from the earlier venture: "There were great fundamentall errors in the former which are like to be avoided in this: ffor: 1:

their mayne end was Carnall and not Religious: 2: They used
unfitt instruments, a multitude of rude and misgoverned persons,
the very scumme of the Land: 3: They did not establish a right
forme of government."[43] The first and seven-time governor of the
Massachusetts Bay Puritans obviously should know. To make
sure the nature of the divine enterprise he heads is properly understood, he invokes the patriarchal precedent of the prophetic era:
"Soe he carried the Isra[e]lites into the wildernesse and made
them forgette the fleshpotts of Egipt . . . Deu 8: 3: 16."[44] Ironically, so intensely zealous and tribally exclusionary was the theo-
cratic government formed by the advanced settlement for the
Massachusetts Bay Colony, in Salem since 1628, that Winthrop
himself had to spend his first sabbath, the day after his arrival,
abroad his ship. He was informed by the Reverend Samuel Skel-
ton, pastor of the Salem church, that not being a signator of the
covenant of a gathered New England church, he was excluded
from communion with its members.[45]

Ironic as this telling exclusion might be, there is something
fitting about it that construes with Winthrop's now legendary
sermon "On Boarde the Arrabella, On the Atlantick Ocean" as
"the great Company of Religious people, of which Christian
Tribes he was the Brave Leader and famous Governor" made its
way to the New England Zion. This is the sermon whose "Citty
vpon a Hill" is still invoked on the swamps of the Potomac on
occasions most convenient and for ends equally incongruous.
Although Winthrop's "A Modell of Christian Charity" is the
convenantal paradigm for governance in an age of Patriarchs that
harken to Abraham, its proemial paragraph, the opening lines
that put forth the sermon's own governing precepts under the
heading of "A Modell Hereof," is unmistakably Aristotelian in its
hierarchical principles of government. One readily recognizes in
this homiletic prolepsis the first book of Aristotle's *Politics* and
the twelveth of the *Metaphysics*. Midway through the previous
century, Juan Ginés de Sepúlveda, the Latin translator of Aristotle and great antagonist of Father Bartolomé de Las Casas's
charitable model of Christianity, had invoked the same texts in
favor of Spanish imperial and colonialist hegemony over the hea-

then natives. The hierarchical criteria echoed by Winthrop simply transmuted in New England, and they did so even before the Bay Colony's Puritan governor could arrive. The standard for a graduated social ordering now is God's grace and church membership that covenanted the faithful with its blessings, making the blessed "highe and eminent in power and dignitie; others meane and in subieccion," as Winthrop's own words at the head of his sermon put it.

PRIMITIVES DIVINED

Divination is a soothing act designed to assuage anxious uncertainty. To meet the requirements of divining one must operate from a precarious ground, a pivotal base always on the verge of coming unhinged. Reality for the divining lies just in sight, rarely in plain view. The divine's discernment is eternally fated to be divisionary. Second sight does not add up except to an ambiguous juncture on which the soothsayer is optically splayed. Because this is the fate of gifted ferrymen caught between one and another world, it is a fate Columbus knew very well. Emphatic perseverance and enthusiastic hyperbole become compensatory gestures for a predicament of such ambivalence and insecurity. And Columbus, as we have seen, wavers rarely, and then only for the sake of self-reaffirmation in the divinely sanctioned surety of conviction. In this, too, Columbus figures as prototype of the blessed New World's cocksure steadfastness.

As divine primitive, Columbus takes the natives of the New World into the ken of his divineness, thereby setting yet another precedent for those who followed him. That precedent is two-fold: first, it consists of an anxious looking both ways on the path of time, now nostalgically, now with impatience, trying to divine the past in the present and to glimpse the imminent presence of the awaited future. Second, Columbus sets the precedent for viewing the natives now as divine ancestors from a revered past, now as incipient anthropoids on the way to a humanity, as Columbus knew it, still in their future. Columbus would be as sure of one as of the other, expressing himself with equal confidence on the primitive as on the prophetic. Knowing himself at midstream in navigation between the two, Columbus would never allow that he was in the limbo of a human comedy, sticking steadfastly to a divine one instead. Keenly aware that he pertained to both and to neither, he adamantly emplaced himself now in the "no longer" of divine primitivism (whether pagan or baptized), now in the "not yet" of divining prophecy. In that tenacious holding to one's ground that betrays the symptoms of displacement, Columbus also stands as paradigm of the modern epic hero who, unlike his classical counterpart from Antiquity, knows that he is firmly planting himself on ground less than firm. Ironically, only fifteen years divides Columbus's debut as transworlding hero and the utter undoing of the grounds he (dis)covered into the groundlessness of the philologist Waldseemüller's American "Nowhereland," as scanned in our third chapter. As much an itinerant between worlds as any of Robert Cushman's "strangers and pilgrims, travellers and soujourners, [whose] dwelling is but a wandering," Columbus had already given the term "pilgrim" a peculiarly American meaning one hundred and thirty years before Cushman's pilgrimage from Plymouth to Plymouth, a sojourn that utterly transformed the Old World place-name and the New World place so named.

Geographical worlds are also, or chiefly, human worlds, and if Columbus opted for coexisting with the conflated duality of Alpha and Omega, of the end of the East and the end of the West, he also could not extricate himself from the human undecidability of this cosmic ambivalence. He thus found himself wracked on the indeterminacy that would have the native Indians be, at once, venerable ancestors and vendible chattel whose history begins with him and his Pilgrim's investment in their hitherto unfolded existence. Columbus's reckoning with regard to the native peoples, then, oscillates between a *tabula radix* and a *tabula rasa*—between a divine genealogy rooted in the common ground of Genesis (whether of the anointed Hebrew Eden or the γένεσις [genesis] of pagan Antiquity's Golden Age) and a blank slate on which prophecy's inexorable future could be indelibly, and profitably, inscribed.

Having sighted fires and made his land fall by 2:00 A.M. on Friday morning, 12 October 1492, Columbus waits for dawn. His first recorded observations concern the natives' nakedness, their amicable disposition and total innocence, their well-built and comely bodies. He is taken by the absence and the natives' ignorance of arms of war, noting that in this Edenic setting, "they have no iron." Clearly, for Columbus, this is an Age of Gold, and in next day's journal entry he will also note that indeed "gold is born here [aquí nace el oro]." The gold-ornamented bodies of these otherwise edenically naked people evokes for the Admiral the Garden of Genesis and the ancients' age of yore. The people's guileless commerce ("they took and gave all they had willingly") corroborates this initial impression. But, at the same time, Columbus articulates, and thereby unveils, the other facet of the natives' ill-fated fall into Europe's history. In the final few sentences of this first commentary on the New World, Columbus's words, at once benign description and, as history would prove, indelible curse, seal the natives' destiny. The confluence of elements in Columbus's pronouncement is ominously telling in view of subsequent history: "Ellos deven de ser buenos servidores y de buen ingenio, que veo que muy presto dizen todo lo que les dezía. Yo creo que ligeramente se harían cristianos, que me pareció que ninguna secta tenían. Yo plaziendo a Nuestro Señor levaré de aquí al tiempo de mi partida seis a Vuestras Altezas para que deprendan fablar. [They must be good servants and intelligent, for I see that they immediately repeat what I said to them. I think that they would readily become Christians, for it seemed to me they had no religion. Our Lord willing, I will take with me six of them upon my return for Your Highnesses so that they may learn to speak]."[46]

A "stranger and pilgrim" on an errand patronized by strangers, Columbus's attitude on this, the New World's first dawn as a New World is strangely assimilationist. And though, as we have seen, by the letter of his third voyage he would be referring to this strange land as "an other world," on the occasion of this initial encounter Columbus takes, literally and figuratively, this world as an idealized version of the world he knew, which is also the

world that preconditioned the way he would know whatever
world he might have encountered. As for the human component
of this New World, in a manner that obviously is second nature
to him, he takes the natives as a secondary humanity in relation
to the primacy of his own human world. Hence the automatic
move from the natives' tractable and edenic innocence to their
serviceability as "good servants," followed by the designation of
these people as mimetic echo, albeit surprisingly intelligent, of his
speech and speaking culture. They readily repeated "what I said
to them." Columbus then moves to a further level of erasure or
conversion of the natives into hollow human chambers ready to
echo his European culture. From the linguistic, Columbus moves
to the metaphysical, assuming outright that he faces a blank sur-
face on which to inscribe the ideology of an entire cosmogony
whose tidal waves belched him unto these shores: "it seemed to
me they had no religion," and, therefore, "they would readily
become Christians." Thus, having rendered this encountered human world blank and mute, Columbus vows that, God willing,
he will take back with him a half dozen of these specimens so that
"they may learn how to speak [para que deprendan fablar]."

I refer to Columbus's attitude as assimilationist, but the unmistakable suppositions that underlie his attitude and his ensuing
actions leave no room to doubt as to who is being assimilated to
and by whom. The situation of these two human elements, native
and European, from this first encounter precludes any symmetry
in the relationship and exchange between them. If the charters we
examined in our fourth chapter, especially the Capitulaciones de
Santa Fe granted to Columbus, had already "conquered" the
geographical world they invented in their inscription, the human
component, as also pointed out, had already been rendered proprietary object, scripted there in those texts as naturalized sub-
ject(s). In this primal encounter, we see clearly how that rhetorical and textual appropriation works out in practice, as rendered,
of course, in textual and rhetorical representation by Columbus
in his journal and, in turn, by the paraphrases of Father Bartolomé de Las Casas. As primal, other-worldly pilgrim and economic journeyman on a worldly sojourn, Columbus *takes* the

New World upon encountering it. He takes it not by storm or surprise but by perplexity, his own and that of the natives. The natives will never overcome theirs since they are overcome by it, and time will give them no opportunity to discern otherwise. A "wonderful plague" visited upon them by God's providence will seal their perplexity with silence for perpetuity. Columbus, on the other hand, may not have been certain of where he was, requiring his crew at one point to sign an affidavit that assured him, Their Highnesses, and posterity otherwise, but such geographical befuddlement did not endanger his cosmological compass in the least. And the greatest certainty of that conviction was the ideological assurance that told him he, on a hierarchical scale of humanity, was first, foremost, and above all, the representative vanguard of humanity's preeminent ranks. Like those who would follow him, whether Papists or Puritans equally convinced of such preeminence as their own rightful condition, Columbus saw his human world and its history as the cosmos' consummate integer whose special dispensation privileged it with the unique opportunity to see (to) the cosmic consummation. For the natives of that initial encounter, the consummation was not long in coming, though their humanity was clearly not nearly as consummate in the dissymmetry of this human exchange.

Prefigured in Columbus's initial reaction to the human world he encountered we find the two principal predispositions toward the Indians that the sixteenth and seventeenth centuries would institutionalize. The first of Columbus's reactions, the assimilationist, belongs, for the most part, to the religious orders of New Spain in the sixteenth century, the Franciscan and Dominican friars who had to account for these natives from within the human cosmology of their own human world. The second, the appropriative (really expropriative and exclusionary, otherwise it would be another form of assimilation), is more readily manifest in the comportment of the clerisy of New England in the seventeenth century. Though there were a number of Puritans, such as John Eliot and Roger Williams, who would essay assimilative explanations of the Indians, more is said by the friars of New Spain than by the divines of New England on the provenance and genealogy of the natives. In general, the sixteenth-century Catholic friars felt compelled to account for the natives. The seventeenth-century Puritans were compelled by their ideological determinations to do otherwise. In short, and at the risk of oversimplification, the Catholic Spirituals took the assimilationist tact prefigured in Columbus's primal example. The Puritans took the "eliminationist" or exclusionary tact. Such exclusiveness was, after all, the underlying impetus of their nonconformist and separatist ethos that led them to preclude any intercourse with the Old World they chose to leave behind. Thus, there is more said by the Dominicans and Franciscans on the subject of the natives. There is less where an ideology of erasure leaves a blank, though it be an articulate silence in its vacuous denial. What the New England divines, for the most part, saw fit to overlook, their nineteenth-century missionary progeny eventually would address, though it was already too late for any redress of the human consequences the forefathers' erasure had wrought. I refer the reader to studies more properly concerned with this later period that falls outside the chronological purview of the present study.[47] It may suffice to remember that even John Winthrop, the Governor of the Massachusetts Bay Company himself, was excluded from the divine communion of the Bay Colony's covenanted divines upon his arrival at Salem on 12 June 1630, much less the "heathenish salvages" so hopelessly far from the divine grace of the Puritans' covenantal God.

In the natives of the New World Columbus finds the embodiment of his divine primitivism and of his incipient Renaissance vision. He sees the Indians as reminiscent of the Golden Age and as the promise of a prophetic future about to become realized as a result of his providential mission. For the missionary apostles of sixteenth-century New Spain, there no longer was a Golden Age of yore, but only the "gold" of an eschatological future and its apocalyptic boon. Their salvationist vision and evangelical primitivism faced with the possibility of a renewed church in the New World, a church that would revive the simplicity and purity of the apostolic age, disposed them toward an explanation of the native peoples in strictly biblical terms. Some felt the Indians were indeed the Ten Lost Tribes of Israel. But even those who did not believe in the Jewishness of the Indians still felt that these people were descended from the same stock as the rest of humanity, as the record of Genesis proclaimed. The Indians, then, were far-flung children of Noah and, as such, divine ancestors whose path after the Flood led them to stray from the rest of humanity and to lapse from the grace of their godly creation.

The compelling need to account for the origin of the natives is grounded in the prophetic tradition. And, most immediately for these latter-day primitive divines who yearned for the earliness of the church and its new covenant, the urgency of such an explanation was apocalyptic. One must underline their pressing necessity since their task originates in the climactic emergency of that apocalyptic moment between the opening of the sixth and seventh seals of Revelation (7: 4–9). This is as close as one comes to the End without being there. And this is the end-time in which all tribes, even those long lost, are gathered for the roll call of cosmic eschatology. The missionary zeal of New Spain's friars had taught them that the Jews were to be converted as Judgment Day closed in and this world prepared to move on to the next. Thus, an explanation based on the prophetic tradition had the double virtue of accounting for the Indians and, for those convinced of the Indians' Jewishness, of reading in this encounter portentous signs that the opening of the seventh seal and the subsequent apocalyptic consummation were imminent. As the Franciscan Gerónimo de Mendieta put it in his *Historia Ecclesiastica Indiana*, "who knows whether we are not so close to the end of the world that the conversion of the Indians is fulfilling the prophecies for which we pray that the Jews may be converted in our time? Because if the Indians descend from the Jews, then the prophecy is already fulfilled."[48] I am inclined to concur then with Phelan's reading of the Franciscan fathers on this point. Phelan noted: "The popularity of the Jewish-Indian myth in the New World was due partly to the fact that it provided a kind of explanation for the origin of American man. But I suggest that the real source of appeal for the spread of this curious legend can be found only in the apocalyptic mood of the Age of Discovery. If the Indians were in reality the lost tribes, such a discovery would be convincing evidence that the world was soon to end."[49]

Don Cameron Allen's *The Legend of Noah: Renaissance Rationalism in Art, Science, and Letters* is close to being a definitive summary of the Renaissance literature on the Indians' origins.[50] In sixteenth-century New Spain, the most convinced of the Indians' Jewish origin was the Dominican Diego Durán who, though Spanish by birth (1537), lived in Mexico from the age of five or six. His familiarity with New Spain and its natives is intimate and detailed, as is his *Historia de las Indias de Nueva España y Islas de la Tierra Firme* (1576–1581). Father Durán, "most likely . . . himself . . . from a family of converted Jews,"[51] loses no time in proclaiming his thesis. On the first page of his *Historia,* declaring that one would need "divine revelation" or "spiritual intelligence" to know the origin of the American natives with certainty, he proceeds confidently with the affirmation that "we could ultimately declare them to be by nature Jews [podríamos ultimadamente afirmar ser naturalmente judíos]."[52] His proof for such certainty is, in fact, "divine revelation" since sacred scripture offers the necessary testimony for his assertion—"para la probación de lo qual será testigo la Sagrada Escriptura, donde clara y abiertamente sacaremos ser verdadera esta opinion [for whose proof Sacred Scripture shall bear witness, from which we shall prove clearly and openly the truth of this opinion]." The scriptural proofs educed by Father Durán range from Deuteronomy to Micah, from Hosea to Zephaniah, from Jeremiah to Ezekiel. He is not always specific about chapter and verse, but the drift of his "proof" clearly points to covenantal law, especially the reiterated commandment of Deuteronomy, and, what is more revealing, to the admonitory jeremiads of those prophetic voices and their terrific clamor against those who would lapse from the laws of the covenant. This particular focus suggests more than mere interest in the Indians' Jewishness. And the Dominican friar is rather explicit in remarks that not only proclaim the Indians to be Jewish, but serve the unmistakable purpose of justifying the Conquest. Thus, if the Franciscan Gerónimo de Mendieta's speculations on the natives' Jewishness do the double duty of explaining their origin and corroborating the imminence of prophecy's apocalypse, Father Durán's proofs, likewise, serve a dual purpose. The Indians are undeniably Jewish because of their "nature," and their state of spiritual declension and social degeneracy constitute the cause and necessary conditions for their foreordained afflictions as prophesied in the admonitions of the visionary Patriarchs. The vicissitudes of the Conquest, then, represent the fulfillment of those monitory injunctions and their implicit curse:

> . . . el curioso letor podrá ver y notar en el Deuteronomio, cap. 4, y 28 y 32, Isaias, 20, 28, 42 capítulos; Jeremías, Ezequías, Miqueas, Sophonías, donde se hallará el castigo rigurosísimo que Dios prometió á estos diez tribus por sus grandes maldades, y abominaciones y nefandas idolatrías, apartándose del culto de su verdadero Dios, De quien tantos beneficios avian recibido: por pago de tal ingratitud les promete Dios, en los lugares acotados, un azote y castigo rigurosísimo qual le vemos cumplido en estas miserables gentes; conviene a saber, que les avian de ser quitadas sus tierras, casas y tesoros, sus joyas y piedras preciosas, sus mugeres é hijos y llevados á vender á tierras estrañas, gozando otros de sus haziendas: paréceme que aunque no diera más autoridad ni raçon para que entendiéramos questos indios son y proceden de los judíos, que lo dicho bastaba, viendo que aviéndose multiplicado como las arenas de la mar, siendo en su trasmigración número breve, y los muchos años de su peregrinación, despues de aver poblado este mundo tan grande, cansado Dios de sufrir sus abominaciones y echos nefandos y idolatrías, trujese Dios gentes estrañas, como águila que viene de los fines de la tierra, que sin tener respeto á los viejos ni á los moços, á los niños ni á las mugeres, los destruyó y consumió sin ninguna piedad, teniéndolos en hambre, en sed y desnudez y en cansancio perpetuo hasta que fuesen apocados.[53]

> . . . the interested reader can see and note in Deuteronomy, chaps. 4, 28, and 32; Isaiah, chaps. 20, 28, 42; Jeremiah, Ezekiel, Micah, Zephaniah, where one will find the most rigorous punishment God promised these ten tribes for their great evils, and abominations, and nefarious idolatries, for straying from the reverence of their true God, from whom they were the recipients of so many blessings: in return for such ingratitude, God promises them, in the cited passages, a calamity and mighty affliction which we see fulfilled in these miserable people; to wit, that their lands, homes, goods, their jewels and precious stones,

their women and children were to be taken away from them and taken
to strange countries to be sold, with others enjoying their estate: It
seems to me that though I cite no other authority and give no other
reason, we should understand that these Indians are Jews and are
descended from Jews. What has been said suffices, seeing that having
multiplied like the sand of the sea, having been few in their migration,
and the years of their wandering many. After having populated this
great world, God, weary of suffering their abominations, nefarious
deeds, and idolatries, should bring strange people, like an eagle that
comes from the ends of the earth, without respecting the old or the
young, the women or children, destroyed and consumed them without
pity, afflicting them with hunger, thirst, and nakedness and endless
weariness until they diminished.]

Like the "wonderful plague" visited by God upon the Indians
of New England, the baneful fate that befalls the natives of New
Spain as a result of the Conquest is the will of Wonder-Working
Providence at work among the strayed tribes of His original fold.
Durán and the Spanish hosts, then, are the instruments of God
visited upon these errant tribes to exact divine retribution and to
redeem them from their errancy by incorporation into a new
covenant and a new dispensation. Father Diego Durán's hopeful-
ness for the natives' future, in fact, leads him to see not only the
violated covenant of Deuteronomy in their past, he also discerns
in their customs and practices elements of the New Covenant
and, surely, he concludes, these people had been proselytized by
some Christian apostle well before the arrival of the Spaniards,
and that evangelist could have been none other than Saint
Thomas whom the Indians called Quetzalcoatl and Topiltzin.[54]
Thus baptized, the natives of New Spain become a distant,
opaque mirror for the Spanish missionary and historian who, if
we follow Todorov's rendition, now seeks to recoup his own
Jewish semblance by polishing that opacity with the grace of
truth and the saving light that guides his pilgrimage.

Between the Dominican Diego Durán's *Historia* (1576–1581)
and the Franciscan Gerónimo de Mendieta's *Historia Ecclesiastica Indiana* (1596/7–1604) intervenes the Aristotelian Jesuit
José de Acosta and his *Historia natural y moral de las Indias*
(1589). This explains, in part, Durán's unconditional certainty

and Mendieta's conjectural, albeit still enthusiastic, attitude toward the Jewish theory on the Indians. Although, as Phelan
points out, Father Acosta "subscribed to the major premise of
apocalyptic mysticism of the Age of Discovery,"[55] acknowledg-
ing that his times were the last age of the world, "the eleventh
hour" (*De temporibus novissimus,* 1590), his Aristotelian rationalism tempered the enthusiastic expectations of the likes of
Mendieta. Acosta's hypotheses on the origin of the Indians rejected their filiation with Israel's Ten Lost Tribes altogether, calling the theory frivolous. In his *Historia natural,* Acosta proposes,
instead, what Don Cameron Allen refers to as "the theory now
accepted by modern anthropologists."[56] This is the theory of the
overland migrations through the northern continental straits. In
the process, Acosta disallows, as well, the Atlantis hypothesis of
Plato's *Timaeus* that still held some fascination, along with Isaiah's prophecies, for Bartolomé de Las Casas earlier in the sixteenth century. Nonetheless, Father Acosta also sees the natives
in a primitive stage but, rather than a lapsed people in a state of
declension, as Durán would have them, for Acosta this is an
unregenerate state of uncivilized earliness, as opposed to a degen-
erate belatedness of a fall from grace. In either case, the native
peoples of the New World are clearly in that primal stage to
which Columbus sentenced them on that initial encounter a century earlier. The Dominican, Jesuit, and Franciscan friars are
representative of the gamut of opinion on the Indians, though
none of the three reflects necessarily the opinions held within his
own religious order.

   Though belated by comparison, the Puritan opinion on the
American natives was equally varied, ranging from the fanciful to
the assimilationist evangelical. For the most part, the English reflect the spectrum of received notions articulated initially by Columbus himself and elaborated by the Catholic friars. Thus, Columbus's "Golden Age" theory has its avatar in Thomas Morton's
New English Canaan (1632). The Admiral's prophetic divinations
on the Indian as ultimate Christian finally reached by Providence
for Its cosmic ends resonate piously in John Eliot and ambiguously
in Roger Williams. The indomitable Thomas Morton bases his

observations and conclusions, as the original title page of his treatise avers, "Upon ten Yeers Knowledge and Experiment of the
Country." Others, his contemporaries and ours, have declaimed
amply on the nature of Morton's "Knowledge and Experiment of
the Country," and there is no need to inflate that Aeolean skin of
righteousness further. Emboldened by "knowledge and experiment," Morton conclusively affirms and conjectures, at once, that
having "bin in those parts any time; besides others lesse, now I am
bold to conclude that the originall of the Natives of New England
may be well conjectured to be from the scattered Trojans after such
time as Brutus departed from Latium."[57] As for the Asiatic or
Tartar origins of the Indians posited in England by, among others,
Edward Brerewood (*Enquiries touching the diversity of languages,
and religions, through the chief parts of the world,* London, 1622,
pp. 94–102), Morton puts no stock in that theory and its conjectures of overland migrations, as originally put forth by Father José
de Acosta. Morton notes that "where as it hath been the opinion of
some men, which shall be nameless, that the Natives of New England may proceede from the race of the Tartars, and come from
Tartaria into these partes, over the frozen Sea, I see no probality
[sic] of any such Conjecture, for as much, as a people once setled
must be remooved by compulsion or else tempted thereunto in
hope of better fortunes, upon commendations of the place, unto
which they should be drawne to remoove."[58] Morton is all too well
"knowledgable and experienced" in such temptations to have his
Trojan theory be read at face value. Though his philological tracing and "proof" of such a theory be symptomatic of the kind of
divination and conjecture the American natives were being subjected to at the time, I am inclined to suspect that Morton's Trojan
genealogy, although valuable as an example, is a Trojan horse in a
polemic with the Founding Fathers of the "New English Canaan."
Clearly, with the last sentence of the passage just cited, Morton
undermines not the theory of the Indians' overland migration necessarily, or solely, but the godly determinacies of providential history. In this sense, he echoes the protean discourse of that other
indomitable New England figure who gave New England its name,
Captain John Smith. I refer to his *Description of New England* and

the passage cited in our last chapter where Smith makes quick to invest human and worldly motives in such enterprises as opposed to divine pred~terminations and providential elections. As for Morton's "bold conclusion" on the Indians' Latin lineage, I do not believe he is adding a thirteenth book to Virgil's *Aeneid*. Rather, he is alluding as much to the founding of England as he is remarking the founding of New England. In doing so, and I shall explain presently, Morton insinuates the insightful observation that the Pilgrim Fathers are taking the American natives as blank and faithful mirrors that echo back to them their own English legends and legendary genealogy, whether these be divined from scriptures' Genesis or from pagan lore. Because the Brutus that Morton would have as the strayed shipwreck whose Trojan progeny multiplied into native Indians is the same legendary founding father of the British race, as documented by Geoffrey of Monmouth (d. 1155) in his *Historia Regum Britanniae* (c. 1136). Geoffrey's source is a "most ancient book in the British tongue" furnished him by Walter, archdeacon of Oxford. Although the veracity of Geoffrey's *Historia* has been disputed often, its substantial contribution to the formation and popularity of the Arthurian legends remains indisputably telling. Morton might or might not have intended it to be so, but in holding up to the Founding Puritans the mirror of their own legendary genealogy and racial mythos through the ruse of a Trojan origin for the Indian natives, Morton is remarking more than the narcissism of any conquering people whose hubris leads them to see inferior and incipient versions of themselves and their own history in those they conquer. Columbus, as we have seen, is the New World's primal example of this predisposition. But, as I suggested, Morton, in his "war" with the orthodox founders, does more in attributing the genealogical paternity of these natives to one who not only sired the British race, but one who is also a filicide and a patricide as well. Brutus, great-grandson of Aeneas, grandson of Ascanius, and son of Sylvius, had the misfortune of killing his father, as he would also slay his children. It was such turn of fortune that, according to Geoffrey of Monmouth, led to his sailing off with a Trojan remnant to an uninhabited island, England, "vacant" at the time, through the

providence of some "wonderful plague" perchance, except for "a
few giants." Surely, the English race would not be sired on runts.
As founding father, Brutus had an earlier career than his British
sojourn, of course, and this is Virgil's version Thomas Morton
obviously knew in his own way. Lucius Junius Brutus drove out
the Tarquin kings in 510 B.C. and founded the Roman republic. He
executed his sons for plotting the restoration of the Tarquins:

> And would you see the Tarquin kings? And, too,
> the haughty spirit of avenging Brutus,
> the fasces he regained? He will be first
> to win the power of a consul, to use
> the cruel axes; though a father, for
> the sake of splendid freedom he will yet
> condemn his very sons who stirred new wars.
> Unhappy man! However later ages
> may tell his acts, his love of country will
> prevail, as will his passion for renown.
>   (*Aeneid*, bk. 4, lines 1083–1092).[59]

It should be clear, I hope, why we can only read Morton on the
origins of the Indians as symptomatic of the philological theoriz-
ing and philogenetic conjecture that compelled his contemporaries. His own ends, beyond the ostensible genealogy he offers for
the Indians, constitute a compelling tale in themselves, but that is
beyond our purview at the moment. That tale's political allegory
as spectral family romance has been long considered, no doubt,
by those who have dared countenance its delightful irreverence.
In Morton's plot, the Puritan pilgrims as Brutus's prosopopoeia
must be read as the image of those Separatists/Nonconformists
who, at once, abandon the fatherland and appropriate/
expropriate the newfound land. But this allegory in Morton's
satirical inversions that would have New England's Founding
Fathers, including Morton himself, reflected as prodigal patri-
cides and filicidal usurpers surely must be the well-trod ground of
innumerable exegetes who have considered this first cultural
iconoclast of the Puritans' New Canaan enterprise.

Even as Morton was "knowing and experimenting" in New
England, an Old England Puritan and apologist for the New

World enterprise, the Reverend John White of Dorchester, specu-
lates on the Jewish origins of the Indians. Though he sought to
remain noncommittal on the conjectures he conveyed, he did
venture a number of his own hypotheses. The title page of his
*The Planters Plea. Or the Grounds of Plantations examined
And vsuall Objections answered* (1630) is graced with II Thessalonians 5:21—"Prove all things, and hold fast that which is
good." There is, obviously, quite a distance between White's
doctrinal "proof" and Morton's knowing "experiment." And
were he forced to seek scriptural sanction in the form of epigram, Morton might have well improvised with "disprove all
things and that which is good shall smile forth upon thee."
Proof through experience, as Morton's usage of experiment denotes, is a process of disconfirmation more in the realm of
worldly investigating than within the ken of doctrinal proving.
Like the rest of the Puritans and the Catholic friars before them,
the Reverend White speaks from other-worldly grounds and, his
circumlocution notwithstanding, he yields to "philological" evidence to see the American natives in prophetic and eschatological light:

> As in New England the Nations beleeve the Creation of the world by
> God, the Creation of one man and woman, their happy condition at
> the first, and seduction by the envy (as they say) of the Cony which
> moves them to abhorre that creature unto this day more then any
> Serpent. It is also reported that they separate their women in the
> times appointed by the Law of *Moses,* counting them and all they
> touch uncleane during that time appointed by the Law: whether
> upon any other ground, or by a tradition received from the *Iewes,* it
> is uncertaine. Some conceive ther Predecessors might have had some
> commerce with the *Iewes* in times past, by what meanes I know not:
> Howsoever it bee, it fals out that the name of the place, which our
> late Colony hath chosen their seat, prooves to be perfect Hebrew,
> being called *Nahum Keike,* by interpretation, *The bosome of consola-
> tion:* which it were pitty that those which observed it not, should
> change into the name of *Salem* [still Hebrew, of course]. . . . Now
> then, if all nations must have Christ tendered unto them, and the
> *Indies* have never yet heard of his name, it must follow, that worke of
> conveighing that knowledge of them, remains to bee undertaken and
> performed by this last age.[60]

"However it bee, it fals out" quite nicely not only in the Hebrew, which the first settlers must have heard in the Indian language as accurately and unmistakably as Columbus heard the language of the Grand Khan in the native Cuban. "It fals out," also that the Reverend White's paragraph begins with Genesis and ends with the Apocalypse. Moving from the Creation and Fall to "this last age," John White sees miraculous providence at work, bringing the cosmic drama to its climactic closure. In the process, there is something reminiscent of both the Dominican friar Diego Durán and the Franciscan Gerónimo de Mendieta in White's conflation of what we saw in Father Diego as theological justification for the travails of the Conquest and in Father Gerónimo as the anxious expectation that prophecy's realization and the covenant's fulfillment might be at hand, at last, if only the Indians were also the Jews. First, the theological strains of Diego Durán's apologia for the Conquest:

> It were little lesse then impietie to conceive that GOD, (whose Will concurres with the lighting of a Sparrow upon the ground) had no hand in directing one of the most difficult and observable workes of this age; and as great folly to imagine, that hee who made all things, and consequently orders and directs them to his owne glory, had no other scope but the satisfing of mens greedy appetites, that thirsted after the riches of the new found world, and to tender unto them the objects of such barbarous cruelties as the world never heard of. Wee cannot then probably conceive that GOD, in that strange discovery, aymed at any other thing but this, that, after hee had punished the Atheisme, and Idolatry of those heathen and bruitish Nation by the Conquerors cruelty, and acquainted them by mixture of some people, with civility, to cause, at length the glorious Gospell of Iesus Christ to shine out unto them.[61]

And, after this salvaging of the "heathen and bruitish Nation" in This World, comes the deliverance unto the Next, as urgently imminent for the Reverend John White as for the Mendicant friar Gerónimo de Mendieta, whom we have already cited:

> . . . to prove that God hath left this great, and glorious worke to this age of the world, is the nearnesse of the *Iewes* conversion; before which, it is conceived by the most, that the fulnes of the *Gentiles* must come in, according to the Apostles prophesie, *Rom.* 11.25.

That this day cannot be farre off appears by the fulfilling of the prophesies, precedent to that great and glorious worke, and the generall expectation thereof by all men, such as was found among the *Iewes* both in *Iudea* and in some other parts of the world before the comming of Christ in the flesh, now then let it bee granted that the *Iewes* conversion is neare, and that the *Gentiles,* and consequently the Indians must needs be gathered in before that day; and any man may make the conclusion that this is the houre for the worke, and consequently of our duty to endeavour the effecting that which God has determined; the opening of the eyes of those poore ignorant soules, and discovering unto them the glorious mystery of Iesus Christ.[62]

John White's exhortation was most earnestly heeded by John Eliot who arrived in New England the year after the Reverend White's tract was published. From 1646 on, Eliot would be the most signaled advocate of Indian catechism. He would become known as the "Apostle to the Indians" and his example would inspire the founding of the Society for the Propagation of the Gospel (1649), London's answer to the Jesuits' evangelic zeal. In his *Christian Commonwealth* (1659), Eliot sees his Christian Indian communities as model societies of a new apostolic age, much like the friars of Minorite orders in New Spain saw theirs a century earlier. Like Mendieta, for example, John Eliot saw his efforts as propitiating the millennial kingdom through the recuperation of the strayed lambs for God's fold. His achievements were so perceived by the expectant Puritans in general. The Puritans' apocalyptic program overlaps unquestionably with the spiritual kingdom of the Franciscans in New Spain inasmuch as Indian evangelism is perceived as the first manifestation of the awaited millennium. A few years before the publication of *The Christian Commonwealth,* and two years following his successful efforts toward the founding of the Society for the Propagation of the Gospel, John Eliot would convey his apostolic vision and his own instrumentality in bringing about God's kingdom on earth in unmistakably hopeful terms: "I intend to direct them [the Indians] according as the Lord shall please to help and assist to set up the Kingdom of Jesus Christ fully, so that Christ shall reigne both in Church and Commonwealth, both in Civil and

Spiritual matters . . . And when everything both Civil & Spiritual
are done by the direction of the word of Christ, then doth Christ
reigne, and the great Kingdom of Jesus Christ which we weight
for, is even this that I do now mention."[63] Eliot's apostolic enterprise and millennialist vision harken to the sixteenth-century spiritual conquest of New Spain that Robert Ricard has so minutely
documented in a book by that title.[64] In the lines that continue
Eliot's just-cited letter, however, the Apostle of the Indians from
Roxbury also echoes Columbus's construction of the New
World's natives as *tabula rasa* awaiting the inscription of a whole
ideological complex that would prove their boon and final deliverance: "As for these poor Indians," Eliot continues, "they have no
principles of their own, nor yet wisdome of their own (I mean as
other Nations have) wherein to stick; and therefore they do most
readily yeeld to any direction from the Lord, so that there will be
no such opposition against the rising Kingdome of Jesus Christ
among them."

Writing some seven or eight years earlier than Eliot, Roger
Williams was neither as sanguine about the role of apostolic
missions nor did he take the natives of New England as
unproblematic receptacles as Eliot did for his cheerful evangelism. The Puritan nonconformist and dissenter from the Bay Colony's theocracy cohabited with the Indians not merely as spiritual
teacher and apostolic father but as sympathetic ethnographer.
His *A Key into the Language of America: Or, An Help to the
Language of the Natives in that part of America, called New
England* (1643) precedes Eliot's linguistic work by twenty years.
Williams rehearses the theories of the natives' Jewish origins in
the prefatory remarks—"To my Deare and Welbeloved Friends
and Coun[t]ry-men, in old and new England"—of *A Key into the
Language of America*.[65] Consulted by Thomas Thorowgood in
1635 on the Jewish origins of the Indians, Williams had no
qualms about the hypothesis. Thorowgood's *Jewes in America,
or, Probabilities That the Americans Are of That Race* (London,
1650) reflects the seventeenth-century discourse on the Indians'
genealogy. In *A Key*, Williams conscientiously reports on the
varied opinion of "wise and judicious men with whom I have

discoursed," relating the Tartar, or Asiatic, hypothesis, as well as the Icelandic, on the Indians' provenance. As for their racial genealogy, Williams moves from hypothesis to observation, allowing the wise, as he says, to draw their own conclusions: "Other opinions I could number up: under favour I shall present (not mine opinion, but) my *Observations* to the judgement of the Wise." He then enumerates his "observations" that run the gamut of criteria rehearsed by the Mendicant friars of New Spain in the previous century: linguistic affinities to Hebrew, customs such as ablutions ("they constantly *annoint* their *heads* as the Jewes did"), the giving of dowries, and a taboo, already mentioned by the Reverend White, "(which I have not so observed amongst other *Nations* as amongst the *Jewes,* and *these:*) they constantly separate their Women (during the time of the monthly sicknesse) in a little house alone by themselves four or five days, and hold it an *Irreligious thing* for either *Father* or *Husband* or any *Male* to come neere them . . . and for their practice they plead *Nature* and *Tradition.*" At this point, as if to keep Columbus's construal of the Indians as Europe's incipient history and yearned Golden Age from disappearing, Williams interjects, on second thought and with no explanation, that as for their speech, "Yet againe I have found a greater Affinity of their Language with the Greek Tongue."

Bewildered and vacillating on his own whereabouts in this wilderness, Williams owns, "I dare not conjecture in these *Vncertainties,* I believe they are *lost,* and yet hope (in the Lords holy season) some of the wildest of them shall be found to share in the blood of the Son of God." And, though he vacillates, one thing is certain for Williams, and that is his earnest expectation of the "Lords holy season" which, he says, "I hope approaching."[66] As W. Clark Gilpin points out however, the conversion of the Indians was not yet as propitious or as propitiating of the desired End. In this Williams differed from John Eliot, but that difference affiliated Williams with the Mendicant friars of New Spain who sought in the *ecclesia indiana* the renascence of the apostolic church, its apostolic poverty and angelic primitivism inspired by the Medieval tradition of the Spirituals and Joachim de Fiore.

Like the primitivist zeal of the apostolic friars, documented extensively, as already noted, by Ricard and Phelan, Roger Williams's
reformationist enthusiasm did not see his times as sufficiently
regenerated into the true spirit of the strayed church, in apostasy
since the Middle Ages, and the conversion of the Indians was not
to be expected to yield the hoped-for end-time, since the real
conversion of the Christians themselves had yet to occur. The
observations and commentary, as well as the intercalated verses
among the lexical lists of *A Key,* clearly convey that by Williams's
reckoning Christian and Indian alike had yet to receive the requi-
site dispensation, or had yet to give themselves over to the spiritual grace of true regeneration, for which he prayed fervently, so
that the End of this world's ends could finally ensue. In this,
Williams differs from a good number of Puritans and Catholics
alike. For whereas the providentialist hopes and messianic aspirations of most, whether English or Iberian, had been linked to a
notion of "chosen people" or "elect nation," Williams ultimately
sees the prophetic ends through this New World not as ends to be
reached by ecclesiastical, national, or racial filiation, but by individual restoration. The vehemence of this conviction led Williams
to question the very legitimacy of the charters and letters patent
that gave proprietary rights to the Europeans in the New World,
a questioning that expedited his departure as suspect dissenter
from the orthodoxy and patriarchy of the Massachusetts Bay
Colony. In this ambiguous displacement, Williams may be closest
to the "pilgrim and stranger" who was Columbus, though God's
"helmsman" without a country but with an unfailing mission
never questioned the legitimacy of his Capitulaciones and of his
privileged capitulation of Europe's enterprise in the New World.

CHAPTER VII

Making Ends Meet

The Dire Unction of Prophecy

. . . me temo que yo no sea bien entendido.
                    Christopher Columbus, 1501.

Christopher Columbus, Admiral of the Ocean Sea, Viceroy and Governor General of Islands and Mainlands of Asia and the Indies, had his last ride on a mule. Simple as that may sound, it was neither effortless nor an unquestionable given. It was the least problematic of the available means to make his way to court, in Segovia at the time. Travel on horseback for the Admiral was out of the question. Forty years at sea made that exertion physically impossible. Columbus returned to Seville in November of 1504 from his fourth and final voyage, which included being marooned for one year and five days on the island of Jamaica. The fifty-three-year-old mariner's body was wracked with gout and arthritis that made even Andalusia's temperate clime unbearable. The jostling of a horse's gait would be excruciating. In a letter to his son Diego, dated 28 November 1504 and still preserved in the Admiral's hand in Seville's Archivo General de Indias (Patronato, 295:51), Columbus alludes to an alternate form of transport. He writes, "Si me escrives, vayan las cartas a Luis de Soria porque me las enbíe al camino donde yo fuere, porque si voy en andas será creo por la Plata [If you write to me, direct the letters to Luis de Soria so that he can send them to me wherever I might be on the road, because if I go by bier, it will be, I believe, by way of La Plata]."[1] This was the easiest road to Valladolid where Spain's itinerant court was quartered at the moment. The "bier" Columbus refers to was a magnificent funeral catafalque on wheels that had recently transported to Seville the corpse of Spain's Grand Cardinal, Diego Hurtado de Mendoza, from the monastery of Tentudia. Columbus had solicited the use of that regal contraption from the Cathedral chapter of Seville and, two days before he writes to Diego, permission had been granted. That was on 26 November, the same day that, unbeknownst to Columbus, Queen Isabel died. For reasons of inclement weather and aggravated ill health (vid. Letter of 1 December 1504), Columbus discarded the surreal idea of having his ailing body rolled on a funeral litter across the plains of Castille. In the same batch of letters in the Archivo General de Indias, there is one dated 21 December 1504, also in the Admiral's hand, in which Columbus requests of his son Diego at court that "if, without much trouble, a permit for travelling on muleback could be obtained, I would endeavor to depart for where you are after January, and I will do so even without it. One cannot hasten enough to see that the Indies are not lost, as they are. [Si sin importunar se obiese licencia de andar en mula, yo trabajaría de partir para allá pasado Henero, y ansí lo haré sin ella. Puriende non se dese de dar priesa porque las Indias non se pierdan, como hazen]."[2] January's "cold" immobilized his body, as he repeatedly complains. On 23 February 1505, King Ferdinand grants the necessary license to travel by mule, "the only favor he ever showed Columbus," according to Samuel Eliot Morison's reading of that ambivalent relationship.[3] Travel by mule had been forbidden to all but women and the clergy by a royal edict of 1494. The prohibition came about at the instance of the Andalusian horse breeders who, citing the scarcity of mounts for the knights-errant of the crusade against Granada two years earlier, sought to increase demand and production. Columbus thus made the three-hundred-mile trek from Seville to Segovia, where the court sat at the time, in May of 1405. A year later, still moving with the itinerant court, Columbus will be in Valladolid where, on Ascension Day, 20 May 1506, a Wednesday, his ailing body succumbs. Death overtakes his pilgrimage even as he tenaciously pursues what he believes are just ends and labors "to see that the Indies are not lost."

I rehearse the circumstances of Columbus's "last ride" in order to highlight the turn of fortune in the Admiral's itinerary, a turn that still retains something of the cosmological sublime from one of the most remarkable careers, but also one that partakes of certain elements of pathos and the ridiculous, thus giving Columbus a greater dimension of humanity than ever. At the end of the day, the Admiral's circumstances speak of an unbreachable gap between the rhetorical formulations, born of a prophetic vision, that gave the enabling ideology of the enterprise of the Indies its conquering impetus and the rather pathetic quandary of the ideology's paradigmatic proponent and earliest practitioner. Having overtaken the ends of the Earth, more earthly ends overtake Columbus. In the process, the ideological enablements and their rhetorical screens with which he is identified fall decidedly out of synchrony with the newly emerged realities. Modified ideological forms and new rhetorical formulations become necessary to suit a new phase of imperial ends and to legitimate a new set of conquering means. By the end of his third voyage, Columbus has more than a premonition that his vision, at once prophetic and pragmatic, no longer coincides with imperial sights set on incorporation of "the other world," not as apocalyptic interlude for eschatological ends, but as hegemonic prelude to colonialist means. This does not mean that prophetic vision and its rhetorical formations outlive their usefulness as instruments of a conquering ideology. On the contrary, as we have seen, the same repertoire of discursive strategies is deployed more than a century later in Virginia and in New England for ends materially not different or differently articulated in the language of their pursuit. And, too, subsequent to the consolidation of the worldly ends pursued in that more northerly arena, those who would persist in the pressing of claims in keeping with their original rhetorical formulations fall out of step and are ruled out of order, either as nonconformists and dissidents (Roger Williams), or as antinomians, literally as "outlaws" (Anne Hutchinson). Although Columbus was neither banished nor outlawed, as were these later avatars of vision's earnestness, he was effectively marginalized. His delivery from the New World in irons at the end of the third voyage, his prolonged displacement as marooned shipwreck during his fourth voyage, and the protracted waiting before being summoned to court to brief Their Highnesses on his final journey may all have their fortuitous turns—whether in bureaucratic over-zealousness, inclement weather, or royal illnesses—that mitigate the idea of deliberate shunning. Nonetheless, the unrecorded infrahistory or the opportunistic capitalization on those reversals of fate make the Admiral's vicissitudes more than symbolic of his precarious predicament in official and institutional circles.

This is why, I believe, Columbus's last writings, primarily his correspondence and drafts of memoranda to court, are so significant. They are poignantly articulate of what happens to the visionary and rhetorical vanguard of a particular ideology when it no longer occupies that forward position in relation to the ends for which it was deployed either as means or as screen. Something of the farcical that Karl Marx discerned in the Eighteenth Brumaire of Louis Bonaparte sets in with the human pathos that accompanies the apprehension of one's caducity. Historiography has not missed the pathetic farce of a waning Columbus unrelentingly clamoring for "my third, my eighth, my tenth" as desperate clutching in an attempt to hold on and as indignant righteousness aiming to recoup what it feels is its due. Historians and biographers of Columbus have uniformly read these final writings very much in this vein.

To my knowledge, however, no one has read these letters and drafts of the Admiral's final five years with an eye to what they may reveal, symptomatically, about the moment when the ideological embodiment of a particular rhetorical formulation falls off, becomes alienated from the ends to which it may have once been put. Columbus, extreme exemplum of anything he ever exemplified, displays the symptoms of this alienation in starkly human terms of bewilderment. He displays greatest urgency in self-recovery, in the recuperation of a personal history and historical deeds, in the recapitulation of the official capitulations that authorized his enterprise, in the enumeration of privileges granted him by patents, in the litany of wrongs he has endured, and in vaunting his endurance in the face of those he proved wrong. But, significantly, Columbus in this process becomes somebody else, an other to himself in the trials and drafts and versions of these memoranda, all aimed at constituting the one final memorandum and the one definitive self that would vindicate him, his cause, and his legacy. The drafts I am referring to are still extant in Columbus's hand, preserved among the holdings of the Archivo de la Casa de Alba in Madrid.[4] Columbus entered the venerable House of Alba posthumously. He did so with the marriage of his son Diego to Doña Maria de Toledo, niece of the Duke of Alba. It was a marriage arranged by King Ferdinand himself.

As drafts for a memorandum, or a *memorial,* as it is known in Spanish, these fragmentary attempts are, literally, trials of memory, rehearsals at self-memorialization. Within these "tryouts" for a constituted whole and in remembrance, the "I," the "you," and the "he" of the self as subject and protagonist are arrayed, made to file before the self-drafting Columbus as in a parade whose point of origin has to be made to coincide with its point of arrival. Columbus's, we might say, is a desperate attempt to make ends meet, an attempt that may have well succeeded totally on Ascension Day of 1506. I say Columbus becomes an other to himself in these scriptive rehearsals, then, because of this essaying of a number of voices in an equally varying number of subject pronouns that run the gamut of grammar's possibilities. There are four drafts in his handwriting, one in the second person, one in the first, one in the third, and one in an admixture. This form of grammatical quandary of the subject is reminiscent of the social and corporate alienation the French sociologist Emile Durkheim designated as *anomie,* literally an existence without law. Columbus's vacillation in grammar is symptomatic of a larger shift of the grounds on which his tenacious vision had previously discerned and legitimated a world-altering endeavor, the enterprise he launched across the Ocean Sea. Now, once more, the master mariner of dead reckoning finds himself in uncharted seas, but with a certain loss of mastery over his reckoner's abacus. Providential history and provident cosmography no longer fit the bill. Prophetic vision and apocalyptic calculus may still set and rhetorically justify the course. But millennialism's expectancy has become inextricably entangled with the economy of "millionism" of a more earthly ledger. Columbus's grammatical anomie, then, evinces the symptoms of a crisis whose pressing exigencies precipitated by certain reality shifts make imperative the re-visioning of vision.

Strong visionaries, particularly those such as Columbus who derive their prescience from the surety of conviction and the prophetic grace of infallible providence, fare rather poorly in times of revisionary imperatives. Their fate, if fading, like Columbus in this final act, is the fluster of puzzlement and righteous clamoring for unswerving steadiness. We can call this quandary a form of anomie precipitated by vision's slippage out of what at that moment might be reality's focus. However, if these visionaries be strong still and vitally commanding, their predicament of anomie becomes transmuted by corporate declaration. The institutional powers that be at the moment render such *anomie* by indictment into *antinomy*. This, in essence, is what differentiates the precarious predicament of Christopher Columbus at the end of his life from, say, the equally precarious situation of someone like Anne Hutchinson who is still dynamic and in full command of her persuasive and prophetic powers. There is a continuity from the "lack of law," or anomie, in Columbus's befuddled state to the lawlessness or antinomy ("against the law") of Hutchinson's enthusiastic subscription to an ideology of a literal and plenary covenant of grace, already compromised by worldly contingency by the time of her arrival in 1634, a scant four years after the Commonwealth's godly founding. The continuity I speak of is not necessarily in the nature of content or essential doctrine. Rather, it is in the character of form and the form of institutional reaction to ideological formulations that may have been outdistanced by newly institutionalized interests. In both cases, that of Columbus at the end of his life and Anne Hutchinson at the beginning of her life in the New World, we see the emergence of a dialogical confrontation. This is a confrontation between, on the one hand, certain formulations within the ideological enablements that made the current institutional state of things possible and, on the other hand, the structures of interest and accommodation that have shifted away from those formulations. The expedient necessity of investing in such shifts rest in the need to consolidate the institutional structures that the original formulations had put into motion. In other words, once the interests in whose service those ideological formulations had been deployed have taken hold, the rhetorical injunctions of prophetic discourse and its ideological forms are deemed out of place and out of synchrony. As such, these are literally conditions of utopia (no-place) and anachronism (out of time). Of course, these are conditions Columbus has always inhabited in good measure since his historical emergence in the Iberian peninsula. His greatest feats were pursued and accomplished even as he lived perennially "out of place," and with another time beyond a this-worldly time always in view. Having thus lived and found vindication for his wildest dreams, he now has some difficulty in reconciling himself to the worldly caprices of a historical situation that would deauthorize his claims and cast his centrality as protagonist to the periphery. Hence his grave preoccupation with the possibility that he might be misunderstood, as the citation I have taken as epigram for this chapter conveys.

Always a stranger, and not oblivious to that fact, Columbus now feels more estranged than ever. And it is wholly appropriate to extend the analogue with Anne Hutchinson also to this point. She, a woman, is no less a phenomenal stranger to the powers that be in the Patriarchal Commonwealth at Massachusetts Bay, a "strangeness" the Anglo-American tradition has flouted through the nineteenth century, Nathaniel Hawthorne's errant "Mrs. Hutchinson" in the Salem *Gazette* of 1830 being a supreme example. Only recently is a critical revaluation of women like Anne Hutchinson being undertaken by historians and cultural critics sensitive to Mrs. Hutchinson as woman in prophecy's patriarchal tradition.[5] After Columbus and before Anne Hutchinson, an analogous disjunction between commonwealth (the state) and ideological vision of foundations befalls the evangelical idealism and apostolic simplicity in New Spain's "millennial kingdom," as John Leddy Phelan has pointed out.[6] The incursion of the earthly commonwealth into the "city of God" through state decrees and official controls, as well as the steady supplanting of

the Mendicant friars and Minorite Orders by the episcopate and
Church bureaucracy, lead Father Gerónimo de Mendieta at the
end of the sixteenth century to see the history of New Spain after
1564 as the "Age of Silver," in contrast to the previous forty
years which he took as the "Age of Gold." Clearly, there is more
than mere reference to the metallurgical capitalization that was
an intricate part of Spain's economic history in New Spain where
Father Gerónimo's pagan nominations for a historical schema are
concerned. The prophetic vision of the Franciscan friar that had
considered the Spanish nation and its imperial monarch, the Holy
Roman Emperor Charles V, as the messianic agents of cosmic
eschatology, is forced to lower its sights in the bureaucratic reign
of Philip II. Philip's official state policy sought to contain the
Ecclesia Indiana that was the idealized restoration of the primitive apostolic Church in the New World, supplanting it, instead,
with the expanding clericy and the state-bound institutions of the
Roman Church and the regular clergy.

Columbus's predicament, not unlike that of the Spiritual Franciscans and the Puritan enthusiasts, is amply articulate in what it
teaches us about the relationship between prophecy and empire.
Whereas prophecy is literally a fore-word, a speaking form that
capitulates history and its events, as ideological figuration it is a
form of (and for) forethought, a fore-structure, if you will, on
whose fundamental provisions (and previsions) the empire is
founded. Once the structural edifice of that founding has taken
form, consolidated its position, and vested its interests with some
degree of firmness, the prophetic precedents either fall off altogether, or, more often, they become transmuted, expediently
metamorphosed as rhetorical formulations that continue to abet
and further imperial investments in the structures and contexts
that have been consolidated. Thus, prophetic rhetoric in the service of an ideology of conquest, colony, and empire passes from
an initial founding stage, in which it serves as *pre*-formative instrument, to the conservative and preservative force of a *per*-
formative discourse. As in the unsettled predicament of Columbus at the end of his life, then, the rhetorical injunctions of prophecy's visions and prophetic ideology that once capitulated (that

once headed) the project of conquest and colonization now serve as mediate instrument of recapitulation, of recovery and incorporation. This may explain why official Spain, now inadvertently, now subtly, sought to displace Columbus, as it would seek to replace the Spiritual visionaries in New Spain who sought the realization of prophecy's visions in Indian *eutopias*. This might explain, too, Columbus's haste and the alertness he would urge on his son Diego "to lose no time in seeing that the Indies are not lost." But, then, as we have seen, he adds, "como hazen,"—"as they are," meaning, as is happening to them. Columbus's self, his own identity, is so inextricably enmeshed with the Indies that his fluctuation and indecisiveness in putting forth a determinate subject pronoun by which to denote himself in this task of memorial recapitulation is clear indication that the Indies are, indeed, deemed lost by their rightful "finder." Clearly, in the founding of empires finders are not necessarily keepers. And Columbus's desperate grammatical flailing speaks of a frantic attempt to recover what he feels he has discovered by the grace of God.

In an undated draft of a letter most likely destined for the Council of the Indies, Columbus reminds the Councilors who now oversee the State's imperial enterprise, "[i]n seven years I carried out this conquest by divine will. When I thought I would enjoy favors and rest, I was unexpectedly seized and brought back loaded with irons. [En siete años hize yo esta conquista por voluntad divina. Al tiempo que yo pensé de haber mercedes y descanso, de improvisto fui preso y traido cargado de fierros]."[7] The draft is in the Admiral's hand and forms part of his documents in the Archivo General de Indias. It is obviously written after his third voyage. It is, understandably, a dark period in his life, perhaps the low point of his career when he might feel that even God-willed achievements and divine intentions may not be altogether immune to worldly travesty. And the measure of loss that creates the chasm between the ends of his prophetic vision and the ends that have befallen his lot is most overtly expressed in Columbus's letter to Pope Alexander VI. Dated February 1502, there is no certainty that it ever reached its destination. But a copy of the letter survives in the hand of Hernando Colón, Columbus's other son. In the letter, Columbus recapitulates the history of his accomplishments, emphasizing the diversity and riches of the island that is the seat of his Viceroyalty and General Governorship, "[e]sta isla es Tharsis, es Cethia, es Ophir y Ophaz e Çipanga," and, he says, "we have called it Española." He recounts, as well, that he has reached a region where "I believed and believe what so many saintly and sacred theologians believed and believe, that there in that region is the Earthly Paradise. [Creí y creo aquello que creyeron y creen tantos sanctos y sacros theólogos, que allí en la comarca es el Paraíso Terrenal]."[8] As he laments to His Holiness the Pope, however, more than the Earthly Paradise may have been lost by fortune's fickleness and human interests. At risk now is the Heavenly Kingdom's millennial reign on Earth, because the ultimate ends of the New World enterprise have been compromised by human temptation and waylaid by the caprices of Satan:

> Esta empresa se tomó con fin de gastar lo que d'ella se oviesse en presidio de la Casa Sancta a la Sancta Iglesia. Después que fui en ella y visto la tierra, escreví al Rey y a la Reina, mis Señores, que dende a siete años yo le pagaría çincuenta mill de pie y cinco mill de cavallo en la conquista d'ella, y dende a cinco años otros cincuenta mill de pie y otros çinco mill de cavallo, que serían dies mill de cavallo e çient mill de pie para esto; Nuestro Señor muy bien amostró que yo compliría, por experiencia amostrar que podía dar este año a Sus Altezas čiento y veinte quintales de oro y çerteça que sería ansí de orto tanto al término de los çinco años. Sathanás ha destorbado todo esto y con sus fuerças ha puesto esto en término que non haya effecto ni el uno ni el otro, si Nuestro Señor no lo ataja. La governación de todo esto me habían dado perpetua, agora con furor fui sacado d'ella. Por muy cierto se ve que fue malicia del enemigo y porque non venga a luç tan sancto propósito.[9]

[This enterprise was undertaken with the purpose of spending whatever accrued from it in restoring the Holy Sepulcher to the Holy Church. Having gone there and seen the land, I wrote to the King and Queen, my Lords, that within seven years I would finance fifty thousand foot soldiers and five thousand horsemen in its conquest; and within five more years, another fifty thousand foot soldiers and another five thousand cavalry, that would be ten thousand horsemen and one hundred thousand foot soldiers to this end. Our Lord showed that I would well accomplish this, showing in practice that I could give Their Highnesses this year one hundred and twenty hundred-weight of gold and certainly that it would be likewise at the end of the next five years. Satan has undone all this, and with his powers will have put an end to this and to the other, if Our Lord does not stop him. I was granted the government of all this for perpetuity; now I have been deprived of it violently. Most certainly one can see that it was the malice of the enemy so that such holy purpose should not come to light.]

Prophecy's own visionary formulation had taught Columbus all too well that one only seeks to recover what one has already lost. And perhaps the most poignant insight of this predicament for the Admiral might well be the recognition that in the clamoring for self-recuperation through drafts and memorial trials, the very object of that attempt, perforce, may have slipped away. When that object would also be, as in this case, the very subject drafting or essaying the pursuit of such redemption, implacable utopia sets in with vehemence and anachronistic derision. A stark sentence from Columbus's *Lettera Rarissima* (7 July 1503), written from Jamaica in the course of the foundered fourth and last voyage, reads: "Yo soy tan perdido como dixe. [I am as lost as I said]." The sentence Columbus passed on himself then, now resonates more suggestively than ever. In a worldly context where prophecy's redemptive rhetoric and enlivening promise have already run their course, u-topia becomes the strangest of the stranger's dwellings, a habitat in Nowhereland, and not just as rhetorical figura or as philological trope, such as Martin Waldseemüller's *Amerige,* discussed in our third chapter. In this regard, the fates do indeed prove implacable when they would have Columbus, in this final act of his drama, meet with his friend Amerigo Vespucci in Seville, probably for the last time, and write to Diego, in a letter for which Amerigo himself served as courier, a letter that reveals as much, or more, about Columbus's own fortunes as those of Vespucci which the Admiral laments here:

fablé con Amerigo Vespuchi, portador d'esta . . . es mucho hombre de bien; la fortuna le ha sido contraria como a otros muchos. Sus

trabajos non le han aprovechado tanto como la razón requiere; él va
por mío y en mucho deseu de hazer cosa que redonde a mi bien, si a
sus manos está. Yo non sey de aquá en qué yo le enponga que a mí
aproveche, porque non sey qué sea lo que alla le queren. El va de-
terminado de hazer por mí todo lo que a él fuere posible. Ved allá en
qué puede aprobechar y trabajad por ello, que él lo hará todo y
fablerá y lo porná en obra, y sea todo secretamente, porque non se
aya d'él sospecha.[10]

[I spoke with Amerigo Vespucci, bearer of the present . . . he is a
good man; fortune has not favored him, as with many others. His
labors have not served him as well as reason would dictate they
might have. He goes on my behalf and is most desirous to do whatever might redound to my good, if it be within his reach. From here, I
do not know what to ask of him that would benefit me, because I do
not know why he is wanted there. He goes determined to do for me
whatever he can. See what he could best do there and aid him in it,
for he will do everything, and he will speak and see to it that it is
done. And let it all be in secret, so that no one should suspect him.]

There is immense irony in this letter, given the treatment Vespucci has received at the hands of history's pundits, from Father
Bartolomé de Las Casas to Ralph Waldo Emerson, as we have
seen in our third chapter. The most ironic of all is Columbus's
language and commendation of his fortunes to the ministry of
Vespucci. Clearly it is a much more prophetic letter than Columbus could have imagined, and in ways he probably could have
imagined less. The letter is dated 5 February 1505 and is one of
Columbus's autographs in the Archivo General de Indias referred
to earlier. But I would like to turn to those earlier drafts, now in
the Archives of the House of Alba, written sometime between the
Admiral's inauspicious, though amply prophetic, third and the
ill-starred fourth voyages.

Self-fashioning has been one of Columbus's most constant oc-
cupations. It begins on record with his official arrival into the
annals of archival history with the Capitulaciones de Santa Fe of
17 April 1492. The titles, entitlements, and charter privileges in
that primal document reveal the conviction of a man with a
mission. But they reveal, too, the unmistakable anxieties of an
outsider, one who feels the immeasurable necessity of having

further to reach. Overreaching, in such circumstances, becomes compensatory gesture for being a stranger. The repeated requests and ensuing reconfirmations of his titles and charter privileges, as we have seen in our fourth chapter, become as much forms of self-confirmation as they serve to reaffirm accomplished deeds and the due emoluments that accrue to them. It is unusual for any of Columbus's letters to the Spanish monarchs not to include an autobiographical sketch or a reminder of his unyielding piety and triumphs over adversity. In his own script, Columbus is definitely the leading character, now heroic, now humble, often obeisant and pious, but never diffident. Even at his most abject, or especially then, as in the letter to the Governess of Prince Don Juan and in the *Lettera Rarissima,* as we have seen in our last chapter, Columbus portrays either a baptized Stoic or an outright Job. And when in utmost dejection and in the most dire straits, as we have also seen, Columbus turns from earthly king and queen directly to God in covenantal dialogue as between contracting parties. Prophetic vision(s), then, have a history as unction for dire straits in Columbus's itinerary. This, of course, should not surprise us. It is part and parcel of the prophetic tradition and of prophecy's cultures, from the Patriarchs of Genesis and Exodus to the patriarchs of New Canaan in New England's wilderness. What is unique in the case of Columbus is the measure and circumstance, the reach and the grandeur of the rhetorical gesture that has always been characteristic and only intensifies in his final years. And, again, the reach is cosmic, the circumstances dire, the conditions incongruous and, though the focus falters, the determination remains unrelenting.

In a letter to Queen Isabel written sometime in August or September 1501, Columbus reiterates what he has always claimed about the source of his strength and daring determination. As much a disclosure of conviction, this letter is a revelation of character, as we shall see. It is unlikely that at the time he was writing to the queen Columbus would have been unaware of the appointment of Nicholás de Ovando as Governor of the West Indies. That official act took effect on 3 September 1501, thereby, as Columbus writes to Pope Alexander VI five or six months later, "depriving me with fury" of the government that "had been granted me for perpetuity." Columbus's letter to the queen, then, could be read as his most immediate response to his now official displacement as "Viceroy and Governor General of Islands and Mainlands" in the Indies. It is clear from his letter (the original has survived—Archivo General de Indias, Autógrafos, 43) that his protest is plaintive, but his determination is relentless. And it is clear, too, that though he may have lost the worldly governance of the Indies, he has yielded no ground either in that geography's other-worldly significance or in the self-apperception as mediate agent for placing the New World in the service of prophecy's greater ends. Thus, rather than worldly honor that has proved so fleeting, Columbus reaches after other-worldly glory. He demurs to monarchical privilege, but he enjoins, in the process, imperial responsibility to transworldly purpose. Worldly government, Columbus implies, remains a mediate instrument of transcendent objectives, and now more so than ever before. Thus, as has been his wont, Columbus not only rises to the occasion, he seeks to rise above it. And, as I noted, he reiterates that the origin of what assures such triumph, or what at least makes him feel triumphant, on such occasions, lies in: "Una confiança grandíssima que yo tengo en Aquel piadoso Redemptor Nuestro [quien] me da esta oxadía, y non abilidad ni esfoerço que de mí cognosca. Yo me di en Barçelona a Vuestra Alteza sin desar de mi cosa, y ansí como fue el ánima, ansí fue la honra y hazienda. [My audacity [that] is given me by the great confidence I have in Our Merciful Redeemer and not by any ability or power of my own. I surrendered myself to Your Highness in Barcelona, holding back nothing, as it was with my soul, so it was with my honor and estate]."[11] It would take Spain's literary tradition nearly a century to dramatize in the honor tragedies, the *Comedias* of the Siglo de Oro, the subtle distinctions Columbus insinuates here. Rhetorical as Columbus's grandiloquent gesture might be, however, unlike those Renaissance plays, it is a lived rhetoric and a vital gesture, not yet a spectacle rehearsed as discursive or as didactic reflection in the staged mirror of the world. Obviously, Columbus's gesture does not lack rhetorical conveyance or theatricality. But his is an existential, a pragmatically lived spectacle, a spectacle of self-essaying. However much self-deluded, Columbus's "geste" has something of the epic's primacy, as opposed to the prosaic's performance, if I may paraphrase Hegel. "Indeed," Marx would say, as he did on Hegel, "but this essayed epic gesture is a rehearsal nonetheless, coming as it does after a season of loss and in the final act of the drama that is Columbus's life, a moment of desperate seeking after recuperation. As such," the Marx of the *Eighteenth Brumaire*'s opening lines might quip, "the quotient of repetition entailed in such an act interjects an element of farce into the geste's would-be grandeur." One would be hard-pressed to contest the claim. But, as already noted, that admixture of farce and tragic pathos is, nevertheless, what humanizes Columbus. And, though a character in his own drama, he remains, at least in his writings, his own human character rather than another human's literary invention. The surrendering of himself to his Monarch "soul, honor, and estate," and his claim to have done so at this greatest moment of triumph—his exultant return from his initial voyage to be received by Their Highnesses in Barcelona—lays bare Columbus entirely. In that extreme divestiture, Her Royal Highness, in turn, is to countenance a higher obligation, one that would make her accede to serve Her servant in the name and by the call of a transcendent duty. Surrendering all to Her mercy, Columbus renders his queen all but duty bound. And the ultimate criterion to adjudicate between his remittent capitulation and Her unremitting sovereignty is the very standard Columbus himself advances as the source of his strength and of his audacity, "la confiança grandíssima que yo tengo en Aquel Piadoso Redemptor Nuestro." Accordingly then, Columbus begins his letter thus: "Christianíssima Reina: Yo soy el siervo de Vuestra Alteza. Las llaves de mi voluntad yo se las di en Barcelona. [Most Christian Queen: I am your Highness's servant. The keys to my will I surrendered to you in Barcelona]." In this utmost self-divestment, Columbus invests proportionately utmost expectations that, in his estimation, should at least have parity with any other royal obligations. In breaching the distance between the two extremes of divestiture and expected return, Columbus brooks no difficulty, nor does he risk the queen's suspicion of his rhetorical gesture and grand geste as gambit of an artful ploy. Thus, he moves artfully to interdict that possibility: "Lo que yo tengo pensado de mi vida yo lo di a Vuestra Alteza en un memorial por mi mano. Si yo creyese que Vuestra Alteza crehe que alí non va maliçia ni arte, sería yo muy alegre. [What I have thought of my life I have conveyed to Your Highness in a memorandum in my own hand. If I could believe that Your Highness believes that there is neither malice nor artifice there, I would be most content]."[12]

Columbus clearly is most anxious to suspend disbelief, both on his part and on Her Majesty's. His other writings, however, would seem to indicate that he had little success, at least as concerns his own qualms toward the sovereigns. And, one suspects, the king's and queen's reservations were not altogether assuaged either. At any rate, having thus sought in the rhetoric of his obeisance to breach the distance between servant and sovereign, Columbus moves to posit what he conceives as his and the queen's common ground. That is, providential history's ends as promised in prophecy's requirements that have made him and the queen equally elect agents of a godly task in pursuit of a God-willed goal:

> Yo veu este negoçio de las Indias muy grande. Los otros muchos que Vuestra Alteza tiene, con su indisposición, non da lugar que el regimiento d'este vaya perfeto. Esto me contrista por dos cabos: el uno es por lo de Yerusalem, de que suplico a Vuestra Alteza que non le tenga en poco, ni que yo fablé en ello por arte; el otro es que yo he miedo que este negoçio se pierda . . . Yo suplico a Vuestra Alteza que non me tenga en esto ni en otra cosa alguna por parte salvo por servidor suyo . . . Vea agora si le aplaz de me experimentar como a tal en esto de las Indias y del otro de la Casa Santa . . . Puédese dar orden con que este negoçio se punga en filo luego sin mucha fatiga.

> [I see this business of the Indies as very great. The many other concerns Your Highness has, begging your pardon, do not allow for the due resolution of this matter. This saddens me on two counts: the one concerning Jerusalem, about which I beg Your Highness not to take it lightly, nor did I speak of it out of cunning. The other is that I fear that this business [of the Indies] be lost . . . I beg Your Highness that you not consider me in this matter or in any other except as your servant . . . I hope it please you to treat me as such in this matter of the

Indies and the other concerning the Holy Sepulcher . . . It could be ordered that this business be put right soon without much trouble.]

Artfully artless, cunningly ingenuous, Columbus sets his "business of the Indies" and the matter of Jerusalem on level terms. In this gambit, Columbus re-invokes the ideological form of prophecy and providential history. He recurs to that ideology's rhetorical formulation, its prophetic rhetoric and eschatological imperatives. This is the formula that conquered the Indies. The question for Columbus now is, Can the unction of prophecy salvage their loss? Can prophetic injunction and its ideological pinions serve, as they did before, in what is now a recuperative enterprise for what was Columbus's "enterprise of the Indies"? History would prove that they could not. But Columbus, indomitable "divine" and incorrigible visionary that he is, though his ways betray an understanding of his recuperative project's impossibility, his acts speak of his refusal to admit to what he may have understood. And any such admission, he gives us to understand, would be tantamount to a different sort of capitulation. He gives himself, instead, to the task of recapitulating, an act of reinvestment of the prophetic self in providential history's waylaid path and travestied futures. It is at this juncture that the self-scattering drafts grasping for integrity and self-reintegration become most shrill and also most revealing. Drafted during this same period, these trials would eventuate in the necessity to undertake a clinching fourth voyage, one which, it was hoped, would put everything right, at last. But, as we have seen, rather than worldly vindication, this was a voyage that would turn as much into a *via dolorosa* as into prophetic pilgrimage through the Ocean's wilderness.

It is not my wish to psychologize the Columbus drafts I have been referring to. I do believe that they offer productive readings of Columbus's own self-fashioning. I deliberately opt for "self-fashioning" rather than "self-portrayal," because I read these drafts as desperate attempts in adverse conditions to forge a self and not just to portray an already securely existing subject. Columbus's is a task undertaken at a disruptive juncture, a critical crossing point when and where the habitual self falls into the

necessity of essaying adversative constructs as venues to an identity. By adversative constructs I mean those procedures most
frequently identified with language devices such as "but,"
"rather," "or," and phrases such as "then again," "on the other
hand," "on second thought," and so forth. All of these elements
represent highly self-conscious instances where Columbus checks
his inadvertent self-characterizations and, in doing so, compounds inadvertence because the instruments and enablements
of self-awareness and calibration are the very gestures of a habitual self. If Columbus seeks in these drafts for a self that would
coincide with a self-perception suited to his predicament, his
ultimate failure is painful evidence that he does not succeed.
However, in his overwrought attempts at self-adequation, at
coming forth with a self adequate to the dire circumstances of
the occasion, Columbus becomes poignantly consubstantial with
those attempts themselves. His task of self-fashioning, then, betrays a self-portrait that is of a piece with the process of this very
task, a portrait that betrays as much inadvertence and self-
consciousness, as it betrays habit and character. In the final
analysis, these drafts, like all drafts or self-rehearsals, are more
articulate than the ultimate portraiture or consequence for
which they were destined. Columbus, then, tells us more about
himself, in spite of his difficulties and vacillations, than he might
have wished us to know. His failure, in this sense, is a greater
success than the success he may have intended. But what
emerges from these tryouts and trials of self-portrayal corroborates what we glimpse of Columbus throughout his career. It is
an emphatic form of corroboration by virtue of the fact that
Columbus's task at this stage has not only the force of assertion
but also the vigor of a counterassertion and the urgency of a
recuperative undertaking. In the reactive and reiterative verve of
Columbus's task, then, whatever is corroborated for us has a
heightened intensity. Having always glimpsed a Columbus with
a providential mission and a divinely elect role in the drama of
prophetic history, we now see Columbus even more magnified in
his self-apperception as key player on the cosmic stage. And
though the oscillation between grandeur and humility still tracks

a pendular swing, the extremes now move farther out, describing an arc of greater proportions. This is the amplified motion we see in the term of self-aggrandizement and self-abjection in the drafts under discussion.

I take first the draft written in the second-person singular. Here, as in most dialogical soliloquies, Columbus takes as interlocutor, really as addressee, his own mirror image, or at least a spectral semblance of his own apperception. A curt sentence at the end of this draft, a sentence that slips into the first person singular, sums the gist of the fragment: "Información de mis privilegios. [Report of my privileges]." Aside from the terse bottom line and the penultimate clause before, to be discussed shortly, the rest of the draft is in the second person. It is a declamatory apostrophe and grandiloquent enumeration. The fragment begins with an invocation to the Virgin, a common practice in Columbus's writings, and proceeds to address the rhetorically evoked second self by the writing self:

> Magnífico Señor: Por vuestro privilegio y capitulación parece que Sus Altezas os fizieron su Almirante del mar Oçéano, el cual fizieron marcar por una raya que pasa de las islas del Cabo Verde [a] aquelas de los Açores de polo a polo, con todas las merçedes y honras que ha y tiene el Señor Almirante de Castilla en su distrito.

> [Magnificent Lord: By your privilege and capitulation it is manifest that Their Highnesses made you their Admiral of the Ocean Sea, which they divided with a line from pole to pole that passes from the isles of Cape Verde to those of the Azores, with all benefices and honors of the Admiral of Castille in his district.]

In the letter of 1500 to the Governess Doña Juana de la Torre, Columbus had essayed a self-portrayal as knight-errant and as chivalric hero of the romance epic. The self-characterization in the passage cited here clearly supersedes that of the passages from the letter to the Governess cited in our last chapter. To look into the mirror of the second-person singular subject and address a "Magnificent Lord" is not exactly an understated magnification.

As already noted, Columbus's aim at this juncture is a recapitulation of his historic deeds in an effort to register, once more, his accomplishments, and to legitimate deeded claims he feels have slipped away. In the process, he becomes entangled in a quagmire of circular reasoning and endless calculation. In the draft under discussion, for example, he asserts the legitimacy of his claims by virtue of the fact that he discovered the Indies. At the same time, he feels that he certainly must have done so because the contracted privileges deeded to him for that purpose have been reconfirmed. Columbus pursues this spectral line of reasoning with such elaborate certainty that he gives the impression of no longer being certain of anything, hence the necessity for its reaffirmations. Here is the fifth clause of this draft where Columbus addresses his second-person self in this circuitous vein:

> Parece por las confirmaciones de vuestros privilegios que habéis descobierto las islas y tierra firme de las Indias, y que si algo se descobre, que es por vuestra industria, ni se puede para con Vuestra Señoría llamar descobrir, porque vos descobristes las Indias sobre que era la profía [sic. for porfía], sobre la cual ansí sabios de letras en tierra como la gente de la mar todos fueron contrarios a vuestra opinión, y todos dezían que era burla y que Dios nunca había dado alí tierra; ansí que non descobren para con Vuestra Señoría, salvo que van o pueden ir adonde no haya andado; mas todo esto non lo hazen ni pueden hazer sin entrar en el dicho almirantado y ir a tierras o mar que habéis descobierto; de manera que en todo lo andado y que se andoviere de aquí en adelante tenéis en la mar vuestra preheminençia de Almirante.

> [It is manifest by the confirmations of your privileges that you have discovered the islands and mainland of the Indies. And that if something is discovered that is by your effort, it cannot be said to have been just discovered in the case of Your Lordship. Because you discovered the Indies over the obstinacy of the learned in letters of the earth as of the sea, all of whom were opposed to your opinion. And they all said it was a joke, and that God had not put any land there. Thus, they do not discover through Your Lordship. Rather, they go or can go where no one has gone. But all this they do not, nor could they, do without entering into the said admiralty and go to lands or sea that you have discovered. So that, in all that has been traversed and is to be traversed from now on, you have your preeminence of Admiral at sea.]

I hope my translation has not overly domesticated the convoluted discourse of this passage. Although the reasoning may be circuitous, it is so, I believe, by virtue of the fact that Columbus's project here is recursive, his aim restorative of what he feels has been lost. His ratiocinations, then, I would say constituted more a de-volution than a convolution. His worldly and other-worldly deeds devolve upon the language that engendered them. If the proverbial wisdom of the Book of Prayer be "ashes to ashes," in the case of Columbus's enterprise it would have to be "words to words." Having begun as language in the productive text of the Capitulaciones de Santa Fe, the New World and its "discovery" (a problematic term, even for Columbus, as we have just seen in the passage above) now return, in the ghastly lucubrations of their protagonist, to a language that wrestles with its mirror image. In these spectral refractions of Columbus's "I" as "You" and historical reality as indomitable words, the ends of the world and the ends of reason, the protagonist's ulterior ends and the circumstances he ends up in resist justification. They just will not add up. That is why Columbus's obsessive harping on claims for "my third, my eighth, my tenth" refuse to construe with reality and fail to convince those who define current reality's configuration. And the invocation of criteria and terms sanctioned by Papal blessing, a blessing whose sanction only a decade earlier had the power to bisect the globe by circumscribing it with an imaginary line, seems to do little good now. Despite his perplexity, Columbus persists, tenacious as ever, more unrelenting than ever before:

> . . . porque sobre el descobrir de las Indias se tomó el asiento y firmó la Capitulaçión y escrituras y en la ora que descobristes la primera isla fue descobierto las Indias y complistes vuestro asiento, y el Santo Padre dio bula de donaçión a Sus Altezas de las Indias y a conçiencia, estando Vuestra Señoría privado de sus oficios, Sus Altezas serían obligados a todo daño y menoscabo que por ello viniese.

> Señores: Yo non demando nada, y todo esto que va aquí dicho, todo lo remito y pongo en las reales manos de la Reina, Nuestra Señora, que lo vea y haga en ello lo que fuere su servicio. Mis privilegios y cartas daré a Vuestra Merçed cada que los quisieren.

> [. . . because agreement was reached on the discovery of the Indies and the Capitulations and writs were signed, and at the moment you discovered the first island the Indies were discovered, and, thus, you

fulfilled your agreement and the Holy Father by Bull of Donation gave the Indies to Their Highnesses and to their conscience, Your Lordship having been deprived of his offices, Their Highnesses would be liable for all ensuing damages and losses.

Lords: I demand nothing. And all I have said here, I take it all back, and put all of it in the royal hands of the Queen, Our Lady, so that she might consider it and do as she please. I shall turn over my privileges and letters to Your Worship as you might desire.]

The unmistakable discrepancy between the two paragraphs cited here is quite telling. The slippage from the second person to the first entails a passage from "You, Magnificent Lord" to "I, supplicant." The strong suit for contracted claims that, in the second person, holds the sovereigns to liability for contractual breach, turns to pathos of entreaty in the palinode that is the "I" of the shrinking self. We have seen this attenuation of ego deployed as cunning strategy in the letter to the queen discussed earlier. The last paragraph cited here may well have served as rehearsal for that letter. The juxtaposition of the two pronouns and their corresponding subjects here, however, makes patent the fact that Columbus as "I, myself" suffers an unmistakable diminution. This is the measure of self-alienation or anomie referred to earlier. Seen in the context of another draft, the one in the first person, this dissipation of self takes on an even more poignant abatement. Because, in that first-person draft, we witness a self that wanes into lacunae, a self whose self-reflexive discourse fades into blank spaces quite literally, as, for example, when Columbus wonders, even as his writing wanders off into space(s), whether he might be running the risk of being misunderstood. I shall indicate his blanks with bracketed ellipses:

Y que todo consiste en esto [. . .] así como de las cartas de marear, y me temo que yo no sea bien entendido, porque en esto yo sirvo asimismo en tener [. . .] pilotos como se [. . .] de mucho [. . .] me que otras generaciones han de ir allá . . .

[And that everything consists in this [. . .] just so, as with the navigational charts, and I fear lest I be misunderstood, because in this I well serve in having [. . .] pilots as [. . .] greatly [. . .] me that other generations must go there . . .]

Perhaps the most telling lacuna in this passage may be the blank space that follows the indexical declaration "And that everything consists in this . . ."

No need to belabor the fact that all indications point to a Columbus who, as first-person subject, as "I, myself," runs into a void, not just into language and its contorted mirrors, but through that spectral refraction and into the gallery of an intermittent space that augurs Néant. Call that augural discernment the ultimate form of dead reckoning. However, as an other to himself, as the second person we have just witnessed, and as the third person of yet another fragment, Columbus is, indeed, somebody else again. The "Magnificent Lord" of the previous draft becomes, in the third person, God's minister and righthand man, and only second to Himself in dispensing the Earth to its conquering occupants. Here is Columbus's third-person portrayal of Columbus:

> Digo que el dicho Almirante descobrió y ganó a Sus Altezas las islas y tierra firme que son allende la línea sobredicha en la mar Océano, y las han habido por su mano e industria y son señores d'ellas, de las cuales non lo eran antes, porque en su mano estaba del dicho Almirante, después de Dios Nuestro Señor, de las dar a cualquer Príncipe con quien él se concertase.

> [I say that the said Admiral discovered and conquered [note the return to the dual verb construct of the founding charter, the Capitulaciones de Santa Fe] for Their Highnesses the islands and mainland beyond the above-said line in the Ocean Sea, and they have acquired them by his hand and industry and they are their owners, which they were not before. Because it was in the hands of said Admiral, after God Our Lord, to give them to any Prince with whom he should concert.]

And, once again, in a fourth draft, also in the third person, a third person that Caesar and Captain John Smith of our fifth chapter could envy, Columbus holds the world's destiny in his hands, much as he is caricatured in patriotic monuments in public parks and plazas, still clamoring for his due and for vindication:

> Las Indias son de Sus Altezas. Descubrióselas y ganó el Almirante contra opinión de todo el mundo y él tiene en ellas la terçia parte, ochavo y diezmo; en su mano parece que estaba a las desobrir y dar a

cualquier otro Príncipe; y pues él servió con ellas, justo es que aya d'ellas la parte que se asentó, la cual ha de gastar en servicio de Dios y de Sus Altezas.

[The Indies belong to Your Highnesses. The Admiral discovered and conquered them for you against the opinion of the whole world. And he has in them the third part, the eighth, and the tenth. It was manifestly in his hands to discover them and give them to any Prince. Thus, he has served with them. It is just that he should have from them the portion agreed upon, a portion which he is to spend in the service of God and of Your Highnesses.]

In the last folio of the *Lettera Rarissima,* his shipwreck's memorandum on his final voyage, Columbus will articulate this compelling necessity for justifying all ends and balancing all books. For, he says, "it is well to give God His due and to Caesar what belongs to him. This is a just sentence, and of the just. [Bueno es de dar a Dios lo suyo y a César lo que le pertenece. Esto es justa sentencia y de justo]."[13] From the beginning of his enterprise, Columbus not only felt that he was "called," but he also held the conviction that he was "justified." Justification, in terms canonical and theological, takes on greatest emphasis when the just feel jilted. So profoundly does Columbus seem to feel that he has been betrayed by justice itself that he can only countenance his own predicament as that of someone else. So thoroughly did he identify himself with his prophetic calling and worldly enterprise that the waylaying of this providential itinerary becomes for him an insurmountable self-negation. His self-fragmentation into drafts that somehow will not cohere, and into subject pronouns that take on referential coherence only in relation to someone else ("you" or "he") is a measure of the abyss that divides the self from the self, the Columbus of scriptures (capitulations, contracts, memoranda, royal directives, epistles) and Scripture (the providential agent of prophetic ends) from the Columbus who is now reduced to reading his scribal other as a second- and third-person character of a paper reality.

At the end of the day, this paper reality proves not only more real, but it also becomes Columbus's most avidly sought connection to the world, his ultimate umbilical cord to reality that he more and more desperately feels must lie elsewhere. Hence the persistent and obsessive leitmotif of his final letters to his son Diego, his last connection to a passing world: on 3 December 1504 he writes, "I marvel greatly at not seeing any letter from you or anyone else. Everyone who knows me is equally amazed at this. Everyone here receives letters, and I who am most entitled to them, see none. It were cause for great worry. [Muy marabillado estoy de non ver carta tuya ni de otro. Esa marabilla tienen todos los que me coñosçen. Todos aca tienen cartas, e yo, a quién más cumplía, non las veo. Era de tener sobre ello gran cuidado]"; then on 29 December he writes, "Let everyone write to me and often, for it grieves me deeply that everybody should have letters every-day from there and I none from so many of you who are there [que cada uno me escriva y muy a menudo, que gran pesar tengo que todo el mundo tiene cada día cartas de allá, y yo nada de tantos como alí estais]"; and on 18 January 1505, "I wait for letters everyday from there. [De alí espero cada día cartas]."

"There" for Columbus is the royal court, but in reality it could be anywhere he himself is not. His presence, like the personal subject pronoun of his writings, passes progressively into legend-ary status, into the impersonal subject of writing. And writing itself as life-extending activity becomes, in Columbus's own words, the plaintive act of a nocturne: on 1 December 1504 he writes, "My illness does not allow me to write except by night, because by day it deprives me of the strength in my hands. [Mi mal non me consinte que escriva salvo de noche, porque el día me priva la fuerça de las manos]." These are, of course, the hands that, as Columbus wrote, held the world and the world's ends, and did so with a discretionary power for their dispensation next only to God's.

Notes

CHAPTER 1: EMERGENT OCCASIONS

1. Frances Yates, *Giordano Bruno and the Hermetic Tradition* (Chicago: University of Chicago Press, 1964), 1.

2. A. Bartlett Giamatti, *The Earthly Paradise and the Renaissance Epic* (Princeton: Princeton University Press, 1966). See especially chap. 2, "The Golden Age."

3. Christopher Columbus, *Libro de las profecías* (folio 5v), in *Raccolta di documenti e studi publicati dalla Real Commissione pel quarto centenario dalla scoperta dell'America. Scriti di Cristoforo Colombo,* ed. Cesare de Lollis (Rome: Real Commissione Colombina, 1892/1894). See pt. 1, 2: 82.

4. Karlfried Froehlich, " 'Always to Keep the Literal Sense in the Holy Scripture Means to Kill One's Soul': The State of Biblical Hermeneutics at the Beginning of the Fifteenth Century," in *Literary Uses of Typology from the Middle Ages to the Present,* ed. Earl Miner (Princeton: Princeton University Press, 1977), 20.

5. Rudolph Bultman, *The Presence of Eternity: History and Eschatology* (New York: Harper and Brothers, 1957), 26.

6. The motives for pseudonymity are a subject of frequent debate. For a summary of the literature and for his own position on the matter see J. J. Collins, "Pseudonimity, Historical Reviews and the Genre of the Revelation of John," *Catholic Bible Quarterly* 39 (1977): 329–343.

7. For the equation of faithful believer and prophet see the discussion by D. Hill, "Prophecy and Prophets in the Revelation of St. John," *New Testament Studies* 18 (1971–1972): 401–418.

8. See, for example, Karl Löwith, *Meaning in History* (Chicago: University of Chicago Press, 1949) and Ernest Tuveson, *Millennium and Utopia: A Study in the Background of the Idea of Progress* (Berkeley: University of California Press, 1949).

9. Karl Löwith keenly observed that the "Christian faith in the incalculable intervention of God's providence, combined with the belief that the world might at any moment come to a sudden end, had the same effect as the Greek theory of recurrent cycles of growth and decay of an inexorable fate—the effect of checking the rise of a belief in an indefinite progress and an ever increasing manageability" (p. 200).

CHAPTER 2: ANXIOUS FOUNDATIONS

1. "Novo Mundo e fim do mundo," *Revista de Historia* (São Paolo) 18 (1954). French original in *L'Education Nationale* 32 (1952): 3–6.

2. Nathaniel Hawthorne, *The English Notebooks of Nathaniel Hawthorne*. Randall Stewart, ed. (New York: Russell and Russell, 1942), 39.

3. Wallace Stevens, "The Idea of Order at Key West," in *The Palm at the End of the Mind: Selected Poems,* ed. Holly Stevens (New York: Random House/Vintage Books, 1972), 97–99.

4. The year 1492 was proclaimed as the time of the *plenitudo temporum* not only by Byzantine prophets but also Florentine Platonists. See Marsilio Ficino's 1492 letter to Paul of Middelburg in which the Renaissance academician declares the arrival of the Golden Age and all its attendant signs for a *renovatio mundi*. Cited in Marjorie Reeves, *The Influence of Prophecy in the Later Middle Ages: A Study in Joachimism* (Oxford: Clarendon Press, 1969), 429.

5. A. Vasiliev, "Medieval Ideas of the End of the World: East and West," *Byzantion* 16 (1942–1943): 462–502.

6. Columbus, *Libro de las profecías,* pt. 1, 2: 108–109.

7. My discussion of millenarianism draws on numerous sources. Chief among them, in addition to the work of Marjorie Reeves already cited, are: Robin B. Barnes, *Prophecy and Gnosis: Apocalypticism in the Wake of the Lutheran Reformation* (Stanford: Stanford University Press, 1988); Norman Cohn, *The Pursuit of the Millennium* (New York: Oxford University Press, 1970;1957); Jean Daniélou, *The Theology of Jewish Christianity,* trans. and ed. John A. Baker (London: Darton, Longman, & Todd, Ltd./Chicago: Henry Regnery Co., 1964); Robert E. Lerner, *The Powers of Prophecy: The Cedar of Lebanon Vision from the Mongol Onslaught to the Dawn of the Enlightenment* (Berkeley, Los Angeles, London: University of California Press, 1983). For primary sources, in addition to the scriptures (Revised Standard Ver-

sion, cited throughout this study), I have relied on two valuable collections by Bernard McGinn, trans. and ed., *Apocalyptic Spirituality: Treatises and Letters of Lactantius, Adso of Montier-En-Der, Joachim of Fiore, the Spiritual Franciscans, Savonarola* (New York: The Paulist Press, 1979) and *Visions of the End: Apocalyptic Traditions in the Middle Ages* (New York: Columbia University Press, 1979).

8. Cited in Daniélou, *Theology of Jewish Christianity*, pp. 396–397.

9. McGinn, *Apocalyptic Spirituality*, p. 22.

10. Daniélou, *Theology of Jewish Christianity*, p. 401.

11. See Werner Goez, *Translatio imperii* (Tübingen: Mohr, 1958).

12. In McGinn, *Visions of the End*, p. 111.

13. Columbus, *Libro de las profecías*, pp. 84, 97, 99, 102, 105.

14. Alain Milhou, *Colón y su mentalidad mesiánica en el ambiente franciscanista español.* Cuadernos Colombinos XI (Valladolid: Museo de Colón y Seminario Americanista de la Universidad de Valladolid, 1983), 437.

15. Cotton Mather, *Magnalia Christi Americana,* 2 vols. (Hartford Edition, 1820). See bk. 2, chap. 11.

16. Columbus, *Libro de las profecías,* p. 71. Translations are my own.

17. Increase Mather, "New Jerusalem" (1687), in William L. Joyce and Michael G. Hall, "Three Manuscripts of Increase Mather," *Proceedings of the Antiquarian Society* vol. 86, pt. 1 (April 1976): 113–123.

18. Germán Arciniegas, *America in Europe: A History of the New World in Reverse* (San Diego, New York, and London: Harcourt Brace Jovanovich, 1986), chap. 1.

19. Luther, Calvin, and Melancthon cited in Arciniegas, *America in Europe,* p. 82.

20. Cited in Mason I. Lowance, Jr., *The Language of Canaan* (Cambridge: Harvard University Press, 1980), 152.

21. Cited in Lowance, p. 313, n. 39.

22. Marjorie Reeves's *Joachim of Fiore and the Prophetic Future* (New York: Harper and Row, 1977) remains the most significant study on Joachim and the prophetic tradition throughout Europe.

23. John Leddy Phelan, *The Millennial Kingdom of the Franciscans in the New World,* 2d ed. rev. (Berkeley, Los Angeles, London: University of California Press, 1970).

CHAPTER 3: NEW WORLDS

1. R. G. Collingwood, *The Idea of History* (Oxford: Oxford University Press, 1946), 49.

2. Norman Cohn, "Medieval Millennarianism: Its Bearing on the Comparative Study of Millennarian Movements," in *Millennial Dreams in Action,* ed. Sylvia L. Thrupp (The Hague: Mouton, 1962), 31–43; Peter Worsley, *The Trumpet Shall Sound: A Study of "Cargo" Cults in Melanesia,* 2d ed. (New York: Schoken Books, 1968), pp. xlii, 225–227, 243.

3. See n. 4, chap. 2, above.

4. On Commodianus, see Norman Cohn, *The Pursuit of the Millennium,* p. 28. On Europe's ambivalent identification of non-European peoples as paradisal, see Henri Baudet, *Paradise on Earth,* trans. E. Wentholt (New Haven: Yale University Press, 1965). On the earliest attempts (1498) to identify the American natives with the ten lost tribes of Israel, see Don Cameron Allen, *The Legend of Noah* (Urbana: University of Illinois Press, 1949), 119–120.

5. Cited in J. B. Bury, *The Idea of Progress: An Inquiry into its Origin and Growth* (London: MacMillan and Co., 1920), 55.

6. Marcel Bataillon, *Erasmo y España: Estudios sobre la historia espiritual del siglo XVI* (Mexico: Fondo de Cultura Económica, 1950; 1937).

7. Bernardo Monsegú, "Erasmo y Vives y la 'Philosophia Christi' como humanismo cristiano," in *Erasmo en España,* ed. Manuel Revuelta Sañudo and Ciriaco Morón Arroyo (Santander: Sociedad Menéndez Pelayo, 1986), 358. My translation.

8. See Daniel Boorstin, *The Discoverers* (New York: Random House, 1983), 225.

9. Ibid., p. 230.

10. Bartolomé de Las Casas, *Historia de las Indias,* ed. Juan Pérez de Tudela and Emilio López Otto (Madrid: BAE, 1957), bk. 1, chap. 2, p. 43. I cite the passage in English from Germán Arciniegas, *America in Europe,* chap. 2, n. 2, p. 268. Emphasis mine.

11. In Albert Hyma, *The Christian Renaissance: A History of the "Devotio Moderna,"* 2d ed. rev. (Hamden, Conn.: Archon Books, 1965; 1924), 311.

12. Cuadernos colombinos XI (Valladolid: Universidad de Valladolid, 1983).

13. Ramón Iglesias, *El hombre Colón y otros ensayos* (Mexico: El Colegio de México, 1944); *Columbus, Cortés, and Other Essays,* trans. and ed. Lesley Byrd Simpson (Berkeley and Los Angeles: University of California Press, 1969).

14. Boorstin, *The Discoverers,* p. 227.

15. Columbus, *Libro de las profecías,* pp. 80, 82.

16. Columbus, *Raccolta di documenti,* 2: 161.

17. See, for example, the Columbus analyzed by Tzvetan Todorov in

The Conquest of America: The Question of the Other, trans. Richard Howard (New York: Harper Colophon Books, 1985), particularly chap. 1, where Todorov discusses Columbus's inability to see things "as they are" rather than as his preconceptions determine them.

18. Columbus, *Libro de las profecías,* p. 82.

19. Amerigo Vespucci, *El Nuevo Mundo: Cartas relativas a sus viajes y descubrimientos. Textos en italiano, español e inglés,* ed. Roberto Leviller (Buenos Aires: Editorial Nova, 1951), 277.

20. Vespucci, *El nuevo mundo,* 290.

21. *Lettera Rarissima* from Jamaica to the queen and king of Spain, 7 July 1503.

22. As early as 1498, a certain licentiate of Salamanca by the name of Francisco Nuñez de la Yerva protests the nomenclature in print in his introduction to the *Cosmographia* of Pomponio Mela. He refers to the new discoveries made in the name of the Spanish monarchs, "que abusive India a quibusdam dicitur." See *Bibliotheca Americana Vetustissima: Ultimas adiciones,* ed. Carlos Sanz, 2 vols. (Madrid: Libreria General Victoriano Suarez, 1960), 1: 245.

23. Vespucci, *El nuevo mundo,* p. 309.

24. Ibid., p. 299.

25. Cited in Germán Arciniegas, *Amerigo and the New World: The Life and Times of Amerigo Vespucci* (New York: Alfred A. Knopf, 1955), 309.

26. *Bibliotheca Americana Vetustissima,* 2: 45–50. I cite from Boorstin, *The Discoverers,* p. 253. Emphasis mine.

27. *Bibliotheca Americana Vetustissima,* 1: 470 ff.

28. For yet another plausible fiction of America's naming, see, in this regard, a discussion by the psychiatrist and psychogeographer William G. Niederland on the psychosexual dynamics that animate Waldseemüller and, according to Dr. Niederland, assure that the name America captures the Renaissance imagination. See William G. Niederland, "The Naming of America," in *Maps from the Mind: Readings in Psychogeography,* ed. Howard F. Stein and William G. Niederland (Norman: University of Oklahoma Press, 1989), 82–96. I am grateful to my wife, Juana Celia, for calling this interesting source to my attention.

29. See, for example, Harold Jantz, "Image of America in the German Renaissance," in *First Images of America: The Impact of the New World on the Old,* ed. Fredi Chiappelli, 2 vols. (Berkeley, Los Angeles, London: University of California Press, 1976), especially pp. 98–99; and Harold J. Cook, "Ancient Wisdom, the Golden Age, and Atlantis: The New World in Sixteenth-Century Cosmography," *Terrae Incognitae* 10 (1978): 24–43, especially p. 38, n. 83.

CHAPTER 4: CHARTING THE CONQUEST

1. Bradford's style is often held up as the epitome of "plain style." In sputtering thus, I obviously wish to convey that I find the plainness of the so-called Puritan "plain style" suspect. So do many others. For a lucid discussion see Larzer Ziff, "The Literary Consequences of Puritanism," in *The American Puritan Imagination: Essays in Revaluation,* ed. Sacvan Bercovitch (London and New York: Cambridge University Press, 1974), 34–44, particularly p. 39 and ff.

2. *Bibliotheca Americana Vetustissima,* 2: 1408.

3. See, for example, the voluminous and elaborately argued treatise by the Spanish historian and emeritus Distinguished Chair of History at the University of Seville Juan Manzano Manzano, *Colón y su secreto: El predescubrimiento* (Madrid: Ediciones Cultura Hispánica, 1982). 780 pp.

4. Cited in Ronald Sanders, *Lost Tribes and Promised Lands* (Boston: Little, Brown, and Co., 1978), 86.

5. Michel de Certeau, *L'écriture de l'histoire* (Paris: Editions Gallimard, 1975). Available in English as *The Writing of History* (New York: Columbia University Press, 1988).

6. Christopher Columbus, *Libro de los privilegios del Almirante Don Cristóbal Colón (1498),* ed. Ciriaco Pérez-Bustamante (Madrid: Real Academia de la Historia, 1951). The transcription of the official document, reproduced also in facsimile later in the volume, is on pp. 41–44. Bracketed translations are my own.

7. Herbert Allen Van Scoy, *A Dictionary of Old Spanish Terms Defined in the Works of Alfonso X,* ed. Ivy Corfis (Madison: The Hispanic Seminary of Medieval Studies, 1986), 6.

8. Columbus, *Libro de los privilegios,* p. xxv.

9. Walter Ullmann, *Medieval Papalism: The Political Theories of the Medieval Canonists* (London: Methuen and Co., Ltd., 1949).

10. Silvio Zavala, *Las instituciones jurídicas en la conquista de America,* 2d ed. rev. and augmented (México: Editorial Porrua, 1971; 1935).

11. In Silvio Zavala, *Las instituciones jurídicas,* pt. 1, chap. 2, p. 38.

12. I translate, once more, from Zavala, *Las instituciones jurídicas.*

13. Marjorie Reeves, *The Influence of Prophecy in the Later Middle Ages: A Study in Joachimism* (Oxford: Clarendon Press, 1969), 503.

14. For their views, in part, recorded mostly by the Spaniards, see Miguel León Portilla, *La visión de los vencidos: Relaciones indígenas de la conquista* (Mexico: UNAM, 1959).

15. Zavala, *Las instituciones jurídicas,* p. 79.

16. Such protestations would become a litany. Perhaps the most influ-

ential in terms of policy would be Richard Hakluyt's *Discourse of Western Planting*, 1584 and the Dutch Hugo Grotius's *More Liberum*, 1609, which Hakluyt translated in English.

17. In Pedro Leturia, "Maior y Vitoria ante la conquista de América," *Anuario de la Asociación Francisco de Vitoria III* (1930–1931): 43–83. My translation.

18. In Ullmann, *Medieval Papalism*, p. 125, n. 5. The English rendering of Innocent is Ullmann's.

19. Sepúlveda's treatise and its premises are discussed at some length most recently by Tzvetan Todorov, as are Las Casas's counterarguments, in his *The Conquest of America*, pp. 151–167. For a more elaborate treatment see Lewis Hanke, *Estudios sobre Fray Bartolomé de Las Casas y sobre la lucha por la justicia en la conquista de América* (Caracas: Universidad Central de Venezuela, 1968).

20. In Ullmann, *Medieval Papalism*, p. 130. I cite, once more, Ullmann's rendering of Innocent's Latin.

21. In Ullmann, *Medieval Papalism*, p. 131.

22. Bartolomé de Las Casas, *Historia*, bk. 3, chap. 57.

23. The document is included in Zavala, *Las institutiones jurídicas*, pp. 215–217. Bracketed translation is my own.

24. Ibid., pp. 216–217.

25. Edmundo O'Gorman, *The Invention of America: An Inquiry into the Historical Nature of the New World and the Meaning of its History* (Bloomington: Indiana University Press, 1961).

26. Beatriz Pastor, *Discursos narrativos de la conquista: mitificación y emergencia*, 2d ed. rev. (Hanover, N.H.: Ediciones del Norte, 1988), especially chap. 1.

27. Zavala, *Las instituciones jurídicas*, p. 488.

28. See references to Gonzalo Fernández de Oviedo's eyewitness accounts as participant in such acts in Todorov, *Conquest of America*, chap. 3, and in Zavala, *Las instituciones jurídicas*, p. 79.

29. I translate from documentation in Zavala, *Las instituciones jurídicas*, p. 79.

30. For a discussion of the papal bull and its repercussions, see Lewis Hanke, "Pope Paul III and the American Indians," *Harvard Theological Review* (1937): 65–97.

31. *Recopilación de leyes de los reynos de las Indias*, bk. 4, title I, law VI. Cited in Hanke, *Estudios*, p. 89. Parenthetical translation is my own.

32. English charters and "letters patent" cited in this study are collected in *Foundations of Colonial America: A Documentary History*, ed. W. Keith Kavenagh, 4 vols., 6 parts (New York: Chelsea House,

1983). "Letters of Patent to Sir Humphrey Gilbert" in vol. 3, part 1, pp. 1690–1693.

33. A. L. Rowse, *The Elizabethans and America* (New York: Harper and Brothers, 1959), 32.

34. Columbus, *Libro de los privilegios*, p. 43.

35. In *Foundations*, vol. 1, pt. 1, p. 18.

36. Peter Hulme, *Colonial Encounters: Europe and the Native Caribbean 1492–1797* (London and New York: Methuen and Co., Ltd., 1986), 156.

37. Samuel Eliot Morison, *Admiral of the Ocean Sea: A Life of Christopher Columbus* (Boston: Little Brown and Co., 1942), 308.

38. Henry Nash Smith, *Virgin Land: The American West as Symbol and Myth* (Cambridge: Harvard University Press, 1970).

39. Annette Kolodny, *The Lay of the Land* (Chapel Hill: University of North Carolina Press, 1975).

40. Peter Hulme remarks the fact that the historiographic foundations of "American Genesis" tend to bracket Virginia's "guiltily acknowledged chronological 'priority' " and invokes Perry Miller's ironic confessions on the "coherence" of Puritan New England with which a historian can "coherently begin." I suspect Hulme would not quibble with the suggestion that "beginnings," as Edward Said taught us not so long ago in a book by that title, can be as dubious as ends could be devious. I would own that "American Genesis" is embedded in scripture, the Genesis of scripture that underlies the foundations of a teleological ideology and an apocalyptic narrative that authorized, in turn, the productive scripture of the charters that engender a territorial reality for their own conquering ends even before its geographic discovery. See Hulme, pp. 138–139.

41. Columbus, *Libro de los privilegios*, p. 43, line 36.

42. In *Foundations*, vol. 1, pt. 1, p. 18.

43. John Winthrop, "General Considerations for the Plantation in New England" in *Winthrop Papers* (Massachusetts Historical Society, 1931), 2: 106–121.

44. Peter Hulme is quite informative on this point. See *Colonial Encounters*, pp. 157–173.

45. In *Foundations*, vol. 3, pt. 1, p. 1690.

46. In this regard, I would beg to differ with Peter Hulme's passing comment on ideology as articulated by Gramsci and Althuser as being irrelevant to the New World's colonial context "because we are dealing not with a consensual model of the social formation in which ideology can be seen as fully pervasive, almost constitutive of social and civil life itself, but rather with a model of division in which ideology is a dis-

course whose mode is largely textual in the narrow sense and whose address is largely internal, towards that group in society most directly concerned with colonial matters." *Colonial Encounters,* p. 7. To begin with, the claims for any text as "textual in the narrow sense whose address is largely internal" I find untenable, particularly when Hulme and I are dealing with texts whose worldly repercussions through the actions of those "most directly concerned with colonial matters" have determined the fate, often the extinction, of whole races of people, changed the imperial frontiers of hegemony among European powers, and continue to have an impact on policy and cultural discourses down to our own day. What Hulme sees as a "model of division," I would consider a practical expediency of ideological insinuation into textual processes that have pragmatic determinations. I do not believe, as Hulme states, that the *Requerimiento* in particular is the exception that proves the rule. Rather, it is a cruder manifestation of a formative ideology, what I have termed an ideology of conquest, whose symptom is the genre of the charter as I have defined it earlier in this chapter, a genre that manifests the ideological symptoms of a consensual and pervasive social formation in a much more refined form in Elizabethan charters. The resurgence of this ideology in cruder, hegemonic form with the Puritans might well constitute proof not only of its pervasiveness and formative determinacy but of its durability. Hulme's chastising observation on Henry Nash Smith's and Annette Kolodny's failure to mention the native inhabitants in their respective books (see nn. 35 and 36 above) may be read as further corroboration of the perdurability and pervasiveness of such an ideological formation through three centuries.

My difference with Hulme may be symptomatic, in turn, of our own respective praxes as readers of colonial texts. He, being British, it seems to me, reads ideology and its social formation as "consensual model" and symptom of its formative context, as manifestation of its conditions of production. I, a former British subject raised in a British colony, concur with Hulme's reading, as far as it goes. But, perforce, I must read ideology not only as symptomatic form and as formative of a consensual model, but also as performative and repercussive, as consequential practice to which accrue ends and results that may or may not be symmetrical to the modeling of the consensual enablements, as "model of division" or otherwise, that empowers those ideological productions.

47. For a succinct commentary on such comparisons see J. H. Parry, "Introduction: The English and the New World," in *The Westward Enterprise: English Activities in Ireland, the Atlantic, and America 1480–1650,* ed. K. R. Andrews, N. P. Canny, and P. E. H. Hair (Detroit: Wayne State University Press, 1979), 1–16.

CHAPTER 5: SALVAGING THE SALVAGES

1. Alfonso Reyes, *The Position of America*, trans. Harriet de Onís (New York: Alfred A. Knopf, 1950), 45. Though he antedates them, neither Perry Miller nor Daniel Boorstin gives any indication in his work of having heard of Alfonso Reyes.

2. A valuable collection of Christopher Columbus's writings have been compiled and annotated by Consuelo Varela in *Cristóbal Colón: Textos y documentos completos* (Madrid: Alianza Editorial, 1982).

3. *Cristóbal Colón: Textos y documentos completos*, p. 101. All English renderings are my own.

4. Ibid., p. 101.

5. Gonzalo Fernández de Oviedo, *Historia general y natural de las Indias, islas y Tierra firme del Mar Oceano* (1535), 5 vols. (Madrid: Biblioteca de Autores Españoles, 1959), bk. 2, chap. 3; bk. 29, chap. 30.

6. In Rafael Diego Fernández, *Capitulaciones Colombinas (1492–1506)* (Michoacan, Mexico: El Colegio de Michoacan, 1987). Includes facsimiles of originals and transcriptions. See pp. 369–373. Translations are my own.

7. For a succinct and lucid historical review of the term *cannibal* and its cultural repercussions see Peter Hulme, *Colonial Encounters*, pp. 16–22, 78–87. For a Latin American perspective, and for the pertinence of this complex phenomenon to contemporary, "postcolonial" culture, see the Cuban Roberto Fernández Retamar's "Caliban," *Casa de las Américas* (Havana) 68 (September–October 1971). Reprinted as title essay in an English collection by the author, *Caliban and Other Essays*, foreword by Fredric Jameson (Minneapolis: University of Minnesota Press, 1989), pp. 3–45.

8. In Rafael Diego Fernández, *Capitulaciones Colombinas*, p. 377.

9. On a discussion of legal issues of cannibalism and slavery see Silvio Zavala, *Las instituciones jurídicas*, pp. 92, 183 et passim.

10. Gonzalo Fernández de Oviedo, *Historia general y natural de las Indias*, bk. 3, chap. 8.

11. Ibid., bk. 8, chap. 2.

12. The *locus classicus* of "barbarism" and "cannibalism" as relative cultural phenomena is still Montaigne's "Des Cannibales." See the facsimile edition in *Essais. Reproduction photographique de l'edition originale de 1580*, ed. Daniel Martin, 2 vols. (Geneva: Slatkin and Paris: Champion, 1976), 1: 31. For a modern edition in English, see "Of Cannibals" in *The Complete Essays of Montaigne*, trans. Donald M. Frame (Stanford: Stanford University Press, 1989; 1958), pp. 150–159.

13. The most serviceable biography is Philip L. Barbour's *The Three Worlds of Captain John Smith* (Boston: Houghton Mifflin, 1964).

14. John Smith, *The Complete Works of Captain John Smith (1580–1631)*, ed. Philip L. Barbour, 3 vols. (Chapel Hill: University of North Carolina Press, 1986), 2: 151. "A True Relation" is in vol. 1, pp. 23–97. "The Generall Historie" is in vol. 2, pp. 33–478. The editor, Philip L. Barbour, offers a useful "Recension of the Narratives of Smith's Captivity" (vol. 1 pp. 9–15), in which the texts of Smith's two works, as well as Samuel Purchas's *Pilgrimage*, relating this episode are juxtaposed. The contrast is telling. Whatever it does tell, however, will by no means curtail the industry spawned by the episode.

15. Smith, *The Complete Works*, vol. 1, p. 346.

16. Ibid., vol. 1, p. 5.

17. Ibid., vol. 1, p. 346.

18. Perry Miller, "The Religious Impulses in the Founding of Virginia: Religion and Society in the Early Literature," *William and Mary Quarterly* 3d series, V (1948): 492–522.

19. Louis B. Wright, *Religion and Empire: The Alliance between Piety and Commerce in English Expansion 1558–1625* (Chapel Hill: University of North Carolina Press, 1943; reprinted, New York: Farrar, Strauss and Giroux, 1965), especially chap. 4.

20. John Parker, "Religion and the Virginia Colony 1609–10," in *The Westward Enterprise: English Activities in Ireland, the Atlantic, and America 1480–1650*, ed. K. R. Andrews, N. P. Canny, and P. E. H. Hair (Detroit: Wayne State University Press, 1979), 245–270.

21. Wright, *Religion and Empire*, pp. 87–88.

22. In his enthusiasm, Wright overshot the significance of this unquestionably significant figure to the occasion when he confuses him with his more obscure namesake, John Done, poet and translator, who authored a commendatory poem at the head of Captain John Smith's *Generall Historie*. See p. 111 of Wright.

23. Parker, "Religion and the Virginia Colony 1609–10," p. 247.

24. Barbour asserts the likelihood of John Healey's authorship of this introduction. See vol. 1, p. 98, n. 11. Should Barbour be right, the ironies of the whole New World enterprise become compounded. John Healey was the translator into English of Joseph Hall's *Mundus alter et idem*, a bawdy satirical novel of the time based on the New World, such as it was then known. Hall introduced Juvenalian satire to England, making the New World its brunt.

25. Smith, *The Complete Works*, vol. 1, p. 25.

26. Both charters are gathered in *Foundations of Colonial America: A Documentary History*, ed. W. Keith Kavenagh (New York: Chelsea House, 1983), vol. 3, pt. 1. The relevant passages are to be found on p. 1698 for the first charter and p. 1715 for the second.

27. Perry Miller, *Errand into the Wilderness* (Cambridge: Harvard

University Press, 1956); Sacvan Bercovitch, *The Puritan Origins of the American Self* (New Haven: Yale University Press, 1975).

28. In Wright, *Religion and Empire,* p. 91. The concerted nature of the pulpit campaign in 1609 is evidenced, in part, by the echoic language and imagery of the sermonists. The likening of the Indians to "troupes like heards of Deer in a Forrest" also occurs in Richard Johnson's *Nova Brittania* (1609). See Roy Harvey Pearce, *The Savages of America: A Study of the Indian and the Idea of Civilization,* rev. ed. (Baltimore: The Johns Hopkins Press, 1965; 1953), 12.

29. In Parker, "Religion and the Virginia Colony," p. 253.

30. In Wright, *Religion and Empire,* p. 98.

31. In Parker, "Religion and the Virginia Colony," p. 253.

32. Ibid., p. 266.

33. Ibid., p. 255.

34. Ibid., p. 256.

35. See chap. 9 of Hernando de Colón's history of his father, *Vida del Almirante Cristóbal Colón* (Mexico: Fondo de Cultura Económica, 1947).

36. In Wright, *Religion and Empire,* p. 98.

37. See Juan Pérez de Tudela, "Vida y escritos de Gonzalo Fernández de Oviedo." Introduction to Oviedo's *Historia,* pp. vii–clxix. On this aspect of Pedrarías, see p. xlix.

38. Pérez de Tudela, "Vida y escritos," p. xlix, n. 143.

CHAPTER 6: DIVINE PRIMITIVES

1. Domingo Faustino Sarmiento, *Civilización y barbarie: Vida de Juan Facundo Quiroga,* 1845. Many modern editions. For one of the most lucid and incisive discussions of this topos and hemispheric allegory in contemporary culture, see Rafael Humberto Moreno Durán, *De la barbarie a la imaginación: La experiencia leída,* 2d ed., augmented (Bogota: Tercer Mundo Editores, 1988). I am most grateful to this accomplished novelist, modern polymath, and fellow pilgrim suspicious of all shrines for many hours of conversation over innumerable bottles of genuine and questionable vintage.

Useful, as well, on the question of culture and colonization as focused through this binomial construct is Roberto Fernández Retamar's discussion, already cited (see n. 7, chap. 5). Fernández Retamar juxtaposes Sarmiento's idolatrous view of "civilization" to José Martí's admonitions as to what such cultism entails in terms of Latin America's neocolonial history. Sarmiento and Martí, or, for that matter, Fernández Retamar himself and Carlos Fuentes, whose treatment of this binary in the Mexican's *La nueva novela hispanoamericana* (Mexico: Joaquin

Mortiz, 1969) he assails, ultimately are the dialectical personifications of the cultural ambivalence in the New World, an ambivalence that begins with the first encounter between Europe and what European's would baptize as the New World.

2. In R. H. Moreno Durán, *De la barbarie*, p. 13.

3. For a lucid and productive recapitulation of the theme of the Noble Savage see Hayden White, "The Noble Savage: Theme as Fetish" in *First Images of America: The Impact of the New World on the Old*, ed. Fredi Chiappelli, 2 vols. (Berkeley, Los Angeles, London: University of California Press, 1976), 121–135. The most thorough study on the treatment of the Indian as theme in the eighteenth and nineteenth centuries is still Antonello Gerbi's *La disputa del Nuovo Mondo: Storia di una polemica, 1750–1900* (Milano: Riccardo Ricciardi Editore, 1955). A revised and augmented edition has been translated by Jeremy Moyle, *The Dispute of the New World* (Pittsburgh: University of Pittsburgh Press, 1973).

4. See chap. 3, n. 18 above.

5. Phelan, *The Millennial Kingdom*, p. 19.

6. *Cristóbal Colón: Textos y documentos completos*, p. 205.

7. Ibid., p. 289.

8. Reproduced in *Raccolta*, Part I, p. 310.

9. *Cristóbal Colón: Textos y documentos completos*, pp. 332–336.

10. Ibid., p. 204.

11. Ibid., p. 205.

12. Ibid., p. 212.

13. Ibid., p. 218.

14. Ibid., p. 215.

15. Ibid., p. 205.

16. See chap. 2, n. 13 above.

17. *Cristóbal Colón: Textos y documentos completos*, p. 243. Also in *Raccolta*, vol. 2, p. 66.

18. *Cristóbal Colón: Textos y documentos completos*, p. 251.

19. Ibid., p. 249.

20. Ibid., p. 243.

21. Ibid., p. 250.

22. Salvador de Madariaga, *Vida del muy magnífico señor Don Cristóbal Colón* (Madrid: Espasa Calpe, 1975), 292.

23. *Cristóbal Colón: Textos y documentos completos*, pp. 297–298. Also in *Raccolta*, vol. 2, p. 192.

24. Alain Milhou, *Colón y su mentalidad mesiánica*, especially pp. 272–286.

25. Claude Kappler, "La vocation messianique de Christophe Colomb," in *Voyage, quête, pélerinage dans la littérature da la*

civilisation médiévales, Senéfiance. Cahiers du CUERMA 2 (Université de Provence, 1976), pp. 255–271, focuses on the millennialist and mystical significance of this and, especially, of Columbus's letter on his third voyage. On the other hand, Alexandre Cioranescu is more suspecting of Columbus's genuine devotion. He considers this passage from the *Lettera Rarissima* as yet another rhetorical ploy by which Columbus, typically, takes the Spanish monarchs to task for their broken promises and his treatment. See Cioranescu's comments in his edition of *Oeuvres de Christophe Colomb* (Paris: Gallimard, 1961), 486, n. 35.

26. In *Foundations*, vol. 1, pt. 1, pp. 23–24.

27. See *Gov. Bradford's History of Plymouth Colony*, in *Chronicles of the Pilgrim Fathers of Plymouth from 1602–1625*, ed. Alexander Young (Boston: Charles C. Little and James Brown, 1841; reprinted New York: Da Capo Press, 1971), 98–99.

28. *Chronicles of the Pilgrim Fathers*, p. 239.

29. For a cursory recapitulation of Columbus's reading culture significant to his visionary pilgrimage, see Pauline Moffitt Watts, "Prophecy and Discovery: On the Spiritual Origins of Christopher Columbus's 'Enterprise of the Indies'," *The American Historical Review* 90 (1985): 73–102.

30. *Chronicles of the Pilgrim Fathers*, p. 240.

31. Ibid., p. 241.

32. Ibid., p. 248.

33. Cushman is referring to the Indians' and their Sachem Massosoit's recognition of King James as their "master and commander." See p. 244 of Cushman, and also Edward Winslow's letter "to a friend," believed to have been George Morton, Gov. Branford's brother-in-law, dated from "Plymouth in New England, 11 December 1621," in *Chronicles of the Pilgrim Fathers*, pp. 230–238, especially, p. 232.

34. *Chronicles of the Pilgrim Fathers*, pp. 245–246.

35. Ibid., pp. 243–244.

36. John Winthrop, *Life and Letters of John Winthrop*, ed. and commentary by Robert C. Winthrop (Boston: Little, Brown, and Company, 1869), 1: 316. I have spelled out the frequent abbreviations employed by Winthrop and transcribed by his descendant in this collection of the governor's correspondence.

37. In addition to Reeves's already cited treatise, see M. W. Bloomfield and M. E. Reeves, "The Penetration of Joachism into Northern Europe," *Speculum* 29 (1954): 772–793. Also see M. W. Bloomfield, "Joachim of Flora: A Critical Survey of His Canon, Teachings, Sources, Biography, and Influence," *Traditio* 13 (1957): 249–311.

38. Winthrop, *Life and Letters*, p. 309.

39. Ibid., p. 311.

40. Ibid., pp. 309–310.

41. Ibid., p. 312.

42. Ibid., p. 312.

43. Ibid., p. 314.

44. Ibid., p. 315.

45. See Larzer Ziff, *The Career of John Cotton* (Princeton: Princeton University Press, 1962), 76, and Richard S. Dunn, "Experiment Holy and Unholy 1630–31," in *The Westward Enterprise: English Activities in Ireland, the Atlantic, and America 1480–1650,* ed. K. R. Andrews, N. P. Canny, P. E. H. Hair (Detroit: Wayne State University Press, 1979), 280–281.

46. *Cristóbal Colón: Textos y documentos completos,* p. 31.

47. For the complete bibliography of Anglo-America's effort to account for the origin of the Indians through the mid-nineteenth century see Samuel F. Haven, *Archaeology of the United States.* Smithsonian Contributions to Knowledge, vol. 8 (Washington, D.C.: Smithsonian Institute, 1856), pp. 3–16. For modern discussions of the issue, see Roy Harvey Pearce, *The Savages of America: A Study of the Indian and the Idea of Civilization,* rev. ed. (Baltimore: Johns Hopkins University Press, 1965; 1953).

48. Cited in John Leddy Phelan, *The Millennial Kingdom of the Franciscans in the New World,* p. 26.

49. Ibid., *The Millennial Kingdom,* pp. 24–25.

50. Don Cameron Allen, *The Legend of Noah: Renaissance Rationalism in Art, Science, and Letters* (Urbana: University of Illinois Press, 1949). For discussion of the origins of the native peoples in the New World, see pp. 113–137.

51. Tzvetan Todorov, *The Conquest of America,* offers an extensive discussion of this Dominican in a chapter entitled "Hybridization of Culture," pp. 185 ff.

52. Diego Durán, *Historia de las Indias de Nueva España y Islas de Tierra Firme,* ed. José F. Ramírez, 2 vols. (Mexico: Editora Nacional, 1951), 1: 1.

53. Durán, vol. 1, p. 3.

54. Tzvetan Todorov traces the parallels and coincidences gleaned by Father Diego that led him to this conclusion, pp. 185 ff.

55. Phelan, *The Millennial Kingdom,* p. 25.

56. Allen, *The Legend of Noah,* pp. 119–121.

57. Thomas Morton, *New English Canaan* (1632) in *Force's Tracts and Other Papers, Relating Principally to the Origin, Settlement, and Progress of the Colonies in North America, from the Discovery of the Country to the Year 1776,* collected by Peter Force, 1836, 4 vols. (re-

printed Gloucester, Mass: Peter Smith, 1963), vol. 2, document V, chap 2, p. 18.

58. Morton, *New English Canaan*, p. 16.

59. I cite from Allen Mandelbaum's inimitable rendering, *The Aeneid of Virgil* (New York: Bantam, 1971; Bantam Classic Edition, 1981).

60. [John White], *The Planters Plea. Or the Grounds of Plantations examined, And vsuall Objections answered,* in *Force's Tracts,* vol. 2, document III, chap. 2, p. 8.

61. *The Planters Plea,* pp. 8–9.

62. Ibid., p. 9.

63. In *The Light Appearing More and More Towards the Perfect Day.* Collections of the Massachusetts Historical Society, 3d series, 4: 127–128 (1834).

64. Robert Ricard, *The Spiritual Conquest of Mexico: An Essay on the Apostolate and the Evangelizing Methods of the Mendicant Orders in New Spain: 1523–1572,* trans. Lesley Byrd Simpson (Berkeley and Los Angeles: University of California Press, 1966).

65. I am consulting the facsimile edition, Menston, England: The Scolar Press, Ltd., 1971, of the original 1643 publication printed by Gregory Dexter of London and now in the Bodleian Library.

66. Roger Williams's eschatological hopes have been discussed by W. Clark Gilpin, *The Millenarian Piety of Roger Williams* (Chicago: University of Chicago Press, 1979).

CHAPTER 7: MAKING ENDS MEET

1. *Cristóbal Colón: Textos y documentos completos,* pp. 312–313.

2. Ibid., pp. 320–321.

3. Samuel Eliot Morison, *Christopher Columbus Mariner* (New York: The New American Library, Inc. A Mentor Book, 1955), 147.

4. A modern transcription of these drafts has also been made by Consuelo de Varela and included in *Cristóbal Colón: Textos y documentos completos,* documents LI–LIV, pp. 266–277.

5. See Amy Schrager Lang, *Prophetic Women: Anne Hutchinson and the Problem of Dissent in the Literature of New England* (Berkeley, Los Angeles, London: University of California Press, 1987). For a more general and canonical view of this phase of early American history through its documents, see *The Antinomian Controversy, 1636–1638: A Documentary History,* ed. David D. Hall (Middletown, Conn.: Wesleyan University Press, 1968). Nathaniel Hawthorne's biographical essay I allude to here can be found in his *Tales and Sketches* (New York:

Library of America, 1982). It is discussed by Amy Schrager Lang at some length.

6. Phelan, *The Millennial Kingdom*. See especially pt. 3, entitled "The Babylonian Captivity of the Indian Church (1564–1596)."

7. *Cristóbal Colón: Textos y documentos completos*, p. 251.

8. Ibid., p. 286.

9. Ibid., pp. 287–288.

10. Ibid., pp. 328–329.

11. Ibid., p. 278.

12. The "memorandum in my own hand" Columbus refers to is more than likely the letter to the Spanish monarchs written from Cadiz or Seville in 1501 and included (folio 4) in the Admiral's *Libro de las profecías*. Father Bartolomé de Las Casas has made a copy of the memorandum, *Historia*, bk. 1, chap. 3, assuring us that these are the words of the Admiral himself, written to Their Highnesses from Seville or Cadiz in 1501. The cover letter of the *Libro de las profecías* is dated 13 September 1501. The *Book of Prophecies* closes with 23 March 1502.

13. *Cristóbal Colón: Textos y documentos completos*, p. 304.

Bibliography

Alfonso X, the Wise. "Siete Partidas." In Herbert Allen Van Scoy, *A Dictionary of Old Spanish Terms Defined in the Works of Alfonso X*, ed. Ivy Corfis. Madison: The Hispanic Seminary of Medieval Studies, 1986.

Allen, Don Cameron. *The Legend of Noah: Renaissance Rationalism in Art, Science, and Letters*. Urbana: University of Illinois Press, 1949.

Andrews, K. R., N. P. Canny, and P. E. H. Hair, eds. *The Westward Enterprise: English Activities in Ireland, the Atlantic, and America 1480–1650*. Detroit: Wayne State University Press, 1979.

Arciniegas, Germán. *America in Europe: A History of the New World in Reverse*. San Diego, New York, and London: Harcourt Brace Jovanovich, 1986.

Barbour, Philip L. *The Three Worlds of Captain John Smith*. Boston: Houghton Mifflin, 1964.

Barnes, Robin B. *Prophecy and Gnosis: Apocalypticism in the Wake of the Lutheran Reformation*. Stanford: Stanford University Press, 1988.

Bataillon, Marcel. "Novo Mundo e fim do mundo." *Revista de Historia* (São Paolo) 18 (1954). French original in *L'Education Nationale* 32 (1952): 3–6.

———. *Erasmo y España: Estudios sobre la historia espiritual del siglo XVI*. Mexico: Fondo de Cultura Económica, 1950; orig. pub. 1937.

Baudet, Henri. *Paradise on Earth*. Trans. E. Wentholt. New Haven: Yale University Press, 1965.

Bercovitch, Sacvan. *The Puritan Origins of the American Self.* New Haven: Yale University Press, 1975.

Bloomfield M. W. "Joachim of Flora: A Critical Survey of His Canon, Teachings, Sources, Biography, and Influence." *Traditio* 13 (1957): 249–311.

Bloomfield, M. W., and M. E. Reeves, "The Penetration of Joachism into Northern Europe." *Speculum* 29 (1954): 772–793.

Boorstin, Daniel. *The Discoverers.* New York: Random House, 1983.

Bradford, William. *Gov. Bradford's History of Plymouth Colony.* In *Chronicles of the Pilgrim Fathers of Plymouth from 1602–1625,* ed. Alexander Young. Boston: Charles C. Little and James Brown, 1841; rprt. New York: Da Capo Press, 1971.

Brant, Sebastian. *Shyp of folys.* Trans. Alexandre Barclay. In *Bibliotheca Americana Vetustissima,* ed. Carlos Sanz, 2: 1408. Madrid: Libreria General Victoriano Suarez, 1960.

Bultman, Rudolph. *The Presence of Eternity: History and Eschatology.* New York: Harper and Brothers, 1957.

Bury, J. B. *The Idea of Progress: An Inquiry into its Origin and Growth.* London: MacMillan and Co., 1920.

Chiappelli, Fredi, ed. *First Images of America: The Impact of the New World on the Old.* 2 vols. Berkeley, Los Angeles, London: University of California Press, 1976.

Cioranescu, Alexandre, ed. *Oeuvres de Christophe Colomb.* Paris: Gallimard, 1961.

Cohn, Norman. *The Pursuit of the Millennium.* New York: Oxford University Press, 1970; orig. pub. 1957.

———. "Medieval Millennarianism: Its Bearing on the Comparative Study of Millennarian Movements." In *Millennial Dreams in Action,* ed. Sylvia L. Thrupp. The Hague: Mouton, 1962, 31–43.

Collingwood, R. G. *The Idea of History.* Oxford: Oxford University Press, 1946.

Collins, J. J. "Pseudonimity, Historical Reviews and the Genre of the Revelation of John." *Catholic Bible Quarterly* 39 (1977): 329–343.

Colón, Hernando de. *Vida del Almirante Cristóbal Colón.* Mexico: Fondo de Cultura Económica, 1947.

Columbus, Christopher. *Cristóbal Colón: Textos y documentos completos.* Ed. Consuelo Varela. Madrid: Alianza Editorial, 1982.

———. *Libro de las profecías.* In *Raccolta di documenti e studi publicati dalla Real Commissione pel quarto centenario dalla scoperta dell'America. Scriti di Cristoforo Colombo,* ed. Cesare de Lollis. Rome: Real Commissione Colombina, 1892/94. Part I, vol. 2.

———. *Libro de los privilegios del Almirante Don Cristóbal Colón*

(1498). Ed. Ciriaco Pérez-Bustamante. Madrid: Real Academia de la Historia, 1951.

Cook, Harold J. "Ancient Wisdom, the Golden Age, and Atlantis: The New World in Sixteenth-Century Cosmography." *Terrae Incognitae* 10 (1978): 24–43.

Cushman, Robert. *Reasons and Considerations Touching the Lawfulness of Removing out of England into the Parts of America* (1622). In *Chronicles of the Pilgrim Fathers of Plymouth from 1602–1625*, ed. Alexander Young. Boston: Charles C. Little and James Brown, 1841; rprt. New York: Da Capo Press, 1971.

Daniélou, Jean. *The Theology of Jewish Christianity*. Trans. and ed. John A. Baker. London: Darton, Longman, & Todd, Ltd./ Chicago: Henry Regnery Co., 1964.

de Certeau, Michel. *L'écriture de l'histoire*. Paris: Editions Gallimard, 1975.

Dunn, Richard S. "Experiment Holy and Unholy 1630–31." In *The Westward Enterprise: English Activities in Ireland, the Atlantic, and America 1480–1650*, ed. K. R. Andrews et al. Detroit: Wayne State University Press, 1979.

Durán, Diego. *Historia de las Indias de Nueva España y Islas de Tierra Firme*. Ed. José F. Ramírez. 2 vols. Mexico: Editora Nacional, 1951.

Fernández, Rafael Diego. *Capitulaciones Colombinas (1492–1506)*. Michoacan, Mexico: El Colegio de Michoacan, 1987.

Fernández de Enciso. *Suma Georgrafía* (Seville, 1519). In *Las instituciones jurídicas,* ed. Silvio Zavala. 2d ed., rev. and augmented. Mexico: Editorial Porrua, 1971; orig. pub. 1935.

Fernández de Oviedo, Gonzalo. *Historia general y natural de las Indias, islas y Tierra firme del Mar Oceano* (1535). 5 vols. Madrid: Biblioteca de Autores Españoles, 1959.

Fernández Retamar, Roberto. "Caliban." *Casa de las Américas* (Havana) 68 (September–October 1971). Reprinted as title essay in an English collection by the author. *Caliban and Other Essays*. Foreword by Fredric Jameson. Minneapolis: University of Minnesota Press, 1989.

Force, Peter. *Force's Tracts and Other Papers, Relating Principally to the Origin, Settlement, and Progress of the Colonies in North America, from the Discovery of the Country to the Year 1776* (1836). 4 vols. Rprt. Gloucester, Mass.: Peter Smith, 1963.

Froehlich, Karlfried. " 'Always to Keep the Literal Sense in the Holy Scripture Means to Kill One's Soul': The State of Biblical Hermeneutics at the Beginning of the Fifteenth Century." In *Literary Uses of Typology from the Middle Ages to the Present,* ed. Earl Miner. Princeton: Princeton University Press, 1977.

Gerbi, Antonello. *La disputa del Nuovo Mondo: Storia di una polemica, 1750–1900.* Milano: Riccardo Ricciardi Editore, 1955; Trans., rev., and aug. Jeremy Moyle. *The Dispute of the New World.* Pittsburgh: University of Pittsburgh Press, 1973.

Giamatti, A. Bartlett. *The Earthly Paradise and the Renaissance Epic.* Princeton: Princeton University Press, 1966.

W. Clark Gilpin, *The Millenarian Piety of Roger Williams.* Chicago: University of Chicago Press, 1979.

Goez, Werner. *Translatio imperii.* Tübingen: Mohr, 1958.

Hall, David D., ed. *The Antinomian Controversy, 1636–1638.* Middletown, Conn.: Wesleyan University Press, 1968.

Hanke, Lewis. "Pope Paul III and the American Indians." *Harvard Theological Review* (1937): 65–97.

———. *Estudios sobre Fray Bartolomé de Las Casas y sobre la lucha por la justicia en la conquista de América.* Caracas: Universidad Central de Venezuela, 1968.

Hawthorne, Nathaniel. *The English Notebooks of Nathaniel Hawthorne.* Ed. Randall Stewart. New York: Russell and Russell, 1942.

Hill, D. "Prophecy and Prophets in the Revelation of St. John." *New Testament Studies* 18 (1971–1972): 401–418.

Hulme, Peter. *Colonial Encounters: Europe and the Native Caribbean 1492–1797.* London and New York: Methuen and Co., Ltd., 1986.

Hyma, Albert. *The Christian Renaissance: A History of the "Devotio Moderna."* 2d ed. rev. Hamden, Conn.: Archon Books, 1965; 1924.

Iglesias, Ramón. *El hombre Colón y otros ensayos.* Mexico: El Colegio de México, 1944; *Columbus, Cortés, and Other Essays.* Trans. and ed. Lesley Byrd Simpson. Berkeley and Los Angeles: University of California Press, 1969.

Jantz, Harold. "Image of America in the German Renaissance." In *First Images of America: The Impact of the New World on the Old,* ed. Fredi Chiappelli. 2 vols. Berkeley, Los Angeles, London: University of California Press, 1976; orig. pub. 1957.

Kappler, Claude. "La vocation messianique de Christophe Colomb." In *Voyage, quête, pélerinage dans la littérature da la civilisation médiévales, Senéfiance. Cahiers du CUERMA* 2. Université de Provence (1976): 255–271.

Kavenagh, W. Keith, ed. *Foundations of Colonial America: A Documentary History.* 4 vols., 6 pts. New York: Chelsea House, 1983.

Kolodny, Annette. *The Lay of the Land.* Chapel Hill: University of North Carolina Press, 1975.

Lang, Amy Schrager. *Prophetic Women: Anne Hutchinson and the Problem of Dissent inthe Literature of New England.* Berkeley, Los Angeles, London: University of California Press, 1989.

Las Casas, Bartolomé de. *Historia de las Indias*. Ed. Juan Pérez de Tudela and Emilio López Otto. Madrid: BAE, 1957.

León Portilla, Miguel. *La visión de los vencidos: Relaciones indígenas de la conquista*. Mexico: UNAM, 1959.

Lerner, Robert E. *The Powers of Prophecy: The Cedar of Lebanon Vision from the Mongol Onslaught to the Dawn of the Enlightenment*. Berkeley, Los Angeles, London: University of California Press, 1983.

Leturia, Pedro. "Maior y Vitoria ante la conquista de América." *Anuario de la Asociación Francisco de Vitoria* III (1930–1931): 43–83.

Lowance, Mason I., Jr. *The Language of Canaan*. Cambridge: Harvard University Press, 1980.

Löwith, Karl. *Meaning in History*. Chicago: University of Chicago Press, 1949.

McGinn, Bernard, trans. and ed. *Apocalyptic Spirituality: Treatises and Letters of Lactantius, Adso of Montier-En-Der, Joachim of Fiore, the Spiritual Franciscans, Savonarola*. New York: The Paulist Press, 1979.

———. *Visions of the End: Apocalyptic Traditions in the Middle Ages*. New York: Columbia University Press, 1979.

Madariaga, Salvador de. *Vida del muy magnífico señor Don Cristóbal Colón*. Madrid: Espasa Calpe, 1975.

Mandelbaum, Allen, trans. *The Aeneid of Virgil*. New York: Bantam, 1971; Bantam Classic Edition, 1981.

Manzano Manzano, Juan. *Colón y su secreto: El predescubrimiento*. Madrid: Ediciones Cultura Hispánica, 1982.

Mather, Cotton. *Magnalia Christi Americana*. 2 vols. Hartford Edition, 1820.

Mather, Increase. "New Jerusalem" (1687). In William L. Joyce and Michael G. Hall, "Three Manuscripts of Increase Mather," *Proceedings of the Antiquarian Society*, vol. 86, pt. 1 (April 1976): 113–123.

Milhou, Alain. *Colón y su mentalidad mesiánica en el ambiente franciscanista español*. Cuadernos Colombinos XI. Valladolid: Museo de Colón y Seminario Americanista de la Universidad de Valladolid, 1983.

Miller, Perry. "The Religious Impulses in the Founding of Virginia: Religion and Society in the Early Literature." *William and Mary Quarterly*, 3d series, V (1948): 492–522.

———. *Errand into the Wilderness*. Cambridge: Harvard University Press, 1956.

Monsegú, Bernardo. "Erasmo y Vives y la 'Philosophia Christi' como humanismo cristiano." In *Erasmo en España*, ed. Manuel Revuelta

Sañudo and Ciriaco Morón Arroyo. Santander: Sociedad Menéndez Pelayo, 1986.

Montaigne, Michel Eyquem. "Des Cannibales." *Essais. Reproduction photographique de l'edition originale de 1580.* Ed. Daniel Martin. 2 vols. Facsimile edition. Geneva: Slatkin and Paris: Champion, 1976; "Of Cannibals." *The Complete Essays of Montaigne.* Trans. Donald M. Frame. Stanford: Stanford University Press, 1989; orig. pub. 1958; pp. 150–159.

Moreno Durán, Rafael Humberto. *De la barbarie a la imaginación: La experiencia leída.* 2d ed., augmented. Bogota: Tercer Mundo Editores, 1988.

Morison, Samuel Eliot. *Admiral of the Ocean Sea: A Life of Christopher Columbus.* Boston: Little Brown and Co., 1942.

———. *Christopher Columbus Mariner.* New York: The New American Library, Inc. A Mentor Book, 1955.

Morton, Thomas. *New English Canaan* (1632). In Peter Force, *Force's Tracts and Other Papers, Relating Principally to the Origin, Settlement, and Progress of the Colonies in North America, from the Discovery of the Country to the Year 1776* (1836), vol. 2, doc. 5. Rprt. Gloucester, Mass.: Peter Smith, 1963.

Morton, Thomas. *The Light Appearing More and More Towards the Perfect Day.* Collections of the Massachusetts Historical Society, 3d series, 4: 127–128 (1834).

Niederland, William G. "The Naming of America." In *Maps from the Mind: Readings in Psychogeography,* eds. Howard F. Stein and William G. Niederland. Norman: University of Oklahoma Press, 1989.

O'Gorman, Edmundo. *The Invention of America: An Inquiry into the Historical Nature of the New World and the Meaning of its History.* Bloomington: Indiana University Press, 1961.

Parker, John. "Religion and the Virginia Colony 1609–10." In *The Westward Enterprise: English Activities in Ireland, the Atlantic, and America 1480–1650,* ed. K. R. Andrews et al. Detroit: Wayne State University Press, 1979.

Parry, J. H. "Introduction: The English and the New World." In *The Westward Enterprise,* ed. K. R. Andrews et al.

Pastor, Beatriz. *Discursos narrativos de la conquista: mitificación y emergencia.* 2d ed. rev. Hanover, N.H.: Ediciones del Norte, 1988.

Pearce, Roy Harvey. *The Savages of America: A Study of the Indian and the Idea of Civilization.* Rev. ed. Baltimore: The Johns Hopkins Press, 1965; orig. pub. 1953.

Pérez de Tudela, Juan. "Vida y escritos de Gonzalo Fernández de Oviedo." Introduction to Oviedo's *Historia,* pp. vii–clxix.

Phelan, John Leddy. *The Millennial Kingdom of the Franciscans in the*

New World. 2d ed. Berkeley, Los Angeles, London: University of California Press, 1970.

Reeves, Marjorie. *Joachim of Fiore and the Prophetic Future.* New York: Harper and Row, 1977.

——. *The Influence of Prophecy in the Later Middle Ages: A Study in Joachimism.* Oxford: Clarendon Press, 1969.

Reyes, Alfonso. *The Position of America.* Trans. Harriet de Onís. New York: Alfred A. Knopf, 1950.

Ricard, Robert. *The Spiritual Conquest of Mexico: An Essay on the Apostolate and the Evangelizing Methods of the Mendicant Orders in New Spain: 1523–1572.* Trans. Lesley Byrd Simpson. Berkeley and Los Angeles: University of California Press, 1966.

Rowse, A. L. *The Elizabethans and America.* New York: Harper and Brothers, 1959.

Sanders, Ronald. *Last Tribes and Promised Lands.* Boston: Little, Brown, and Co., 1978.

Sanz, Carlos, ed. *Bibliotheca Americana Vetustissima: Ultimas adiciones.* 2 vols. Madrid: Libreria General Victoriano Suarez, 1960.

Smith, Captain John. *The Complete Works of Captain John Smith (1580–1631).* Ed. Philip L. Barbour. 3 vols. Chapel Hill: University of North Carolina Press, 1986.

Smith, Henry Nash. *Virgin Land: The American West as Symbol and Myth.* Cambridge: Harvard University Press, 1970.

Stevens, Wallace. "The Idea of Order at Key West." In *The Palm at the End of the Mind. Selected Poems.* Ed. Holly Stevens. New York: Random House/Vintage Books, 1972.

Todorov, Tzvetan. *The Conquest of America: The Question of the Other.* Trans. Richard Howard. New York: Harper Colophon Books, 1985.

Tuveson, Ernest. *Millennium and Utopia: A Study in the Background of the Idea of Progress.* Berkeley and Los Angeles: University of California Press, 1949.

Ullmann, Walter. *Medieval Papalism: The Political Theories of the Medieval Canonists.* London: Methuen and Co., Ltd., 1949.

Van Scoy, Herbert Allan. A Dictionary of Old Spanish Terms Defined in the Works of Alfonso X. Ed. Ivy Corfis. Madison: The Hispanic Seminary of Medieval Studies, 1986.

Vasiliev, A. "Medieval Ideas of the End of the World: East and West." *Byzantion* 16 (1942–1943): 462–502.

Vespucci, Amerigo. *El Nuevo Mundo: Cartas relativas a sus viajes y descubrimientos. Textos en italiano, español e inglés.* Ed. Roberto Leviller. Buenos Aires: Editorial Nova, 1951.

Waldseemüller, Martin. *Cosmographia Introductio.* In *Bibliotheca*

Americana Vetustissima, ed. Carlos Sanz, 2:45–50. Madrid: Libreria General Victoriano Suarez, 1960.

Watts, Pauline Moffitt. "Prophecy and Discovery: On the Spiritual Origins of Christopher Columbus's 'Enterprise of the Indies,' " *The American Historical Review* 90 (1985): 73–102.

White, Hayden. "The Noble Savage: Theme as Fetish." In *First Images of America: The Impact of the New World on the Old,* 1:121–35. ed. Fredi Chiappelli, Berkeley, Los Angeles, London: University of California Press, 1976.

White, John. *The Planters Plea. Or the Grounds of Plantations examined, And vsuall Objections answered.* In Peter Force, *Force's Tracts and Other Papers, Relating Principally to the Origin, Settlement, and Progress of the Colonies in North America, from the Discovery of the Country to the Year 1776* (1836), vol. 2, doc. 3. Rprt. Gloucester, Mass.: Peter Smith, 1963.

Williams, Roger. *A Key into the Language of America: Or, An Help to the Language of the Natives in that part of America, called New England* (1643). Menston, England: The Scolar Press, Ltd., 1971. Facsimile edition, of the original 1643 publication printed by Gregory Dexter of London and now in the Bodleian Library, Oxford.

Winthrop, John. "General Considerations for the Plantation in New England." In *Winthrop Papers,* II (Massachusetts Historical Society, 1931).

———. *Life and Letters of John Winthrop.* Ed. and commentary by Robert C. Winthrop. Boston: Little, Brown, and Company, 1869.

———. *Reasons and Considerations.* In *Chronicles of the Pilgrim Fathers of Plymouth from 1602–1625,* ed. Alexander Young. Boston: Charles C. Little and James Brown, 1841; rprt. New York: Da Capo Press, 1971.

Worsley, Peter. *The Trumpet Shall Sound: A Study of "Cargo" Cults in Melanesia.* 2d ed. New York: Schoken Books, 1968.

Wright, Louis B. *Religion and Empire: The Alliance between Piety and Commerce in English Expansion 1558–1625.* Chapel Hill: University of North Carolina Press, 1943; rpt., New York: Farrar, Strauss and Giroux, 1965.

Yates, Frances. *Giordano Bruno and the Hermetic Tradition.* Chicago: University of Chicago Press, 1964.

Young, Alexander, ed. *Chronicles of the Pilgrim Fathers of Plymouth from 1602–1625.* Boston: Charles C. Little and James Brown, 1841; rprt. New York: Da Capo Press, 1971.

Zavala, Silvio, ed. *Las institutiones jurídicas in la Conquista de América.* 2d ed., rev. and augmented. México: Editorial Porrua, 1971; orig. pub. 1935.

Ziff, Larzer. "The Literary Consequences of Puritanism." In *The American Puritan Imagination: Essays in Revaluation,* ed. Sacvan Bercovitch. London and New York: Cambridge University Press, 1974.

———. *The Career of John Cotton.* Princeton: Princeton University Press, 1962.

Index

Designer:	U.C. Press Staff
Compositor:	Huron Valley Graphics
Text:	11/14 Sabon
Display:	Sabon
Printer:	Edwards Brothers, Inc.
Binder:	Edwards Brothers, Inc.